Rattles And Steadies

Memoirs of a Gander River Man

retold by

Gary L. Saunders

Canadian Cataloguing in Publication Data

Saunders, Gary L.
    Rattles and steadies : memoirs of a Gander River man

(Canada's Atlantic Folklore-Folklife Series)
ISSN 0708-4226 ; no. 12

ISBN 0-919519-75-X (bound)
ISBN 0-919519-73-3 (paper)

1. Saunders, Brett.   2. Outdoor life – Newfoundland – Biography.   3. Guides for hunters, fishermen, etc. – Newfoundland – Gander River – Biography.   I. Title.

FC2195.G35Z49 1985   971.8'09'24   C85-099524-8
F1124.G35S38 1985

Cover: The author's brother Calvin steaming up Big Chute on the Gander River. Photo by Gary Saunders.

Unless otherwise credited, all photographs are reproduced with permission from the family albums of the late Frank and Mary Saunders, Brett and the late Winifred Saunders, Calvin and Catherine Saunders, and of the author.

Breakwater gratefully acknowledges the support of The Canada Council

Contents

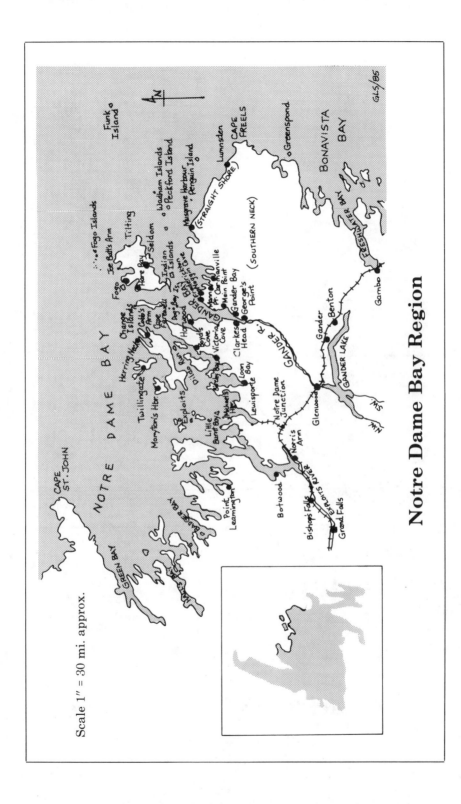

Scale 1″ = 30 mi. approx.

Notre Dame Bay Region

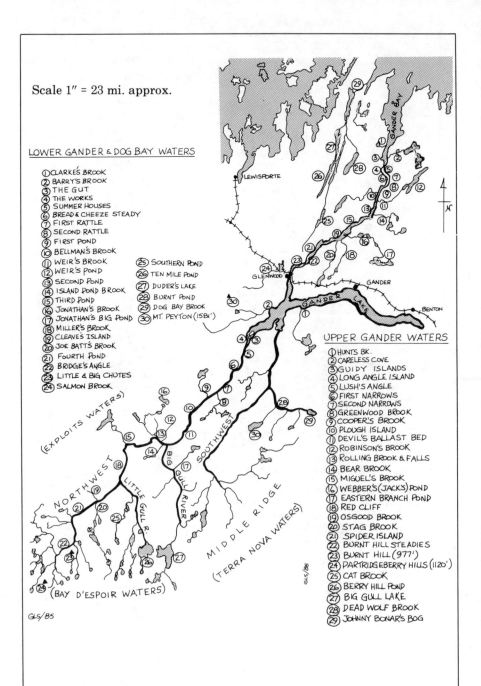

Scale 1″ = 23 mi. approx.

LOWER GANDER & DOG BAY WATERS

1 CLARKE'S BROOK
2 BARRY'S BROOK
3 THE GUT
4 THE WORKS
5 SUMMER HOUSES
6 BREAD & CHEEZE STEADY
7 FIRST RATTLE
8 SECOND RATTLE
9 FIRST POND
10 BELLMAN'S BROOK
11 WEIR'S BROOK
12 WEIR'S POND
13 SECOND POND
14 ISLAND POND BROOK
15 THIRD POND
16 JONATHAN'S BROOK
17 JONATHAN'S BIG POND
18 MILLER'S BROOK
19 CLEAVE'S ISLAND
20 JOE BATT'S BROOK
21 FOURTH POND
22 BRIDGE'S ANGLE
23 LITTLE & BIG CHUTES
24 SALMON BROOK

25 SOUTHERN POND
26 TEN MILE POND
27 DUDER'S LAKE
28 BURNT POND
29 DOG BAY BROOK
30 MT. PEYTON (1581')

UPPER GANDER WATERS

1 HUNTS BK.
2 CARELESS COVE
3 GUIDY ISLANDS
4 LONG ANGLE ISLAND
5 LUSH'S ANGLE
6 FIRST NARROWS
7 SECOND NARROWS
8 GREENWOOD BROOK
9 COOPER'S BROOK
10 PLOUGH ISLAND
11 DEVIL'S BALLAST BED
12 ROBINSON'S BROOK
13 ROLLING BROOK & FALLS
14 BEAR BROOK
15 MIGUEL'S BROOK
16 WEBBER'S (JACK'S) POND
17 EASTERN BRANCH POND
18 RED CLIFF
19 OSGOOD BROOK
20 STAG BROOK
21 SPIDER ISLAND
22 BURNT HILL STEADIES
23 BURNT HILL (977')
24 PARTRIDGEBERRY HILLS (1120')
25 CAT BROOK
26 BERRY HILL POND
27 BIG GULL LAKE
28 DEAD WOLF BROOK
29 JOHNNY BONAR'S BOG

(EXPLOITS WATERS)

(BAY D'ESPOIR WATERS)

NORTHWEST

LITTLE GULL R.

BIG GULL RIVER

SOUTHWEST

MIDDLE RIDGE

(TERRA NOVA WATERS)

LEWISPORTE

GANDER BAY

GLENWOOD

GANDER

BENTON

GANDER LK.

GLS/85

GLS/85

Gander River & Related Waters

Dedication

This book is dedicated to the woman behind the man who told these stories, she who kept hearth and home through many a stormy winter's night "not knowing if he was dead or alive," my mother Winifred Jane, who passed away on June 9, 1984.

"...the Newfoundlander...has always been unable to build light draught canoes of tough wood, because no wood capable of withstanding the rocks of the rivers is to be found in the island. He is also clumsy in the rivers, and unable to use a pole like the Indians.... He has any amount of pluck, but no skill on the rivers. Though at home at sea, he is all at sea at home."

J.G. Millais
Newfoundland and Its Untrodden Ways
1907

Acknowledgements

At least two dozen people helped make this book. Near the top of the list is David Quinton of the CBC who first saw, in a windy piece of nostalgia I wrote about the Gander River in the early 1970s, the makings of a television script for his *Land and Sea* programme. "The Riverman" was aired in 1974. From it came the idea.

After collecting more material from my father I needed uninterrupted writing time. Charles and Agnes Blackie, longtime friends and neighbours of my parents in Gander, urged me to try for a Canada Council grant. In 1978, with Sheila Cotton, Don MacLean and Dave Quinton vouching for me, I was awarded a $3,000 Explorations grant which bought me ten precious weeks away from my job. The resultant first draft caught the interest of Clyde Rose of Breakwater Books, and his subsequent encouragement kept me plugging away through several years of part-time writing.

To gain a wider perspective on my father's doings I turned to three of his former hunting colleagues, namely Dr. John M. Olds of Twillingate, the Hon. Beaton J. Abbott, and historian Jac Weller. All were generous with information. So was salmon angler Dr. Richard TeLinde. For background on the Beothuk I contacted Dr. Fred W. Rowe, Dr. Ingeborg Marshall, and Edgar Baird, all of whom were helpful. *Them Days* editor Doris Saunders of Happy Valley gave Dad and me leads on the Labrador sojourn of Esau Gillingham, the "White Eskimo," as did A.R. Penney of Manuels, Conception Bay.

To fill in some blanks in our family tree and track down the doings of our ancestors, I turned to my Aunt Kathleen and Uncle Harold Saunders of Gander Bay. My father's youngest brother Donald took me upriver in canoe to have another look at Summer Houses and The Works, and Uncles Aubrey Saunders and Roy Reccord added useful details. Jabez Hodder — great-grandson of William Hodder, one of Gander Bay's first settlers — kindly allowed me to study the gravestones in their family plot on Salt Island. From him I learned that my grandparents, Frank and Mary Saunders, were his godparents, and that when he was small they regularly "rowed across the Bay on fine Sunday evenings to visit and bring [him] a treat." My second cousin Otis Gillingham of Glenwood took time to discuss the newspaper columns of his late father Stanley, a frequent trapping partner of my father's in Depression days.

Meeting my mother's brother Harry Layman in 1984 — the first time in thirty years — was a pleasure, especially when, after an evening of spirited story-telling, he agreed to write the Foreword. Fellow Notre Dame Bay author Aubrey Tizzard, who died in Port Hope, Ontario last summer, boosted my morale at a critical point. Toward the end of the project my older brother Calvin has been a trusty editorial companion. And my wife and children? Quite simply, without their forebearance during many a workaholic weekend and many a late night, the job would have remained unfinished.

I wish to acknowledge permission to reprint published material from *Outdoor Canada* Magazine Limited, Newfoundland Book Publishers (1967) Limited, and *The American Rifleman*; and to excerpt from the personal correspondence of Dr. Richard W. TeLinde, Kenneth and Blair Davis, and Jac Weller.

My special thanks to all those mentioned and to any others I may have overlooked. Above all I thank my father — for telling the stories again and so well.

Gary Lloyd Saunders
Old Barns, Nova Scotia
November 1984

Author's Preface

Until my tenth birthday I never doubted I would be a riverman like my father. Growing up with the Gander River only three miles from our doorstep and the canoes coming and going all summer and the men talking around the kitchen stove on winter nights of salmon and caribou and lynx, how could I doubt? It seemed only a matter of time until I would have my own canoe and dog team and trapline and go guiding in the summer and fall and furring in the wintertime.

But in 1945, the year I was ten, we moved to St. John's. In the next seven years we moved five more times — from St. John's to Lewisporte to St. John's to Toronto to Clarke's Head to St. John's — one winter at home and six away. These moves were made partly for the sake of better schooling for my brother and me, partly so my mother, never robust and forever nervous about tuberculosis, diptheria and polio, could have a doctor handy. A third reason was so that we could be reasonably central to my father's winter travels. From 1945 to 1947 he was an inspector for the Newfoundland Fisheries Board, serving first in Placentia Bay, then in Notre Dame Bay, and the third winter in Bay of Islands on the west coast. Beyond such practical reasons, however, I sensed in my father a tremendous restlessness, a dissatisfaction with city life, a distaste for any kind of occupation not connected with the woods or the sea. Even our few years in St. John's were spread among five different addresses. And whenever possible we went back to Gander Bay for the summer.

Although enjoying some aspects of our many moves, I was often lonesome and at times wondered who I really was — a bayman or a townie or what? The thing that consoled me and preserved my identity was the stories I had heard as a child. Looking at snapshots of myself when I was four or five, I am struck by the expression of wonder on my face. Certainly I was all ears for anything concerning Up the River or In the Country, those mysterious worlds into which my father regularly disappeared to return a week or a month later, bewhiskered and smelling deliciously (I thought) of woodsmoke and fir boughs. The best part for me was when, after the hugs were over and the dogs were unharnessed and fed and the family was back to normal and I had my bag of fresh frankgum (spruce gum) knobs to chew, the old men of the community would amble in to hear news of The Country. They didn't mean Newfoundland. They meant the Gander River and its hinterland, and they sought information about such things as the thickness of the ice, the depth of snow and the abundance or scarcity of "sign" in this or that trapping area.

It so happened that in our house at Clarke's Head my bedroom adjoined the kitchen. This bedroom was chilly, so in order to let in the warm air off the *Bridgewall* range my father cut a heat register through the wall above my bed. This worked better than he knew. Not only did it soften the chill, it let me hear what was being said in the kitchen after my bedtime. All I had to do was stand on the head of the bed. As long as my feet could bear the discomfort of the cold cast iron rod I would perch under that lamplit, magical aperture, listening to the soft murmur of their voices, distant yet near, hearing the fire crackle and the kettle hiss, smelling the fragrance of spruce wood, *HiPlane* and *Beaver* pipe tobacco and the kerosene lamp, absorbing the stories. Slowly, a picture of my world emerged. But always before I could get all the places and characters straight, one of our moves would intervene. Four times Dad bought lumber for a new house in Gander Bay and four times he sold it.

The event that finally led me to weave the seemingly tangled threads of my parents' life and times into a pattern was the chance in 1973 to script a programme about the Gander River for the CBC television series *Land and Sea*. "The Riverman" was aired in Atlantic Canada in 1974, and afterward on the national programme *This Land*. Since then it has appeared several times on both shows, and recently the Newfoundland Department of Education put it in their school film library. I like to think it struck a chord.

But film images fade. The idea of a book came. First it was to be merely my personal "Roots" project. Then I saw it as a family record. Finally it grew into a documentation of the lifeways of the Gander Bay woodsman in general and of my father in particular. Originally conceived as a third person narrative, it soon shifted to the first person. At times I had trouble remembering who was speaking. When I felt his voice slipping away I would play the tapes again and mentally stand on the headboard until it sounded right. If the reader sometimes hears two voices, it can't be helped. After all, my father's stories are now mine — and yours.

A more serious problem in a book of recollections is that someone with inside information may feel this or that story is wrong. While he or she may be right, it is well be bear in mind three things which bedevil the labours of any collector of stories. First, the selectivity of the storyteller's memory. Any event witnessed by several persons will invariably generate several versions in the retelling. Second, the same event may happen more than once in similar circumstances. And third, good story-tellers embroider the truth.

While I have tried for accuracy throughout this work, it was folklore I was after, not history — the folklore hidden in one man's treasury of tales. Stories are the stuff of culture, but until recently Newfoundland stories have almost all been about the sea. This book is about the men and women who left the salt water for the fresh, who learned to make a living from the forest.

If few women figure in these stories it is because in those days they considered the river and the woods a male domain. They stayed home to look after the children and grandparents, to tend the livestock and keep house. When their menfolk returned they baked and sewed and mended for the next expedition. As a boy I recall seeing Mom mending pair after pair of socks and mitts worn out or accidentally scorched on the trail. And before each trip I remember her filling a large cotton flour bag with a whole day's baking of fresh bread, which Dad would carefully stow under canvas on his dogsled. Once while working on the television script I remarked to her that I realized there was another side to the story, and that perhaps we would do hers next. "Thanks for the thought, my son," she said with a smile, "but I doubt that you could tell it in twenty-eight minutes." So if men seem to dominate this narrative, remember that in the background the women were doing, as Hilda Chaulk Murray so aptly phrased it, *More Than 50%*.

At the outset of this preface I said my boyhood ambition to be a riverman was frustrated. Now I can see that writing this book was a kind of substitute. If I have succeeded in paying the rivermen of the Gander the respect I feel, then perhaps being born too late was a good thing after all.

G.L.S.

Foreword

To write a foreword to this book about my brother-in-law, the riverman, is no easy task. Apart from his involvement with immediate family and very close friends, Brett Saunders was somewhat removed from a lot of things with which we are involved daily. This is not to say he lived hermit-style — as I've known a lot of trappers to do — nor that he isolated himself from the world and from current events. Nothing could be further from the truth. He is a man of exceptional intelligence and a superb conversationalist.

Having graduated from the esteemed Bishop Feild College in the early twenties with a coveted record, he was academically qualified to fill most positions being offered at the time. But the blood of his ancestors the Gillinghams and the Saunders, both of whom had migrated from the Old Country long before, trickled through his veins, and the instinct to outdo the wily fox, to jig cod on Fogo's Offer Grounds, and above all his love of the rivers and forests, were too strong.

There are two distinct sides to Brett, and to really appreciate him one would have to be in direct contact with him in the forest and in more urban settings. I have known him in both. But during the winter of 1936 I had the pleasure and privilege — forgetting the discomforts, as I was a tenderfoot youth — of spending two months with him in the woods.

The first stage of my journey took me some thirty miles over mostly Arctic ice from my hometown of Fogo to Clarke's Head in Gander Bay. It was to be a trapping expedition. With only two dogs to haul everything, our food was necessarily restricted as we had to take along canvas tent, tin stove, stovepiping, axe, bucksaw, et cetera. The food we did take consisted of flour, tea, sugar, baking powder, potatoes — and the inevitable fat back pork. Rabbits, caribou and moose supplied the protein on such expeditions, along with trout from the numerous brooks along the way. Our journey took us from Clarke's Head to a cabin above Little Gull River, a distance of some eighty miles over the ice of Gander River and Gander Lake.

It was an unusually stormy winter. But regardless of blinding snow or darkness, Brett would find his intended place to camp, or locate a snare drifted over. He carried no compass. If in doubt, and when visibility was favourable, he would climb a tree and set his course from there. His accuracy always impressed me. Many a stormy night we spent under canvas when the trapline took us away from base camp. While the blizzard raged without, we were quite comfortable within, and following a meal of Indian brewis or damper dumplings Brett's rendition of "Home on the Range" would be my lullaby.

On our way to Little Gull Brett spotted a herd of caribou crossing the Base Line Bogs. It was a bitter cold day with a low drift. He ordered — and I mean ordered — me to lie flat on the snow while he stalked. A kill would mean meat for the month ahead. I was soon petrified with cold. Hearing a rifle shot I looked up and was horrified to find myself surrounded by the stampeding herd, some thirty in all. Minutes later Brett dragged the dead caribou to where I was and quickly opened it up. He told me to remove my clothing from the waist up, then forced me to put my arms to the shoulders in the body of the still steaming animal. Washing was out of the question until I reached camp. There was no alternative but to put my clothes back on over blood-stained arms and chest. But the heat which penetrated my whole body compensated for any discomfort, and a wash and a good feed of fresh venison that night completed the cure.

During the trip I managed to get a severe face infection from shaving with an unsterilized razor. At length there was every indication of blood poisoning setting in. We carried no medication, and of course medical help was out of the question. Brett was very concerned, and after taking a good look went to work on some concoction which he applied to my face. After two or three applications this poultice resulted in a perfect cure. I have no idea what he used. But I do recall 'twas damn hot and there was more than water involved.

Although Brett isn't over-endowed with patience, I cannot recall ever seeing him in a vexed mood. Yet he would sometimes do unpredictable things. One Sunday he and I were walking out the cemetery road in Clarke's Head. It was springtime and he was wearing a pair of new shoes. I noticed he was limping. After a while he stopped and, without comment, removed one shoe and threw it in the surrounding trees, after which we continued on our way. When I asked why he didn't throw away the other one too, he replied, "Because it wasn't hurting me." Another time I saw him do the same thing with a pocket watch that wouldn't go. Such incidents sometimes gave me the feeling that if for sufficient reason I ever failed him I would meet a similar fate.

Riverman always seemed to be in command of any situation. Late one bitterly cold afternoon I had the misfortune of experiencing immerse baptism in Gander Lake when I fell through the ice. Chilled to the marrow, I was immediately taken ashore where Brett pitched the tent and got a fire going while I changed to dry clothes. Seeing I was still shivering and my teeth chattering, he hurriedly cut boughs and made a bed on the snow, over which he placed his bearskin rug. He then called in the two dogs and got me to lie down between them. While not the most desirable of bedfellows, their warmth soon drove the cold from my body. The next morning found me feeling fine and ready for another thirty-mile trek.

I don't believe Brett had a superstitious bone in his body. Late one dark night, in the country by himself, he was caught in a severe rain and wind storm. He knew of a camp not a mile away, but he also knew it had a reputation for being haunted. Legend said that a Beothuk had been murdered nearby in a storm, and that ever since it was built the camp would toss and sway. Tonight he had no choice but go there and take shelter. He found the roof tight, but no sooner had he bedded down than the floor began to rise and fall and the walls to creak and rent. Taking his flashlight, Riverman went out and inspected the surrounding area. He soon discovered that the roots of a huge pine tree extended directly underneath the camp, and that when the tree swayed the camp would move too. For the rest of that night, he said, he slept like a baby rocked in a cradle.

At eighty, Brett is gradually and reluctantly severing his relationship to the things he so loves. The floral-carpeted forest floor will miss his footfall. The ever-present and bold jay, which I've so often seen being fed crumbs while perched on Riverman's shoulder, will look in vain, and the fox, muskrat and beaver, whilst his victims, would, if they could communicate with us, speak in admiration of how they were so often outwitted by his superb trapping skills. The turbulent rapids of Gander River and the placid reaches of Gander Lake are missing the purr of his outboard motor. Those are things which, were it possible for me to capture them on paper, would do justice to the foreword of this book.

Harry Layman
St. John's, Newfoundland
September 1984

PART I

Growing Up

Adrift in a Packing Crate
and Other Boyhood Adventures

I was born on February 15, 1904* in Clarke's Head, Gander Bay, near
where the Gander River empties out. Like most Newfoundland
communities of that time, Clarke's Head was a wonderful place in which
to grow up. When we got big enough we dodged along the landwash
looking for interesting shells and rocks and especially fool's gold. The Bay
never seemed to get very loppy. Up the road a short piece from our house
was a shallow cove where we would wade, and beyond that was the round,
cliffy knoll we called Point Head, with a fenced-in meadow at its foot and
beyond that the beach where we could capture barneystickles with our
hands in the rock pools and cast for sea trout with homemade spruce poles.
In back of the houses and meadows was Clarke's Brook and the woods.
We never went there until we were older, just the same as we were never
allowed on the wharf or out in boat. But we boys watched the men, we
heard them talk of trips to Fogo or Twillingate, trips to Glenwood and
Big Gull River, and we wondered. And in the wintertime we watched
them harness up the horses and go in the Portage Road with bobsleds
to haul out sawlogs or firewood. Other men harnessed teams of dogs to
loaded slides and went "in the country" to trap lynx and otter and fox.
We wondered about this too. And there were the old men and women
who told stories of when they were youngsters, and what they had seen
and done, and even about the days long ago, when the Red Indians roamed
the woods and took a scattered white man's head.

That really happened: Mother told me the story more than once.
Her great-grandfather Robert Gillingham Sr. and a crew of fishermen
had been dipping salmon out of their "rakeworks" or rock weir near the

*For a short family history, see "Afterword," p. 271.

21

mouth of the Gander River when a party of Beothuk braves burst out of the woods and attacked them, killed one of the men, and ran away with his head. And she would relate how Uncle Jack Gillingham's father, who always had the salmon berth down to Sandy Cove, came early to his nets one morning and found some Beothuk taking salmon; how all but a lame woman ran away, and how, when they caught up to her, she reached inside her deerskin tunic and pulled out a black duck and offered it to him if he would spare her; how she wouldn't eat molasses bread, but relished blubber. I liked those stories.

My own earliest memories are of our sawmill, the sounds and the smells: I grew up with those. Every morning early Uncle Hezekiah or another man would walk in the Portage Road and open the sluice gate, as well as a second gate in on Clarke's Pond, and every evening he would walk back and close them. When the water was running good our parents charged us to stay off the flume for fear of being washed into the turbine — or so they said. But on Sundays when everything was shut down we used to climb up and walk the flume. One day Francis Thistle and I rolled an orange the whole length of the flume, from Steady Water to the mill, without having to push it once. That's how even the slope was.

The summer I was six they were finishing the Anglican church in Clarke's Head. Ten years in the planning, it was framed up by Reuben Peckford and others and completed by Robert Small of Summerford, who also built St. Peter's Anglican Church in Victoria Cove around the same time. Father sawed the lumber and the various Church of England families in Clarke's Head donated either twenty-five logs or $2.50 apiece, and free labour. This was a major event because it meant that they no longer had to travel to Fogo for baptisms and weddings, and they wouldn't have to worship in the schoolhouse any more. I can't recall any of this, nor the dedication on April 24, 1910, nor the death of young Aunt Victoria a few days before, but something else happened that spring which I can mind very well. I tried to pole across the mouth of Clarke's Brook in a wooden box and nearly drowned.

The box was lying on the landwash by the church. Perhaps the font or the organ came in it. After some prising and scoting I got it in the water and afloat. Climbing aboard, and using a piece of mill edging — what we called crip — for a pole, I pushed out into the current. The brook was in spring flood and top high, and the current was stronger than I bargained for. Pretty soon I lost bottom. Halfway across the brook — which at that point wasn't much over thirty feet — the tide took me and my box and away we went, out past the lumber piles, past the end of the wharf, out beyond the big rock with the ringbolt where the log boom was chained, and on into the main channel of the Bay.

22

By this time the box had settled in the water, which was up to my knees and bitter cold. If I moved at all she would list, which would send me scrambling to the high side, which would only make it tip again. I tell you, I was some frightened by the time they found me. It was Uncle Jack Gillingham heard my screams as he rowed back from tending his salmon nets at Sandy Cove on the south side. He took me aboard his punt, wrapped me in his big warm sweater, and rowed me home.

When I was eight Gander Bay North was just about burned out by a forest fire. It started east of Glenwood — they said it was sparks from the train — and a strong southwest wind drove it down country forty miles, from Salmon Pond alongside the tracks, on past South Pond and Bellman's and Burnt Pond, right toward Dog Bay. We knew what was coming, for the sky was yellow and hazy the day before, the smell of burning moss was in the air, and the sun set red as blood. They said it all depended on the wind. If it veered even a few compass points to the west, every house on the north side would be in danger because it was woods all the way down. Some families moved out on Big Salt Island to escape. One woman went into labour there that night and they took her to nearby Little Salt Island to have her baby. That baby was Moses Hurley. When the fire got close enough to see the smoke rolling up in the daytime, we were all shifted out on Point Head, the next safest place. There we huddled all one night, men and women and children, watching the flames and flankers going up along the whole western sky, listening to the dull roar of it like the rote of the sea on a far shore, wondering what would happen. It passed us by, coming down in back of Clarke's Pond; but five miles north, in Victoria Cove, it took a few houses. One was Mr. Reccord's; another was a new one belonging to Nath Webb, who had to postpone his wedding because of this. Although it stopped short of Horwood, this fire dealt a hard blow to the lumbermen of the area, especially the Horwood Lumber Company which had limits all up through Dog Bay waters and several dams and a big mill in Dog Bay that they built in 1911. My Uncle Stanley Gillingham was working on the Dog Bay drive that spring, and it's a wonder the whole crew wasn't roasted like caplin. He was only a young man then, twenty years of age, but it was all they could do to outrun the flames. He said they spent the night in the water at the lower end of South Pond with fire on either side, with them splashing water on the dam to keep it from burning. This he told me years later when we trapped on the Northwest together.

Horwood's never had a mill in Gander Bay, though in later years they used to drive wood off Bellman's and other brooks emptying into the Gander, move it down to tidewater, and tow it out around Dog Bay

Point with their tug the *Beatty*, to the mill in Horwood. In 1902 they had acquired 250 square miles of timberland on the Dog Bay watershed and around this time they started operations in the Bay by setting up a large supply depot called Gander Stores and a barn big enough to hold about twenty horses. This was just below Burnt Point in Clarke's Head; the barn was opposite the store on the inside of the road. The man who tended the horses was a pleasant Irishman named Bobby Walsh. We loved Bobby. He was a wonderful man with a story. Better still, he lived right in the barn in a little room with a stove and a cot. In the summertime when there wasn't much for him to do we used to hang around to watch the horses and listen to his yarns.

Horses were his world. He measured everything by horses. One of his favourite stories was about "The Seventh of April Batch," a snowfall so heavy that one of the Horwood Lumber Company's horses perished in the stable before the teamsters could dig it out, and to get out the Portage Road from Burnt Point to Gander Bay, a distance of five miles, it took them several days of steady shovelling. The snow on the level was so deep, he said, you could lay a plank across the top of the cut and big Clydesdales could walk underneath without touching their hames. On the south side of the Bay it drifted so deep, he said, people had trouble getting at their firewood piles, and Mrs. Hodder tied her garter to the top of a tall fir for a mark. That's what he said. This storm took place in 1907.

Bobby had around two dozen horses to tend, big work animals every one. His job was to feed and water them and doctor them in the summertime when they weren't working. In the wintertime their own teamsters would look after them. There was plenty of grass growing handy Horwood's barn, so Bobby would just open the door in the early morning and out they would go, out onto Burnt Point where the school is now, in around Clarke's Brook, places like that. And in the evening he never had to round them up. No, all he had to do was sing out and they would come from wherever they were on the stretch gallop to get their few handfuls of oats for the night.

Well, one evening I was hanging around the empty barn, looking at this and that, not paying much heed, and I didn't hear Bobby leave. The next thing I knew there was a rumble and the barn started to shake. And I saw the horses coming. They came through the door on the trot, two abreast — and me standing fair in their way. I thought for sure I'd be trampled to death. Jumping behind a post I hung on with both arms while they went by, their iron shoes chewing into the wooden planks. My heart was in my mouth. But when he saw me Bobby just laughed. "Now, lad," he said, "you just watch and ye'll see how well Bobby's horses are trained." And sure enough, every horse knew his own stall. In no time at all everything was peaceful again and all I could hear was a scattered nicker and whinny as Bobby walked among them, and the sound of them chewing their oats. That, and the pounding of my heart. After that I made sure I was outside the barn when Bobby called his charges to supper.

When I was small a good many families in Gander Bay kept a horse or a pony, and so did we. His name was Beaver. Beaver was what you'd call a Newfoundland pony. He was five to six hundred pounds, about halfway in size between a Shetland and a regular horse, with a thick black coat that was shaggy in winter, and a knowing look in his eye. Beaver was a pet and a work horse both. At first I wasn't allowed to take him out by myself. But that was all right, for Father would harness him up to the sleigh on a fine Sunday afternoon in the winter and take Mother and me and my younger brothers, Harold and Aubrey, for a jaunt up the road or in the Portage Road. I can still see the coloured tassels on Beaver's collar bobbing, and hear the cheerful tinkle of the four brass bells — each a different size and sound — on his collar, and the thump of the clods of snow flying off his hooves and striking the front of the cutter.

By and by I was old enough to take him out by myself. I don't recall ever carting sawdust away from the mill with him, though this was a job that had to be done by wheelbarrow or horse-and-cart all summer while the mill was sawing. I do remember hauling feed for the foxes. In 1912 there were two fairly large fox ranches started in Gander Bay North. One was up by Arthur's (or Thistle's) Mill — which was what they called the Nova Scotia Steel Company sawmill. This was just above where the causeway comes ashore now, and Ned Francis was the ranchman or caretaker. The other was down by Burnt Point. There were some smaller fox farms too. All those hungry foxes in cages had to be fed, so the company that owned the ranches hired local men to supply rabbits in winter and fish in summer. Father, always quick to make a dollar, was one of the suppliers, and it was my job to go around with horse and cart and collect fox feed. I forget what they paid, but one load Beaver and I delivered counted out to two hundred rabbits. And many's the load of stinking flatfish, sculpins and salmon peps I hauled on hot summer days when I could have been swimming in the brook.

For a short time around 1915 Pop tried his hand at fox farming. Not only did he purchase a $50 share in the Garia Bay Fox and Trapping Company Limited of North Sydney, Nova Scotia, but he paid out $150 for a silver fox male, built four cages, and got three female cross foxes for breeder stock. This was how the mainland companies did it; they paid local trappers to trap live females and then caged them with imported silver fox studs. A prime silver fox pelt might be worth $1,500 or more, and in this way you could breed them hand over fist, whereas a good trapper might be fortunate to catch one or two in his lifetime. Or so the promoters said. For a while most every able-bodied man in the Bay left all other jobs to trap live foxes for these ranches. They would go in the woods in teams and ring cow bells in likely places and then smoke the poor things out of their hiding places and catch them in brin bags. So Pop set himself up, and one night when Father judged his three vixen to be in heat he slipped the male in and went away to plan the future expansion of his ranch. A day or so later Parson Gosse, the Church of England minister, making his rounds of the parish by motor boat, came to stay at the house. Proudly my father invited him to inspect his fox farm. Mother feared the smell might offend the Reverend, but Mr. Gosse said he didn't mind. What he minded more, I daresay, was the language Pop used when they looked in the foxes' master bedroom and saw the handsome male torn in three parts! Either each vixen wanted the silver fox for herself or else neither of them wanted him at all. At any rate, it was the end of our fox farming. On top of that the other fox ranches went bankrupt, along with the Garia Bay outfit. The share he had bought was in my name, but I'll never get to cash it now. But I remember that for a few years after that we had a red fox for a pet, a vixen that we called Purv. As tame as a dog, she used to run up and down the road and go in the shop and jump up on the counter. One time she had pups upstairs in our house. We found out when Mother caught her taking cakes of hard bread from the pantry to carry up to them.

Even though fox farming failed in Gander Bay as in many other places, there was plenty else for Beaver and me to do. There was water to haul in barrels from the brook winter and summer, and slabs to bring from the mill for firewood. Sometimes we would be sent on an errand. On one of those errands Beaver and I had a falling out. Well, it was me that fell out — of the sleigh. This happened one winter during the First World War, when pitprops were in strong demand for the coal mines of Britain and Father got a contract from Uriah Freake of Lewisporte to supply 1,500 cords, to be picked up by ship the following spring. He built a camp on the north side of Clarke's Pond and hired a crew of twenty men, mostly from Tilting Harbour (now Tilting) on Fogo Island. Broaders is one surname I recall — two brothers, big strapping men. Joe Edwards and his wife cooked for that camp, and so did Tom Torraville from Victoria Cove, and his wife. So perhaps my father was in this business more than one winter. Some of the timber they cut had been killed in the fire of 1912.

Anyway, one morning Dad told me the cook was out of lard and would I mind harnessing Beaver and taking a few pails in to him. Would I mind! It was the first time I was ever allowed to take him in the woods that far — over two miles. I was determined to make a good job of it. "And dress warm now," he said as he handed me the four five-pound pails with their wire handles. "It'll be nippy today out on the pond." Up the road we trotted that bright January morning, harness bells jingling, snow flying, clouds of steam coming from Beaver's nostrils. In past Jim Allen's, where the Portage Road takes to the woods, up Big Hill and over Cow House Brook where great-great-grandmother Eliza Gillingham killed the wolf, then easterly to Clarke's Pond we went. In less than an hour we reached the shore and struck out across the ice for the camp on the far side. In the morning sun the ice shone like gun metal, with here and there a ribbon of hardpacked snow. My father was right, the wind cut like a knife. Beaver felt it too and quickened his pace to a fast trot. In fact, the closer he got to the camp, the faster he went. I was having a hard time keeping the sleigh straight on the glare ice when all of a sudden it slewed sideways, struck a drift and capsized, sending me and the lard tins tumbling across the ice. I sung out for Beaver to stop till I was hoarse, but he never looked back. He just trotted on with the empty sleigh — which righted itself with the strain on the shafts — until he was up the bank and out of sight in the woods. Seeing him arrive without a driver, Tom the cook got quite a start. But when I came in camp a while later, red in the face and lugging those heavy lard tins with the wire handles cutting into my fingers that were scrammed with the cold, Tom had a good laugh. For a while I was so crooked at Beaver that I wanted to cut an alder switch and beat him, but Tom said it was no use now and quieted me down with a ginger bun and some hot tea.

Another time Dad had sent my cousin Hezekiah Gillingham and me down to Gander Stores to fetch some flour and sugar. Because the ice was getting soft we were charged to stay on the road. But Hezekiah, six years older than me, was very strong-willed — he once threatened to chop off his big toe if he didn't get his way, and then did so — and decided to cut across the cove and see how fast his father's horse could go on the level ice. When we came abreast of Clarke's Brook the horse fell in. One minute we were flying along with Hezekiah slapping the reins to make him go faster and me riding on the horse's back holding on to the hames, and the next minute I felt myself falling, and I turned a complete somersault over the horse's head and landed in front of him on my backside. Turning around, I saw him in the water up to his neck, pawing with his front hooves, trying to get up on the ice, with the sleigh sinking behind him and my cousin jumping off. I grabbed the reins just as the horse

27

found bottom — for we were handy shore — and after we got the sleigh unhitched and hauled back to safety we managed, with much scoting and swearing, to get him up on solid ice. If the tide had been higher I doubt if we could have saved him. And luckily we were not far from Uncle John's barn. With a heavy blanket and some warm mash we soon had the horse as good as new.

The fastest thing that ever we saw in Gander Bay in those days was Doff Gillingham's tame caribou. Doff — his real name was Theophilus — was Hezekiah's younger brother. In 1923 Hezekiah took sick with pneumonia and died. It was in January and he was only twenty-four. I sat by his bed as he was dying. Doff was so heartbroken that their father John (my mother's half-brother) brought home a little doe caribou for him when he came back from the lumberwoods. Uncle John had been cutting pulp for the Anglo-Newfoundland Development Company up to Red Indian Lake that winter. One day in the spring they frightened a small herd of caribou crossing the lake, stampeding them so that some fell through the rotten ice. This calf got left behind, so Uncle John brought her home with him on the train from Millertown and down the River. They put her out in the hayfield tied to a long rope on a stake so she wouldn't jump the fence. Doff named her Nan, and she took to him right away. He would stand for hours by the fence, rubbing her neck and scratching her forehead, passing her bits of moldow or old man's beard off the fir trees. I helped pick a good many brin bagsfull of it for her; she liked it better than grass.

Another thing she liked very well was homemade soap. We found that out one day when Aunt Lizzie Gillingham — she was Uncle John's oldest daughter, who died in her nineties at Barr'd Islands in the early 1980s — came after us shouting that we had swiped a whole batch of soap she had put out on the doorstep to cool. Turned out it was Nan. Pulling out her stake, she had jumped the fence and finished off those cakes in short order.

By fall Nan was almost full-grown. At that time her shoulders came just about to a man's waist and her coat was thick and gray. Around her neck and shoulders she was nearly white. She would follow Doff around like a dog. One day he sawed two discs from a big pine log, made a two-wheeled cart or sulky, and harnessed her to it. Training Nan to haul this rig took patience, but after a spell he did it. And could she go! She was just like a racehorse. She didn't have much grace; her big hooves went every which way when she ran. But we didn't care. We vied for the privilege of driving her, lining up to take turns. One day when Doff was driving her full tilt she came to a fork in the road — it was just before you came

28

to the big split rock below Uncle Joe Gillingham's — and she never bothered to take the turn at all, but left the road and plowed into a thick droke of spruce until the cart brought up against a stump. The wheels flew off, and Doff was pitched in a mud hole. Nan was a barrel of fun.

But she had a sad ending. Perhaps it was the mating urge brought on by fall weather, but one night she broke her rope, jumped the five-foot fence and disappeared. Uncle John and Doff tracked her to the beach only to find she had waded in. They figured she must have decided to swim the Bay — which of course would be nothing for a caribou. So they gave her up for lost. For a long time Doff was broken-hearted.

In many parts of Newfoundland it was and is the custom to let horses roam free all summer, trusting them to come home by themselves in the fall. Now and then one or two will linger. Then you have to go with a halter and rope and search for them, hoping all the time they are not stogged in a marsh somewhere. A few weeks after Nan broke out, Eli Hillier and Eli Downer were in to Main Point Bog on the south side looking for their horses when they came across the track of a caribou. Knowing nothing of the tame one and excited by this discovery, they lost no time in trailing it. In their fathers' day it was nothing to meet large herds of deer, as they called them, migrating from the upper Gander to the Southern Neck. But forest fires and overhunting had changed all that.

A few hundred yards down the bog and there she was, browsing contentedly on the white caribou moss. Seeing her snap to attention and raise her flag, they expected her to run away. Instead she turned toward them and broke into a trot. The two were baffled but stood their ground. If she for some strange reason meant to attack, it was no use trying to outrun her. She had no antlers, but they knew how sharp a caribou's hooves were. All they had was an axe. Nan never slackened her pace until one of them brought the poll of the axe down on her head.

I never heard about this until one winter in the thirties when Harold and I logged in on Barry's Brook waters with one of the men involved. He said that when they found out they had killed Doff's pet caribou they felt so bad that they never told a soul about it in all those years. Telling us that night in camp seemed to ease his mind. I don't know whether Doff ever found out the rights of it or no — I know I never told him.

Once during the war Dad tried to tame a lynk or lynx for a pet. He was trapping — or trying to, I don't think he was much of a hand at it — with his brother-in-law Stanley when they found this female alive in a trap, held only by a couple of toes. My father never had a knapsack, only a small trunk for his dry clothes and the like. Somehow they managed to get this lynx into the trunk and brought it home. She was a pretty animal to look at, grey and fluffy as a snow cloud, with great big paws and tufted ears and faint tabby markings along her back. They put her in a cage, and if anyone so much as looked at her she would tiss and growl and strike at the wire with her talons. The prospects for taming her looked slim. For safety's sake Pop moved her to the store loft, where I fed and watered her every day and tried to make friends. One morning when I climbed up with her ration of salted bullbirds I found the cage empty. My first thought was to run out and bar the door behind me. The dim light from two cobwebby gable windows was hardly enough to see by. I decided to go tell my father. As I backed toward the door I happened to look up. There, right above me on the window ledge, sat our lynx. Only her eyes, glowing like small green lamps and tracking my every move, showed she was alive. I ran and got Uncle Stan and Dad. Using a small trap wired to a long pole they caught her by the paw. Not long after that she escaped again, this time for good.

I always liked ships. I liked them in my *Boy's Book of Ships and Trains* that Father bought me on one of his buying trips to St. John's, and I liked them even better in the water. In 1916, on one of those trips, he took me along. I don't remember much about the trip, but I think we must have gone by coastal boat. What I do remember is going aboard H.M.S. *Calypso* in St. John's harbour. For a twelve-year-old boy to be going aboard a real warship was like dying and going to heaven. She was tied up at a pier on the Southside and the public were invited to come aboard. She had eight gun ports down each side, with two jutting out so she could shoot fore and aft. An officer took you around and you could have a cup of tea. The *Calypso* was the biggest ship I was ever aboard, certainly bigger than the coastal boat *Dundee* that brought our mail and summer supplies every fortnight. *Calypso* had a fine square bow that slanted back as it went up, which was the style for battleships then. A three-masted ship with auxiliary steam power, she was made of steel, they told us, but looked like a wooden ship because her sides were sheathed in oak planking to withstand the ice. Inside there was lots of shiny brown teak and mahogany. And her saloon was full of flowers.

Father was on the *Dundee* when she was lost in 1919 at Noggin Cove Islands. He was coming home from another buying trip to St. John's. There was a snowstorm on, and he was playing cards in the saloon when the ship shuddered and stopped. Everyone that was standing fell down; everything that was loose went flying. Then she took a slow list and the seas started to pound her and the engines stopped. He often told us the story of how he and the other passengers and the crew went to the bow, climbed over the rail in an orderly fashion on the low side, and jumped to safety. So far as he knew, nobody was hurt. The only person to his knowledge that panicked was a Jewish peddler who, when she struck, ran off shouting "My pack, my pack!" Before dark a flotilla of boats came out from nearby Carmanville and Frederickton and Noggin Cove and ferried them in to Carmanville to await a relief vessel. They had it a lot easier than the people aboard her sister ship, the *Ethie*, which ran ashore at Martin's Point near Bonne Bay that same year. Still, the *Dundee* was a total loss. For years afterwards she was a rich source of salvage for the people around about. Her rusting hulk is still there today.

The only other ships I can recall from my childhood are the *Gullpool* and the *Willowpool*, which came from England to Gander Bay during the Great War to load pitprops. The pitprops that Father's crew cut had to be in lengths of six, nine and thirteen feet. In late April they drove them out Clarke's Brook and down to tidewater, then assembled them in a boom in the cove opposite the church. These two vessels, and one other which I forget, drew too much water to anchor off Clarke's Head and had to stay down in Tibby's Cove. Our boom was towed and loaded there. They were steamships from three to five thousand tons, registered in Hartlepool, England.

And of course there was Father's little schooner or bulley boat that he used for carrying lumber. I forget her name, but I know she was forty feet long and about eighteen tons. Some years later he bought a smaller boat, a former sailing yacht made over into a motor boat with a cabin and wheelhouse. My memory of her is a lot sharper. She was part of my school years. Yet the bulley boat must have made a big impression on me as a youngster. All my life I've thought how nice having a schooner would be.

School Days

When I started school in 1910 I went to a one-room white frame building thirty by forty feet that had also served as a chapel until that year. It stood near the mouth of Clarke's Brook on the east side where the Anglican Church is now. We had a small grassy playground on the Bay side which the sheep and goats kept close-cropped, and which later washed away in a big storm along with part of the cemetery. Leading from the playground was a path to the toilet or privy, a slant-roofed structure about six by eight feet built out over the landwash. It had two doors with a partition between, one side for girls and one for boys, and inside each was a closed-in seat running across the back end with a round hole and a cover with a handle. The tides flushed everything away.

The school as you entered had a porch on one end with a door in the centre. Inside the porch there was firewood piled on one side and on the other a row of hooks for hanging up coats. Inside the second door was the schoolroom itself, well-lit by windows along each wall. On the one side we could look out and see the Bay, and on the south side there was the brook, the road, then a meadow and the woods. Between the windows and at both ends of the room were kerosene lamps mounted high in metal brackets, each with a round mirror reflector.

In the centre of the room was a woodstove with the word "Giant" on the front and in bold letters on each side. It was about two feet long, fourteen inches high, and about a foot wide, with a damper that pulled out in front to control the draft. The stovepipe also had a damper. Every pupil had to bring a junk of wood a day to keep the school warm, and one of the older boys would be hired for a dollar a month to tend the stove and make sure the fire was lit every morning before the pupils came. The desks were arranged in two rows on either side of the stove, girls on one side, boys on the other, with two to a desk. The desk was just a plank to sit on and a sloping top with a groove near the top for our slate pencil and a little ridge at the bottom to keep our slates from sliding off. The slate was dark grey in colour, about a foot long by ten inches wide by one-eighth inch thick and framed in hardwood. There was a small length of round slate like a pencil for marking, and we used a rag and a small bottle of water for cleaning off old work. Sometimes in the morning the rags would be frozen stiff, and in such cold weather it was wise to empty the bottles before going home. Through the winter months the room never got really comfortable until recess time — half past ten. School took in at half past nine. We had one hour for dinner and a second fifteen-minute recess at quarter to three.

Across the far end of the room as you came in was a raised platform. It was eighteen inches or so high and I suppose eight feet from front to back, with two steps cut in the centre. This platform was for concerts and recitations. The rest of the time it held the teacher's desk — there was never any doubt who was in charge.

Except for Miss Payne, who had a withered hand, all my teachers were men. My first was Nelson Shave, son of Constable Shave of Fogo who used to come sometimes on court business with Magistrate Cook. Nelson Shave was a kind of cocky young fellow, tall and thin. He knew how to keep order and he was pretty good to learn from.

We studied reading, writing, arithmetic and grammar and that was about it. Our books were the *Royal Readers*, Primer to Six, published by Thomas Nelson and Sons. Spelling was a big part of the first few books, and the Primer was nothing but spelling. The way we were tested was to be stood in a row and asked to spell words. If you couldn't, someone who could would be moved in front of you. After that happened once or twice you made sure you knew it next time. Meanings came in the second book, along with more spelling of harder words, and after that came Useful Knowledge and Memory Verses. The latter were memorized a verse at a time until we knew the whole poem by heart. Some of the poems went on for many, many verses. I didn't mind; I had a good memory. I can still recite parts of "Lucy Gray" and "The Wreck of the Hesperus."

If we did something bad we were stood in the corner for a certain length of time. This was the punishment for the younger children. For the older ones who were supposed to know better there was the birch cane or the strap. The strap might be the teacher's belt, but usually it was a special piece of leather about two inches wide and eighteen inches long, worn shiny and dark with use. Two or three blows from it would turn a boy's hand quite red, and he would have a hard time holding back the tears. If a pupil was saucy or drew his hand back before the blow he would get still more, perhaps six or seven. A man teacher could strap harder than a woman teacher and we knew it. On rare occasions a big girl would be strapped. They nearly always cried, whereas most boys tried hard not to even flinch. Before we got through all six books, nearly all of us knew what a strap felt like, and those who didn't were considered teachers' pets.

Compared to Mother's early school days mine were pretty tame. As a young girl she went to the first teacher Gander Bay ever had, James Rowsell by name, an Englishman from Poole in Dorsetshire. I remember him, a tall, white-haired gentleman with a flowing Father Christmas beard, leaning on a cane. Often in his last years I would bring him a meal of trout or help him saw wood. In his younger days he worked as a bookkeeper for the fishing firm of Robert Slade and Company — Slade was also from Poole — and when Slades closed out their Fogo operations in the late 1800s Mr. Rowsell came to Clarke's Head to become the teacher, lay reader, postmaster, and Justice of the Peace.

Mother often told me stories about him. She said he was a very strict teacher. I imagine he had to be. Her step-brother John and her brother Hezekiah, and some others of her time, started school as young men. Sitting in a desk, learning how to read and write and cipher, was more or less a joke to them then, starting so late. They went as much for the sport as for an education. Yet some of them learned enough to take up trades in Phillip's Mill across the Bay and elsewhere that did him proud. Uncle Hezekiah must have done well at mathematics, for he later became tallyman in that mill and then sawyer in Father's mill. He also laid out the flume that brought the water to that mill, a quarter of a mile through the woods, over hill and hollow, dropping one inch in every four feet.

Although a sturdy birch rod was Mr. Rowsell's standby, when necessary he'd take more drastic measures. One day, said Mother, he grabbed the iron poker from the stove and whacked Louis Francis, the oldest of Tom's sons, about the shoulders with it. Louis went home and told his father. Tom challenged the teacher to a fist fight the next day. It rained, but they went ahead anyway. Mr. Rowsell won, and that was that.

The smell of rabbit stew always reminded Mother of school, she said, because whenever he felt like it Mr. Rowsell would send the older boys to the nearby woods to snare a rabbit. The next day when they brought one in he would skin it and cook it in school, then eat it at his desk.

He lived across the road from the little schoolhouse. He lived in poverty, for a teacher's salary in those days was very poor and there was likely no pension at all. It was said that he slept on a feather mattress with another feather mattress over him to keep warm. As often happened in my day with an old person who lived alone, he was aggravated very much by the young men and older boys. On dark nights they would torment him by rapping to his door and running away. Sometimes he would lie in wait with his old muzzle-loader crammed with two or three fingers of black powder and a handful of split peas. As the sleveens raced from his doorstep and up the road he would let fly at them in the dark. The noise and the spurt of yellow flame alone were enough to frighten the daylights out of them, but if he heard yelps of pain Mr. Rowsell would scramble after them, waving his gun and singing out, "Oho, ye nasty beggars, I caught you on the hop that time!" And they would leave him in peace for a spell. The worst thing they did was to drop a bag of gunpowder down his stovepipe one night when he was asleep. When he bent to light his fire the next morning the explosion blew the stove lids all over the kitchen and set his beard ablaze. It's a wonder he wasn't killed. As it was, he had to run and drive his head in the water barrel to douse the flames.

Once, after I helped him saw wood, he showed me his walking sticks. One was crooked and one was straight. The crooked one was just an ordinary cane for everyday use; I had seen him use it when he went to Pop's store for tobacco or provisions. The straight one, seen only on the Sabbath and other special occasions, was made of some dark tropical wood and was done out in little figures, leaves and berries and such, all very finely carved by hand.

James Rowsell was a pioneer in education for our area. Some of the men and women who came out of his small classes developed a respect for learning, and insisted that their youngsters go to school too. For close on twenty years he was schoolmaster to the families of the north side, the Francises, Gillinghams, Burseys, Harbins, Heads, Coates, Squires, Snows, and others. With his other duties he became an important figure, consulted on many matters. He was also a fine violin player. At dances or "times" he often played into the small hours. Always a bachelor, he lived a lonely life after he retired. That would be around 1904, because Gander Bay's second teacher, Emma Russell, came in 1905. She belonged to Fogo too. He was still alive in 1907, for he signed my cousin Stanley Gillingham's birth certificate that year. He outlived his longtime housekeeper, Harriet Gillingham — Walter George Gillingham's sister — and ended his days on the south side where Mr. and Mrs. Henry George Peckford of Harris Point took him in and cared for him until he died sometime during the Great War.

My own teachers after Nelson Shave I don't recall very well, but the routine was much the same. From fall to spring we attended the same school and sat in the same classroom. The only things that changed were our school books as we went from one *Royal Reader* to the next, the seating arrangements, and the teachers. Some of my classmates were Howard and Francis Thistle, Walter, Effie and Hezekiah Gillingham, Arthur Hoffe and Levi Harbin. Every day we had to bring our junk of wood from home, sometimes two if the weather was cold or the pile was getting low. Almost every November, usually on a storm of easterly wind and rain, the carey chicks (petrels) would come skimming in along the landwash and we would sling rocks at them, and always miss.

Our favourite boy's game was called 'Cat'. We played Cat on fine days spring and fall, at recess time and before and after school. We played it with two small holes in the ground about fifty feet apart, two bats, and two short sticks which took the place of balls. Each hole was home base to one team, and after batting a stick the players tried in turn to reach home without being struck out. Although Cat resembled baseball, I believe most of the rules came from cricket. It could be that Mr. Rowsell taught the game to our parents. In the wintertime we didn't play hockey, though we skated a lot. In those days the older girls and boys had homemade skates made from a file or other piece of hard metal reworked and set in a wooden stock, called stock skates. Stock skates were tied on with leather thongs threaded through holes in the wood. In later years some of us had store-bought skates, such as "Star" skates from Nova Scotia. Sometimes after a January thaw the whole bay would be a sheet of smooth ice and it was hard to go to school at all.

In April or May the Bay ice would gradually break up, leaving cakes or pans in all the coves. The cove by our school would have a good supply too and when the tide wasn high these would float and drift around in a most enticing way, making it hard to concentrate on anything else. We weren't allowed on them during recess time, but after school we would make for the pans and copy from one to the other behind a leader, back and forth, showing off for the girls and occasionally falling in. It was great sport. Girls sometimes ventured onto the bigger, safer pans; but copying was considered boy's work. Girls mostly played among the ballycators around the shore.

The chief pastime for girls was ring games. Ring games came into their own in the springtime, and the favourite place was some nice level spot like a bridge on the road. While bigger boys seldom took part, it was common for the younger ones to join in — or be dragged in. The games I remember best are 'The Farmer in the Dell' and 'King William'. In the first game someone chosen as the farmer would stand in the middle while those in the ring would circle around, singing:

36

The farmer in the dell, the farmer in the dell,
Heigh-ho, the dairy-o, the farmer in the dell.

Then they would sing, still circling with hands joined:

The farmer takes a wife, the farmer takes a wife,
Heigh-ho, the dairy-o, the farmer takes a wife.

The person in the middle would pick a 'wife', and the game would go on as the wife took a child, the child took a dog, the dog took a cat, and so on. At the end it went,

The cheese stands alone, the cheese stands alone,
Heigh-ho, the dairy-o, the cheese stands alone.

The other ring game started out much the same way, with someone in the centre and the rest circling as they sang:

King William was King George's son,
All the royal race is won;
On his breast a star he wore
Pointing to the governor's door.

Come choose to the east,
Come choose to the west;
Choose the very one you love best.
If she's not there to take your part,
Choose another one with all your heart.

As soon as the centre person chose someone from the ring that person would join him or her and they would kneel down, as the song went on:

Down on this carpet you must kneel,
As the grass grows in the field;
Kiss your partner, kiss her sweet;
You may rise upon your feet.

Then the new person would choose a partner from the ring, and so on until all had a turn, or until the recess bell rang. These were old games our parents and grandparents had played long before.

At age eleven or twelve I graduated from *Royal Reader* Number Six and launched into higher studies. I don't recall much about the books we had, but I seem to recollect that the first year was called Primary, the second Preliminary, and the third Intermediate. The three of them were more or less equivalent to junior high school I suppose. It was in those grades that, for one reason and another, many of my classmates dropped out: the boys to work in the lumberwoods, the girls to get married or to "go in service." Those who got married at fifteen or so usually had no

37

choice because they were "in the family way" and the child's father was expected to look after them. To go in service meant to get a job as a servant girl with some family and learn housekeeping skills. It was good training, and some from very humble homes went on to become expert housekeepers whose services were in demand in places like St. John's, Toronto, and New York. In those days to go in service with the right family was considered a step up in the world, especially if a girl was not doing well at school. About the only other careers open to an outport girl of that day seemed to be teaching and nursing, or perhaps telegraphy.

For a boy it was the lumberwoods or the fishing boat or, if he had some education, a life in business or teaching. Going into business meant getting on as a junior clerk with some lumbering or fishing firm and working your way up. The big G.L. Phillips sawmill at Georges Point where my Uncle Hezekiah had been tallyman was already shut down when we were in school. As I got older I often helped Father in the shop. It didn't appeal to me.

What did appeal to me was being a soldier. In 1917 my buddy Francis Thistle and I tried to enlist. He was sixteen; I had just turned fourteen. It was Francis's idea. His brother Howard had joined up two years before, along with Ken Blake from the south side. Howard and Ken sent home postcards of themselves in uniform, and that was enough. We copied down the address of the recruitment office from a war poster in the post office and sent away for the forms. As soon as we got them we filled them out — faking our ages — and rushed them back. At that time all winter mail travelled overland by horse and sleigh every fortnight to and from Boyd's Cove. We knew it would take a good while to hear back. The first week we hardly slept. A month later Francis got accepted — but no letter for me. It turned out that my application never left the post office. My father found out about it and stopped it. But Francis, who was big for his age, soon went overseas. Somewhere in France, on the thirtieth day of April 1917, he was killed in action and Howard and Ken came home without him.

About this time I started going to dances, and to fancy myself a lady's man. Pride goeth before a fall! I'll always remember one particular dance, the one that climaxed the annual parade and tea of our local Orange Association in March month. It was the year I was sixteen. The tea was held in the Orange Hall and consisted of a fine supper of salt beef and cabbage, potatoes, carrots and turnips, served on long tables in the lamplight, with strong tea to wash down large helpings of cake and pie. After the women of the community had served everybody, the tables and chairs were hauled out of the way so the dancing could begin. Pretty soon the lamps were jiggling in their brackets to the beat of the accordian and the fiddle, while the dancers stepped through the "Virginia Reel" or "The Lancers" or "Mussels in the Corner." It was the first time I had been allowed to stay out after midnight, and I was having a grand time.

Part of the reason for my new freedom was that Father was away. That afternoon he had harnessed up the horse and left for Noggin Cove, fifteen miles away toward Carmanville, to bring back the new servant girl. Mother had to have a new maid because the previous one had got married to a soldier some months before. Dad had arrived back with the girl around dark, and as the weather was cold Mother decided to put her in the room over the kitchen, the warmest room in the house and the room where my brother Harold and I were sleeping together that winter.

I got home around 4:00 a.m., unaware of the new arrangement. With the fire out in the kitchen stove and the house cold, I didn't bother to light the lamp but slipped upstairs and into bed in my longjohns in the dark. Now my brother Harold was, at this time, ten years old and much shorter than I. But this person in bed with me was as tall as I. I put out my hand and felt long silky hair. At that moment a girl's voice began to plead "No, no, no," very softly. I jumped out of bed and took off upstairs to the attic where I found Harold sleeping. That morning I was late coming downstairs. The strange girl was sitting at the table. "Brett," said my mother, "I'd like you to meet our new servant girl, Jessie Collins." Blushing, we said hello, and that was that. She was kind enough not to tell Mother.

Jessie was pretty with dark hair and a quiet manner. She later married Aquila Warrick of Fogo. When by chance I bumped into her in 1977 I asked if she remembered the episode. "Indeed I do," she said, and we had a good laugh.

That fall there was no teacher in Clarke's Head. At least I think there wasn't because my parents shipped me off to Carmanville, about twenty miles to the east, to board at the home of Mr. and Mrs. Alfred Hicks for the winter. I was in what today would be called grade ten. My teacher there was a Miss White, a prim woman in her mid-thirties and rather strict. Carmanville was at that time mostly Methodist, and I soon found that my new interest in dancing would have to be shelved. To ease the boredom, myself and Harold Parsons and Ralph Russell made up a song called "The Girls of Carmanville." Sung to the tune of "The Star of Logy Bay," it remarked about each girl in turn, according to where she lived around the harbour. Here's a sample:

And now it's for Miss Bessie
I think I'll make a start;
When she combines with other girls
Sure she can do her part.

When they do get together
All kinds of things they'll say;
May the heavens above protect our love,
She's the star of Rocky Bay.

In spite of Ralph's part in writing this, Bessie Ellsworth later married him.

Around this time Dad bought a motor boat. He and Uncle Stan had gone up to Exploits — where my maternal grandmother Sarah Ann Gillingham had family — and brought back this lovely thirty-two-foot former sailing yacht, a sixty-mile trip through the Bay of Exploits to his wharf. He bought her from Jonathan Burtt there and named her the *Matilda* after Mother's middle name. The *Matilda* had a forecastle for sleeping, a wheelhouse against the weather, and a seven horsepower Mianus make-and-break engine to push her along. She soon became Dad's pride and joy, taking the place of the schooner in his affections. And the thing he was most proud of was her mast.

That spring my parents decided to come and visit me before exams. To my surprise they came in the *Matilda*, which Dad had given a fresh coat of white paint. He had also varnished the slender spar so that its wood shone like new. As soon as they were on the wharf I introduced my companion Flossie Chaulk and persuaded Dad to let me take her for a spin around Carmanville Arm while they caught up on the news with Mr. and Mrs. Hicks. Away we went in the motor boat, Flossie and me, with a bunch of our chums watching on the wharf. And we were having a wonderful time until I decided to show off. We were steaming back toward the wharf — one of those wharves built of separate, rock-filled piers — and naturally I had her opened out. And I got the idea to come at the wharf full speed and then at the last minute shut off the engine and throw her in reverse. This I had seen my Uncle Stan do many times.

It was a trait of those old make-and-break marine engines — which had no spark plug, only two points controlled by a rocker device that worked off the water pump lever — that if after you shut off the spark you turned it back on just as the engine died, you could catch the flywheel on the rebound and she would start in reverse. It looked easy when my uncle did it. I told Flossie, and as we bore down on the wharf with its small crowd of spectators, I flipped the off switch, at the same time watching the flywheel to gauge the moment. The moment never came. The Mianus kept put-putting at full throttle. I looked up. The wharf loomed towards us. Father was waving his arms. Mother had her hands over her mouth. Flossie's eyes were like saucers.

"Flossie, duck!" I shouted, and hove the tiller hard to port. With only a boatlength to spare the *Matilda* swerved in time to miss the pier itself. As we shot under the decking of the wharf the onlookers overhead cheered. The racket of the engine in that dark, confined space between the two piers was so deafening that I didn't hear the crash. But when we came out into the sunshine the *Matilda* looked different. Her lovely spar was smashed, its top trailing by the shrouds in the water. And the sad part was that this was a special mast made to fold down for going under low bridges and wharves. Father sputtered and got red in the face and asked when I planned to grow up. Mother pointed out that nobody was hurt and that he could get a new mast. The Hicks thought it was all in a day's fun. But Flossie didn't think much of me after that.

When exams came in June I went to board for a week or so with Enos Hicks who lived closer to the school where the Provincial examinations were being held that year. Enos was a fisherman who operated a cod trap between Carmanville and Change Islands. He had two sons about my age, Frank and Cyril, and Frank used to take the fits — what they call epilepsy today. Enos wouldn't risk him in the fishing boat.

One day that spring Frank and I went trouting along the shore, me in my long rubbers and Frank on a big rock he had jumped onto. We were about fifty yards apart, fishing away, not saying much. Then I caught a trout, a nice sea trout. I got it ashore, baited my hook again, and had turned around to wade out, when all of a sudden I noticed Frank was gone. Dropping my pole, I waded as fast as I could toward the rock, the water up to my waist and the going slow, and as I came abreast of it I saw his pole floating. I knew he must be handy, but there was just enough breeze to ruffle the water's surface so I couldn't see bottom. I was just climbing up on the rock to get a better look when he burst out of the water, coughing and thrashing, a few yards away and then went under again. A few minutes later I had him on the beach, working the water out of him over a round boulder and trying to keep him from rolling into the bay again or hurting himself, and he moaned and gnashed his teeth and foamed at the mouth the whole time. It was the first time I had ever seen someone in an epileptic seizure. I was frightened and didn't know what to do. After a while he lay still, breathing normally as if in a deep sleep. Covering him with my jacket, I ran and got his mother and we brought him safely home.

Except for this incident and breaking the *Matilda*'s mast I enjoyed my time in Carmanville. It was my first trip away from home to stay with another family. The Hicks were good, God-fearing Methodist people who treated me like a son. Among the young people I made some good and lasting friendships. And in August when my marks came I found that I had passed in all subjects — which helped my relations with Dad when it came time to help him step the new mast.

41

My last year of school was in St. John's. Dad had it in his mind for me to go into business or some profession — not to hang around Gander Bay and be a trapper and woodsman like Uncle Stanley. He was bound and determined to give me all the education he could afford. And in those days if you were a Church of England businessman from the outports the choice of school was simple: Bishop Feild College. So to Bishop Feild I went in the fall of 1921.

Uncle Stan took me upriver to the train. Our two days of poling and paddling gave me time to think. Would I ever come back to the River? Much as I liked reading and learning, there was no place I would rather be. Paddling up Fourth Pond on our second morning, with the aps and birch bright yellow against the dark spruce on either side and the sun lighting up Mount Peyton all blue in the distance, I got a lump in my throat. I decided then and there that wherever I went, I would always come back.

The night trip from Glenwood to St. John's by train would have been more exciting if I could have stayed awake. I had barely waved goodbye to my uncle and found my berth than I dropped off to sleep. I was dead tired. and besides, in Glenwood Ellen and Jim John had stuffed me with one last meal of fresh venison and potatoes and gravy. The long ride down along Gander Lake to Gambo, and beyond that to Port Blandford, Clarenville and Come-by-Chance, was lost on me. All I can mind of that part of the trip is the sound of a lonesome mouth organ somewhere, the sound rising and falling with the clacking of the wheels and the chuffing of the engine, and now and then the long sad wail of the whistle far up ahead.

The first thing I saw next morning was the Brigus barrens in the fog. My first thought was, it's even bleaker than Fogo. Mount Pearl and the Waterford River made up for it though, with their green farms dotted with cows and sheep and haystacks — the first real farmland I ever saw. Then ahead, rising in the glare of the morning sun as I stood in the brake between two cars and leaned out, I saw Signal Hill with its tower. The harbour as we drew nearer bristled with the masts of schooners and the funnels of steamships. The next thing I knew we were swallowed up in the noise and confusion of the big railway station, and then I was in a taxi climbing the steep grimy streets to the Upper Levels.

The college consisted of a large old building facing Colonial Street near Bannerman Park and a new piece almost as big added on. The new piece was called Feild Hall and had been built three years before to relieve the crowding in the Colonial Street building, where even the gymnasium and assembly hall had been converted into classrooms. Feild Hall had separate classrooms for each grade, a science room, an assembly hall, a mess hall and a dormitory. Everything was the very best — though the buildings were all of wood and there was some fear of fire. The College also had a manual training department where a boy could learn carpentry, mechanics or other skills.

The proper title of my grade was Grade Eleven and Junior Association. And to tell the truth I was a bit nervous, starting in. Bishop Feild College had a reputation as one of the best schools in the Dominion of Newfoundland, sending graduates to universities in England and the United States. To graduate you had to pass the next grade, which was called Associate of Arts, or "AA": I figured I'd be lucky to make the "JA" level. The other thing I wondered about was the town students. "Townies" or "Corner Boys" were said to be wonderful down on "Baymen." I soon found out that we baymen outnumbered the St. John's boys, and because most of them lived at home, the Hall was more or less outport territory.

The subjects we studied were arithmetic, geometry, algebra, history, geography and hygiene. The only teachers whose names I can recall are I.J. Sampson from Flat Islands, Bonavista Bay who taught geometry, and George House who taught algebra. Discipline was strict and there was plenty of homework to be done before lights-out at ten o'clock. We all ate together in a big dining hall. The dormitory overhead was as big as a barn, with rows of double bunks on either side and two coal stoves in the centre. Before we turned in each night Chaplain Pike led us in prayer, and every morning before breakfast it was to the ice-cold chapel for devotions. Since it didn't pay to heat the chapel for fifteen minutes a day, there were mornings that winter when our teeth chattered as we read and sang from the *Book of Common Prayer*. Saturday was our only night out, and we had to be back at eleven or find the doors locked. Headmaster R.R. Wood ran a tight ship.

Going to school in town wasn't so bad, once I got used to it. The only thing I had no use for was drill. Every spare minute seemed to be taken up with it. If the weather was fine we marched outside; if it was dirty we did it in the gym. It wouldn't have been so bad if we had had uniforms. Khaki puttees wrapped around our shins were all we had. We did have real rifles though — Lee Enfields left over from the War, I suppose. We got so we could handle them on parade like real soldiers. But the pleasure from that only stretched so far, and one sunny afternoon in October when the air was warm with the last heat of summer and the Southside Hills beckoned, I took someone's bicycle without permission and sneaked away berrypicking with a girl.

My punishment was swift. Directly I got back Headmaster Wood haled me into his office. First he gave me a tongue-banging, then he took me to detention. There the old man angrily pointed to a long rack of dirty rifles and told me to oil and clean them all. One of his flunkies brought me a rag, some string, and a bottle of gun oil, then sat near the door with arms folded to watch. I didn't mind; it was better than drill. I worked so hard, cutting the rag into neat patches, oiling them and hauling them through each barrel that the flunky got bored. First he yawned, then he got up and went to look out the window. Quickly I poured the rest of my oil down the barrel of the rifle I was working on.

"Sir," I said in a serious voice, "I'm out of oil here."

"Let me see that bottle," he said. He held it up to the light, frowned, then went for more, locking the door behind him. While he was gone I checked the windows, but they were locked. Before supper time I made him go for several more bottles of oil. I never did finish those rifles — though the ones I oiled were *very* well oiled — and for that I was kept in after school for a week. On top of that I had to apologize to the owner of the bike, even though the front wheel came off as I was speeding down a hill, causing me to skin both my palms on the hard gravel.

Ten o'clock was pretty early for young men to turn in and go to sleep. Sometimes we older boys ignored the curfew and stayed up to play poker. Poker was strictly forbidden at any time, so we were breaking two rules, which added to the excitement. Each bunk had an electric reading lamp and we all had a trunk or suitcase, so it didn't take much to rig up a playing table between two adjoining bunks. Because Headmaster Wood was known to prowl about after curfew, we always posted a lookout at the stairhead. A low whistle meant douse the light and dive for cover.

This night a bunch of us were playing on my bunk for money when we heard the whistle. Out went the light, all hands ran for their bunks, and I was left in the dark to pick up the cards and hide the money. By and by there came a heavy tread on the steps, then the beam of a flashlight darting from bunk to bunk. As luck would have it, our bunks were handy the stairs, and before I could hide the evidence the spotlight fell on me. Blind as a bat in that bright beam — it must have been a five-cell flashlight he had — I knew I was in for it.

"Well, well, well," came Headmaster Wood's sarcastic voice, "what have we here?"

"A game of penny poker, Sir," I said. No sense trying to hide what he could plainly see. The spotlight swept across my neighbours' bunks and beyond. The boys all looked dead to the world. One was even quietly snoring. I scooped up the rest of the money as the beam came to rest on me again.

"Saunders, you know very well we don't allow cards and gambling at the College. To wilfully and deliberately break the rules is a very serious matter." He went on more severely: "In fact, it may be grounds for expulsion, did you realize that?" I nodded. "But I am well aware," he said in a lower tone, "that you are not alone in this deed. If...."

"If you want me to squeal on my buddies to save my own skin, Sir, forget it," I said. I was getting vexed at him for making such a fuss about a little game of cards and I didn't care what I said. I figured he had it in for me over the rifles anyway.

That did it. I knew he was crooked because the light in his hand commenced to quiver. In a shaking voice he told me that I was a disgrace to the College, that I would be expelled forthwith, and that I should pack my bags in the morning for he would be wiring my parents to meet me at Lewisporte the following day. Wiring my parents was the last thing I wanted to happen, especially over something so small as this. I knew he meant business, so I hit him with the only thing I had. It was common knowledge around the school that Mr. Wood was seeing the matron of Feild Hall, a Mrs. Collie on the sly. I brought this up. There was a long silence. Then Headmaster Wood turned on his heel and went downstairs and never troubled me again.

In June — much to my surprise, though I had good marks — Bishop Feild graduated me. But all of a sudden I felt homesick, homesick and fed up with city life and books and rules and all the rest of it. With my Grade XI diploma in my suitcase, I was only a year away from university in England or elsewhere, yet the prospect of more school turned my stomach. I wanted to go home. Above all, I wanted to see the River.

Jim John
First Caribou Hunting Trip

It was Jim John, a full-blooded Micmac, who had taken me on my first real trip in the country, all the way up the Northwest, when I was fifteen. We came back two weeks later with three caribou. I went up a boy and came back a man, that's all there is to it. Oh, I knew a bit about boats and guns and the woods, like any Gander Bay boy, but I had never been up the River any farther than Third Pond. I had never seen a wild caribou, let alone hunted one. I thought I was strong, but I didn't know what strength was. I knew the meaning of the word patience, but that was all I knew until Jim took me in hand. All my life I had heard stories about "The Country," but until August 1919 it was only hearsay, only a faraway place like India. The difference was, I never wanted to go to India. Going in the country was always on my mind. If I'd known what Jim would put me through on that trip, I daresay I would have balked. For months I had pestered Mother and Dad to let me go with somebody, and when the chance came, I jumped at it.

In those days caribou season opened August the first and you could take three caribou — two stags and one doe — and sell the meat if you wanted to. One day that summer of 1919 Jim paddled down from Glenwood and came in the shop to see Father. I was helping behind the counter when he walked in, a heavyset, dark-skinned man of nearly fifty, about six feet tall, wearing a battered felt hat, a faded red shirt, wool pants with braces and sealskin leggings and moccasins. Except for a thin moustache and a few wispy hairs on his cheeks, his face was smooth. It wore a pleasant expression as if he found the world amusing. I knew right away it was Jim John, and at the first opportunity I followed him into Dad's office where they were talking. Jim was well known in central Newfoundland as a guide and hunter, and I soon realized that he had come to ask Dad if he wanted to buy some venison. As soon as Dad said yes, I waited my chance and asked Jim if I could go caribou hunting with him. Just like that. It was a brazen thing to do. Jim looked at me, then at Dad.

"I suppose it's all right," said Dad.

"Is he any good in boat?" said Jim, eyeing me doubtfully.

"Well, he spends enough time in them," said Dad. "And he loves the woods. He's just like his Uncle Stan that way."

"Very good then," laughed Jim, "He can come." So that was that.

Mother wasn't fussy about the idea and said so. Going so far from home for the first time was part of it — the dangers of the River and of hunting — but I think the worst part for her was the thought of her boy going off in the wilds with an Indian. It took some doing to persuade her. As soon as she consented, though, she worked with a will to get me ready. We only had that evening because Jim was going back to Glenwood early the next morning. When my bedroll and clothes were packed she took a flour bag and stuffed it with two or three buns of bread, a bottle of bakeapple jam carefully wrapped in two wool socks, a great wedge of cheese, some tea and sugar, a bag of dried caplin — food for a month. Although it was August and hot by times, she put in wool mitts, a heavy sweater and the like of that until I had to stop her and tie up the bag while I could still lift it. Dad gave me his .30-.30 Winchester half-magazine rifle and a box of shells. That night I hardly slept a wink.

The trip upriver to Glenwood took two days and I was in heaven. Jim had an eighteen-foot cedar canoe made in Old Town, Maine. It was the first I was ever in, and a beautiful thing it was. We paddled and poled the thirty miles. Happy as I was, sometimes I thought for sure my two arms would fall off. We paddled the steadies and poled or portaged the rattles, and even before we crossed The Gut and struck the tide at Dawson's Point my shoulders were aching. By the time we passed Summer Houses a mile or so upstream, the paddle felt like a lead weight. But Jim kept on paddling, never slacking, past The Works, through Bread and Cheese Steady (as we call it now), and on through Jim Brown's Rattle until we came to the foot of First Rattle. Long before that I had to take a spell a couple of times. He said nothing, didn't seem to mind. Poling, though a welcome change from paddling, was hard at first. You had to be able to keep your balance standing up in the canoe in loppy water — much different than fooling around with a punt in the cove. And you had to be able to find a good footing for the pole in places with a slippery bottom and strong tide without taking your eyes off where you were going. We got up First Rattle all right, though I nearly fell in once, leaning out too far. Jim just laughed. He was always laughing at one thing or another, a deep, hearty laugh that made you feel good just to hear it. Second Rattle was too rough, so we went up on the back of the main island. Another stint of poling brought us by the Burnt Stump and past The Boilers — two big boulders mostly under water — to Booming Point where First Pond begins. We turned right, went on for a piece, and swung in to a nice pebbly beach.

"Time for a mug-up," said Jim. Sweeter words I never heard. After tea and bread and molasses and caplin we lay on the beach for a nap. But I couldn't sleep. While Jim snored I sat up and listened to the wind rustling the leaves of the small aps and birch on the bank behind us, the distant sounds of salmon jumping and a kingfisher scolding. I sniffed deeply of the sweet breeze off the pond, and mused on what lay beyond the blue haze where the water met the land, and whether the overcast sky meant rain. After a while Jim stirred and got up, and soon we were on our way once more. Now the paddling was easier. There was hardly any current, just gliding along, mile after mile, up a long valley about a half mile wide between low hills of spruce and fir scarred on the north side by the fire three years before; just paddling and paddling. After four miles we came to a sort of narrows which widened into Second Pond.

By and by a breeze came up behind us. Using his blanket and a pole and some rope, Jim rigged a sail. We fairly skimmed along, and never had to paddle again until the River took a sharp turn to the northwest and we were back in the current, threading our way among big and small islands covered in aps and white birch with sometimes a tall pine that leaned out over the water. One or two of the pines had a bed of dry sticks in the top that Jim said was an eagle's nest, but the young were gone by now. In one place the run was so narrow we paddled right in under the trees, and when I clunked the paddle on the gunwale the sound echoed like inside a tunnel, and you could hear the breeze in the leaves overhead. So peaceful was it that when a family of black ducks skittered away, quacking loudly, they gave me a start.

Around duckish we pulled in to the shore of a large island opposite a brook with a low sandbar in front of it. "Cleaves Island," he said. "We camp here." I mentioned that it looked like a meadow and he told me that Ol' Cleaves, who used to drive wood for Phillips thirty years before, once had a drivers' camp here and grew potatoes and hay. He showed me some mouldering logs where the camp had been. No sooner had we landed and unloaded our stuff than he was pushing off again. Puzzled, I asked where he was going. "You pick up some wood now, like a good feller," he said, "and make in a little fire. Jim'll be back by and by." Kneeling in the canoe, he spun it around and was soon out of sight behind the bar. The sun burst out under a bank of low clouds behind me, flooding everything with a light like gold: the river with its flecks of white fob, the birches, the sandbar, the tall spruce on the far shore.

As dusk gathered, I busied myself with the fire and the kettle, wondering whether I could make it home if he never came back. While I stared at the river a dark form appeared and his canoe took shape. He stepped ashore and held up seven fine brook trout strung on a forked alder twig. "There's always a meal of trout in Miller's Brook," he said.

"But how, without a rod or line?" I asked, trying not to let on how glad I was to see him.

He grinned and took from his shirt pocket a spool of fine line with a hook baited in red worsted. "Fools 'em every time...long enough to catch a meal, anyways."

After cleaning the trout at water's edge he made a paste of clayey mud, packed each trout in it, scooped a hole alongside the campfire for them, and carefully covered them with the live coals. I figured our supper was ruined — and me famished. "You never had trout cooked this way?" he said. I shook my head. "Oh, you wait," he said, beaming, " 'tis the very best, better than frying or boiling." A half hour later we uncovered them. The mud peeled off cleanly with the skin, and I never tasted better trout. When the fire died down to coals and it was time to turn in, we felt a few drops of rain, so we hauled the canoe up on the bank and crawled under it. I was so tired I slept like a baby.

The next day we travelled much the same — poling and paddling, working our way past Joe Batt's Brook and Burnt Wood Rattle, sailing with the help of a blanket up Fourth Pond, boiling the kettle at Nut Brook before paddling up Bear Cliff Steadies into the last hard stretch of water at Long Rattle. From there we portaged over Big and Little Chutes and poled up Salmon Brook Rattle, arriving at Glenwood in time for a late supper at Jim's. His wife Ellen, a light-complexioned woman about five feet tall, treated me like one of the family. She served up steaming plates of salt beef and cabbage followed by raspberry jam on fresh bread. After the supper dishes were cleared and Jim was smoking his pipe, she sat down with us and talked. Her maiden name was Benoit, she said, and she told how in 1895, the year she and Jim got married, they had walked with some friends from their home in Bay D'Espoir to Glenwood where they planned to settle because of the railway. "On the way," she said, "between Little Gull River and Stag Brook on the Nor'west, one of the women went into labour and I had to be midwife to her. I told the men to leave us be for a while, and I jus' did what had to be done. The mother and baby came out of it just fine. We stayed there that night for to rest them, and the next day we dodged on. That's how we did things then."

"And that place is called Child Brook to this day," said Jim.

Ellen lit a pipe and puffed away too. "How far did you walk that time?" I asked.

"Oh, from Conne River, counting all the twists and turns, I s'pose over a hundred and forty miles," she said. "'Twas hard goin' too — plenty of bogs and thick spruce. We followed the caribou trails wherever we could." For a time she seemed lost in thought. "Ahh, but in those days I didn't mind."

We talked for a spell longer. They told me Jim's branch of the John family originally came from Nova Scotia. By this time I was so drowsy I could hardly keep my eyes open. "Show him to his bunk, Ellen," said Jim. "The boy's had a long day."

About three in the morning a noise like the end of the world brought me awake and to the open window. It was the eastbound freight train crossing the trestle over the River a few hundred yards away, her headlight reaching away down the shiny tracks, the sparks flying from her firebox, clouds of smoke and steam streaming behind. Watching all this, hearing that mournful whistle echo from the hills, I felt the cold shivers run up my back.

The next morning we were in luck — there was a light northwest wind. Gander Lake is all of thirty miles from west to east, and it doesn't take much of a breeze to build up a lop. A strong northeaster can keep you windbound for days. Starting at daylight and using the sail again, in less than two hours we reached King's Head. Then, instead of hugging the westerly shore we struck off across Careless Cove for the mouth of the Northwest. A while later Jim lifted his paddle to point out the high ridge of Mount Peyton to our right. From Fourth Pond he had done the same. Then it had reminded me of the tooth of a saw, blue in the distance. Now, looking at it side-on, I could see a high barren ridge of rock about ten miles away.

When the sun was halfway up the sky we entered the shallow, winding channels of the Guidy Islands that hid the mouth of the Northwest. For a while I thought we would never get clear of them. That evening we pulled in toward an island larger than the rest. "This is Long Angle Island," said Jim, stepping ashore and holding the canoe for me, "and I got a camp here; let's go see what shape she's in." We had paddled and poled all day and needed a stopping place soon. We found that a bear had torn a hole in the birch rind roof and tipped over the stove. "Too bad they can't learn to use the door, eh?" said Jim with a chuckle. But we had

50

supper there anyway, and as it was fine, bedded down for the night on the floor.

We spent the next night at Second Narrows where his nephew Billy John had a trapping camp. After a supper of rounders and bread and jam washed down with hot tea, we turned in early. Some time in the night I thought I heard rain on the roof, but other than that I was dead to the world again until I woke to the sounds of the Indian frying pancakes. "How much farther to the hunting grounds, Jim?" I asked while splashing my face in the River. "Will we get there today?"

"Oh, 'tis a nice piece yet," was all he said. I could see that the River was getting narrower and shallower. We had to pole most of the time now. And we hadn't seen a single caribou. To keep my mind off this and the ache in my shoulders I'd ask Jim the name of any place that stood out. He didn't mind. That's how I first learned them. It was the best geography lesson I ever had, because they were the names I had heard ever since I was a youngster: places like Greenwood Brook, Man O' War Island, Cooper's Brook and Dick's Angle; Webb's Island — where a log driver spent a day and a night in a tree when his camp was flooded out; the Plough Island, pointed like a ploughshare on the upstream end; the Devil's Ballast Bed above that, with boulders so thick together in some places that we had to wade the canoe; then the Doughboy Islands, shaped like dumplings because of the way the trees and bushes grew on them; and finally, late in the day, Gull Island opposite the mouth of Big Gull River. Here he said we would camp for the night. Joe Gillingham and Uncle John Gillingham and one of the Hodders had a nice wigwam there then.

But instead of landing on the island he steered for a sandbar in midstream, landed, and started to make camp. When I asked why, he simply said, "No flies." Afterwards, when I went ashore to pick up some deadwood for the fire, I found out what he meant. The nippers or mosquitoes there nearly ate me alive. It had rained a little and there was no wind — whatever the reason, the woods were humming with them. So we slept on the sand under the canoe with a light breeze on our faces all night, and the sounds of the River in our ears — and no flies.

The next morning I saw my first wild caribou. Waking at the crack of dawn, I was just rubbing the sleep out of my eyes when I looked out under the gunwale toward Big Gull and there it was, dodging along the far shore — just a small moving patch of gray and white, but I was positive. "Jim!" I whispered hoarsely. Jim's snoring stopped. The animal was climbing the bank now. I shook Jim's shoulder and he rose up on one elbow and squinted at me in the half-dark under the canoe. "Caribou!" I said proudly, pointing.

51

Jim looked. "Where?" he said. But it was gone. I tried to explain, but his head fell back and he started to snore again.

When he got up I persuaded him to paddle over and look for tracks and, sure enough, there in the wet sand were caribou prints. Even the little half-moon marks of the dew-claws showed, and the water was still welling up in the hollows. "Good," said Jim. "A doe, and she's likely headin' up Bear Brook. After a mugup we go same way, see what we can find." I felt proud. I was a caribou hunter! Little did I know.

With a good meal of baked trout under our belts we took our rifles, ammunition, grub bag and axe and walked two miles uphill along the south side of the brook through open spruce woods and alder beds. Every time he spotted a fresh print in the moss or a dark mound of droppings he would point it out. Leaving the brook trail, we walked without speaking. I had on knee rubbers but Jim wore skin boots — sealskin leggings handsewn to rawhide moccasins. Watching him move so easily along the trail, I felt clumsy. By and by we broke out into a high open bog. I could see scattered drokes of black spruce and small ponds the colour of tea. The yellow water lilies were just coming in blossom. But no sign of my doe.

"We're a bit too late," said Jim. "She's bedded down by now. But this is good crossin' place." He nodded toward a muddy trail worn down into the grass and moss. In spots it was over a foot deep. Farther on it merged with two more trails to become a regular road. "When I was a boy," said Jim, "Newfoundland was alive wit' caribou. But that damn railroad of Mr. Reid's, and them Englishman hunters pretty near wiped 'em out. Ol' Man Phillips and his son George did their share too. Phillips stocked his camps with venison; hunters like Millais took five, six big heads every trip, all the racks they could lug, but leave the meat to rot; the railway carries trainloads of meat and hides to St. John's to sell. Makes it tough for the likes o' we." It was the most I'd heard Jim John say on the whole trip, and the closest I'd seen him come to anger. "We wait here a spell," he concluded.

For a long time we sat still, rifles across our knees, watching the bog for any movement, waiting while the sun rose higher behind the tall spruce. But I was discontented. If this was caribou hunting, I would just as soon shoot rabbits or something. I was just going to say so when Jim leaned forward. Following his gaze, after a time I saw a moving grey spot against the far trees. The spot slowly took the form of a caribou, a small doe — whether my doe of the morning or no I couldn't make out — grazing and drifting toward us. The wind was in our faces, so it should be easy, said Jim. He would tell me when to fire. My heart was thumping loudly as I laid down on a hummock and steadied the .30-.30 with my elbows and tried to draw a bead.

"Now," said he, "she's plenty handy." I fired. The blast made my ears ring. The doe took a short run and froze in her tracks. While I levered another shell up, she hunched and made water. My palms felt damp and my scalp prickled. I fired again. She broke into a trot, away from us now. My next two shots must have gone completely wild, and then I heard Jim laughing. He laughed until the tears rolled down his cheeks, he slapped his thighs with merriment. That made me crooked. I asked him what was so funny. "Why," he said, still chuckling, "you no good to shoot. You'll never get a caribou that way!" and he laughed some more. I threw the rifle down and walked away. After a while he came and put his hand gently on my shoulder and said, "Young feller, do you know how far away that doe was when you fired?" I shook my head without facing him. "A good five hundred yards! That's a long piece for any rifle, let alone a .30-.30."

"That so? Then why tell me to fire?" I said.

"Jim was jus' havin' a bit of fun wit' you," he said. So we laughed and I felt better, and after a spell we dodged on along the trail. But it was getting too hot to walk. Our shirts were stuck to our backs. We came to this small brook, laid down our guns and splashed our faces and had a drink. We went a short ways farther and he left the trail and went off to one side about 150 feet to a shady spot and lay down on his back with his .38-55 leaned against a tree. "Time for a nap now," was all he said as he pulled his hat brim down over his eyes. I wanted to keep hunting, even in the heat, but there was nothing I could do. I would only get lost. So I lay down too and closed my eyes and listened to the sounds. A few birds twittered in the deep woods. A bumble bee droned by. Nippers whined around my ears. By and by I started to doze off.

It must have been two or three hours later when I heard Jim whisper one word. "Caribou," he said, and motioned for quiet. He rose and took his gun and stole away. He couldn't have walked more than a few yards toward the trail when there was a shot. I ran to find him standing over a large doe, her legs still jerking, bright blood spurting from her neck. How he knew a caribou was coming along that trail I'll never understand. Perhaps he wasn't really asleep, or perhaps he felt some vibration through the ground. At any rate, there she was, our first caribou. The greyness of the hair surprised me. It looked just the same as the bleached old juniper starrigans and weathered rock around us. The doe had one small antler. Jim flashed a broad grin.

After bleeding and paunching the carcass with his sheath knife, he took his axe and chopped it in half for carrying, dividing it at the third rib from the rump end and removing the head. The tongue he kept, wrapping it carefully in birch rind and putting it in our bag, which he

53

slung on his back. "Now we start to earn our money," he said. "You take the front half and I take this." With a grunt he hoisted his half over his head so that the hind quarters rested on his shoulders, and the back part hung down behind with the shanks sticking out in front. The load was so well balanced he could steady it with one hand while carrying his rifle in the other.

And now he was waiting for me to pick up the other half. Even though it was about thirty pounds lighter than his, and even though I managed to get it on my back, there was no way I could carry that load. When I let it fall for the second time, Jim told me I was no damned good, took his axe and cut the load in half, added one of the fore quarters to his load and started off, leaving me to catch up as best I could. I took the one quarter and we travelled the two miles back out to the River. It was now late afternoon.

When we topped the last ridge and looked down on the river where the canoe was, what should we see standing on the beach nearby but a small stag. With the load still on his back, Jim raised his rifle and shot it right there. A difficult shot too, downhill and into the sun. That load, with the bones and all like that, must have been close to 140 pounds. After that I never questioned anything he said.

"That's one we won't have to lug!" he shouted in high glee. "I hope I didn't strike the canoe!" That night we had a delicious feed of liver and onions and potatoes I will never forget.

The next day we took the canoe and went upstream about three miles to Rolling Falls and scouted around. And while we were eating our lunch at the mouth of Rolling Brook another stag came walking down the shore toward us. You talk about luck. And Jim shot that one. So now we had our limit, and I wouldn't get to shoot one after all. But I didn't care, I was under age anyway, and I couldn't blame Jim for not taking a chance when the caribou were coming right to us like that. It was certainly better than lugging the meat two or three miles on our backs through the woods.

This happened on a Saturday. By the time we got the stag cleaned up it would be too late to leave for home that day. The day being hot, Jim said he was worried our other meat would go bad, even though it was in the shade and hung up. "If the damn fish flies get into it we'll have maggoty venison," he said. While he honed his knife on a soft piece of blue slate in preparation for paunching, he instructed me to walk back to camp and wash and smoke the meat. "Hang it up on a scaffold of spruce poles," he said. "Make it like a woodhorse" — he sketched one in the sand with a twig — "then make in a smokey fire from green var boughs and moldow off the trees." So I did as I was told, tending the fire and flicking the bluebottle flies off the meat with a willow switch and moving around to keep the smoke out of my eyes.

I must have dozed off, because the next thing I knew something was poking my shoulder. I looked and there was a tall Indian standing over me, getting ready to give me another thump with the butt of a shotgun. I rolled away pretty quick and scrambled to my feet. "Who're you?" I asked, trying to hide my fright.

"Stride," he said. "Abe Stride." I asked him what he was doing there, without a canoe or anything. He motioned upriver with the gun. "Walkin' home to Conne River from Badger," he said. "Me and my brother Ben. He waved the gun toward the west shore and I saw another young Indian sitting on a rock. They were in their mid-twenties and both of them wore crumpled felt hats and red-checked shirts and torn khaki pants. I wondered what they wanted. "Where's Jim?" said Abe. "Seen his canoe the other day coming up."

"Up to Rolling Falls paunching a stag," I said.

"You got any grub?" he said. "Ben and me is kinda hungry. We shot a nice doe down to the Ballast Bed this morning, but we got no bread. You give us some bread, you and Jim can have the meat. It's hung up in a tree on the north side."

"I s'pose Jim won't mind," I said. Then I remembered the extra loaves Mother had given me. I gave him one of them and a handful of caplin and he was tickled. Wading slowly back across the shallows he joined the other man and soon they were out of sight in the woods, on the long trail to Bay D'Espoir.

In those days it was nothing for the Micmac people to walk across from Bay D'Espoir to Glenwood or some other place on the northeast coast or on the railway. I remember one May morning in the 1940s when Howard Thistle and I were muskrat trapping on the Northwest. Tending my traps alone, I heard someone whistling. First I thought it was Howard, but then I saw this young Micmac walking towards me in his shirtsleeves, no pack or anything, whittling an alder with a pocket knife.

"Where you headed?" I asked after we said hello.

"Oh, over there," he said, pointing north.

"Where from?" I said, sure he must be lost.

"Back there," he said, pointing up Little Gull River. Then he dodged on, whistling to himself as contented as could be. What he lived on during that four- or five-day journey I don't know, just marshberries and a scattered trout, I suppose. In those days Little Gull was always the route the Indians used on their way to and from Bay D'Espoir. Later I learned this was Ellen's nephew going to Glenwood to pay her a visit.

55

When Jim returned I told him about the Strides, and how Ben had stayed on shore. "Oh, that's Ben all right," he laughed, "and I know why he wouldn't come out. The bugger owes me $10 since last year now, and he was afeared I might make him pay up!" He explained that they had gone on the Badger Drive that spring and stayed to cut pulp. But he couldn't figure why they were going home so soon. Later we found out their camp was going to be quarantined for typhoid.

Around duckish, as we sat watching the sun sink behind the islands, a red canoe with two men aboard appeared downstream and drew in to shore on the north side. It so happened they were Henry George Gillingham and Fred Hurley from Gander Bay, on their way to Little Gull for venison. After they got their tent up and cut some boughs to sleep on they had a cup of tea with us. Fred was dark and short with the stout frame and rolling gait of a sailor. A grey fedora hat was clamped tight on his head. They said he never took it off, even in bed. He was a top river driver who worked with Uncle Stan and other Gander Bay men every spring. Henry George was the talkative one, entertaining us far into the night with jokes and tales of tricks he had played.

Sunday morning Jim decided to go back upriver with them as far as the Falls, for Henry George bet five dollars he couldn't pole them. It was a well-nigh impossible feat that Jim was said to have performed when he was younger. Rolling Falls is not really a waterfall, but a series of drops and ledges with standing waves two and three feet high, and very treacherous that time of year. Henry George knew he himself couldn't do it, but he tried it anyway just for sport, falling back each time and almost capsizing his canoe.

Jim took his place at the foot of the Falls. The canoe shot forward out of the steady water along shore, it seemed to dance over the lower waves like a leaf; his pole flew forward and back like a weaver's shuttle, driving the boat higher and higher up the foaming ledges to the very lip — and there it hung for I don't know how long while we clapped and sung out encouragement and his pole quivered with the strain. At last he fell back and came safely to shore, his shirt soaked with spray and his face one broad grin. "That's how it is when a feller gets old," he said to me, wiping the sweat from his forehead with his shirtsleeve. "It costs him money too." But Henry George wouldn't take the money, saying it was all in fun, and with that they left for Little Gull and we headed back downstream to pack for the trip home.

Running with the tide for the first time in a week, I felt a slight longing for Clarke's Head. It seemed we had been away a long time, that I was five years older. The feeling soon passed. I looked at Gull Island and the mouth of Big Gull, the low rolling hills yellow with birch and aps amid the dark spruce, and vowed I'd be back.

Right after having a bite to eat we stowed the venison and gear and started downriver. With no rain for a week, the River was several inches lower than when we came up. And even though thunderheads were building up, the coming rain would take effect too late to do us much good. Now I understood why we had travelled so light. Even so, we only had three inches of freeboard. Any rough water on the Lake could swamp us. For the rest of that day we hauled and portaged most of the time. But it was all downhill now, and by dark we had reached Billy John's camp at Second Narrows. That night it rained torrents.

The next day, the Lake being civil, we got to Glenwood before supper. Right afterward we left for the Bay. The load was a bit lighter now because Jim had taken out a fore quarter for his family and friends. The lower Gander was also pretty shallow, since the rain on the Northwest could not take effect until the Lake had risen. We had to portage Big and Little Chutes again, and the same with First Rattle, the boat was loaded so deep.

It was a funny thing. I never felt real homesick until we passed The Works. All of a sudden I wanted very much to see my parents. Rounding the wide bend at Summer Houses, I kept craning my neck for the first glimpse of Clarke's Head. One by one the houses came into view, then the big Horwood Lumber Company store and barn on Burnt Point, the school, the white church, our mill, and our house. When we drew in to the wharf there was nobody around and I was glad. I wanted to savour it alone for a few minutes. Everything — the grey-blue sand and pebbles on the beach, the smell of the mud-flats and the wet lumber, the look of the white picket fences and the houses behind — seemed the same; yet everything seemed different.

Soon my brothers Harold and Aubrey saw the canoe and came running down, then raced off to tell Mother. I can't mind much of what happened next, except that Mother fussed over Jim and me, stuffing us with fresh pie and tea, and bringing me a change of clothes and rushing me off upstairs to wash because she said I stank of wood smoke and my hands were grimy. Jim regarded all this as a big joke on me; but I had been in The Country at last, and I didn't care. Dad was delighted to hear we had bagged our limit of caribou and immediately made plans for selling it. Mother confided later that she had never expected to see me alive again, that for the first few nights after we left she had cried herself to sleep.

When Jim left for home the next day, having been paid for his portion of the meat, I wished I was going back with him. Nobody could have taught me as much in a week as this fine man did, especially at that stage of my life. Being the oldest in our family, I was used to having my own way too much. By taking me down a few pegs at first, then sharing his knowledge with a mixture of roughness and humour, he gave me exactly what I needed. And he bonded me to the River for life.

My father figured he could sell the meat in Fogo to a merchant named William Furze who had a large icehouse. Fogo Island had no native caribou then — though they have been introduced there since — and the people were generally eager for a taste of venison. Mr. Furze answered Dad's telegram the same day with "Will Take All You Can Supply." It so happened that Fred Hurley and Henry George Gillingham also got back that evening, each with meat to sell. It was decided to make one shipment of it, fifteen quarters in all, and that Fred and Uncle Stan would leave the next morning in the motor boat. The going price was fifteen cents a pound and they were pretty sure the two saltfish firms in Fogo would buy some as well.

"School's still a week away, so you might as well go too," said my father. "You've seen The Country; now you can see how the Fogo Jumpers live. And if you're lucky you might even get stop in Change Islands, where the real fishermen be." Change Islands was his birthplace, and I knew he wished he was coming too. It surprised me because he was mostly gruff and business-like, with no time for anything but work. But he was wonderful fond of the sea and boats.

The good weather held, and early the next morning we were on our way down the Bay with the meat packed in brin bags stowed under a tarp on the roof of the cabin where the breeze would keep it cool. Below, we had a few armloads of dry wood and some splits and birch rind for the little stove, enough grub and fresh water for a few days, and about five gallons of gasoline. Soon after we left the wharf Uncle Stan gave me the wheel, saying it was about time I learned the way to Fogo. Fred tended the engine and checked the punt now and then as it rode our wake on a long rope, swinging now to one side, now to the other. "Keep her off the Point, Skipper," said my uncle, laying his hand over mine and turning the wheel to starboard. "We don't want to run over Uncle John's salmon nets now, do we?" Except for his blue eyes, I fancied his high cheek bones made him look like an Indian; but he didn't have Jim's height or dark skin. Jim would be somewhere near First or maybe Second Pond now, perhaps using his blanket for a sail.

After we had passed Tibby's Point with Victoria Cove tucked behind it, the Bay widened out and I forgot the River. Gander Bay Island loomed — the same island you can barely see from Clarke's Head, but now tall with rugged reddish cliffs falling sheer to the sea and dark woods on top. From there on everything was new to me. I asked Uncle Stan to take back the wheel, but he said he'd tell me what to do. "Just hold her steady on the Dog Bay Islands," he said, and so I did.

He showed me how to avoid the shoals of Bonds Island Tickle by slipping through the gap between the middle and south islands, how with a westerly wind you could hug the east side of Change Islands, because there was plenty of water to take you to where you could make a run for Hare Bay Head, and then across Hare Bay into the lun of Brimstone Head and home free. At the last of it we had to put on our oilskins for the spray and we shipped a little water, but we never struck once. And that was how I learned the way to Fogo. Years later when Allan Peckford and I were out cod jigging there one summer we drove our boat right fair over a bad ledge and didn't even know it because it was high tide. But when we landed, a fisherman who had been watching from his stagehead smiled and said, "You come pretty close to the sunker, skipper!" That always stuck in my mind; he knew his rocks better from a half mile away than we did right on top of them.

Next to St. John's, Fogo was the busiest place I had ever seen. After we slipped through the canal between Seal Cove and Fogo Harbour, everything widened out I saw that we were in an anchorage as big or bigger than St. John's harbour, and that it was almost as crowded with vessels of all sizes — schooners, square-riggers and bulley boats all mingled along the wharves and moored off from the stages. There were hardly any trees on the high hills that encircled the main harbour. To the north I could see two openings half-barred by low islands and reefs over which the sea was breaking — Middle and Eastern Tickle. Western Tickle was hidden by a hill. Back the way we had come, Brimstone Head now looked like a round dome hiding Change Islands. Right around the harbour there was a winding gravel road, and above and below it the houses clung to the grey and purple cliffs, some on stilts, some on a bit of level garden. They looked bright and clean with maroon, white and yellow ochre paint and white picket fences. Except for clumps of alders and juniper here and there, Fogo didn't seem to have any woods at all — a strange sight to a Gander Bay man. Around the cliffy shore every space that was fit was filled with wharves, fish rooms and stages up on longers or poles, and right behind or beside them were the flakes, snowy white with salt cod drying. As we drew closer the smell of this cod, mixed with that of fish guts from the stages and landwash and that of blubber barrels in the sun, made you wonder whether you could hold down your last meal. But then a fresh sea breeze would waft it all away for a while.

Messrs. Earl Sons and Company Limited consisted of four or five buildings as big as barns, clapboarded and shingled and painted in red ochre with white trim, behind several hundred feet of wharves. At the wharf where we tied up were several square-rigged sailing ships, their sails furled, loading fish for overseas. From one of the lower yardarms a young fellow, probably a cabin boy, was diving for pennies thrown from the wharf. The minute somebody tossed one he would be right behind it, and in the clear greenish water he usually caught it before it struck bottom.

Fair across the harbour was another large group of buildings marked Labrador Export Company Limited. As we steamed across after selling two quarters at Earl's we could see more ships being loaded. The barrels of fish were being rolled up ramps and lowered by block and tackle into the holds. At other wharves green fish was being forked from skiffs and punts onto stageheads where men were busy at the splitting table. On some of the flakes women and girls in bright kerchiefs and dresses bent over the fish, turning it to catch the sun. (I have often wondered since whether Winnie Layman — my future wife, who was then fourteen — was among them. Her father Harry Layman Sr. was a cooper who married William Waterman's daughter Prudence and settled in Little Harbour, just around the point from the Labrador Export Company's premises.) As we lugged ashore two more quarters of venison I recalled that all my life I had heard people jokingly called "Fogo Jumpers." Now I knew why. Compared to Fogo, Clarke's Head was Sleepy Hollow. No wonder Fogo people called us "The Gander Bay Noddies." I began to understand why my father was always in such a hurry. He came from an area where you had only a few short months to catch and cure and pack and ship the fish that fed you through the winter.

We were now at Mr. Furze's wharf. Presently a small wiry man with glasses came down and greeted us. Quickly William Furze rounded up some young fellows to help us move the meat to his ice-house. He bought eight of the remaining eleven quarters. "Ye should be able to sell the rest in Change Islands on the way home," he said. That night we slept in the boat, which had a double bunk on either side of the cabin, a drop-down hinged table toward the bow, and a small "Cod" stove in the middle for cooking and warmth. After that night I decided that to hear water chuckling inches from your ear, and feel the boat swinging gently and bumping the wharf every now and then, is even nicer than sleeping under canvas in the rain.

The first sound I heard next morning was the fire crackling as Uncle Stan got breakfast. Soon the little cabin got so hot I had to scramble from my bunk and go on deck for a breath of air. The eastern sky was a bleary yellow and the wind was in the southwest. Fred joined me on deck.

"Northeaster comin'," he said, tugging on the peak of his cap. "And by the look of those mares' tails" — he waved his hand toward a bank of long, wispy clouds advancing from the south — "we're in for a breeze of wind." We lost no time over breakfast. By nine o'clock we entered Main Tickle of Change Islands, a much smaller place with houses strung out along both sides of a narrow channel between two islands. Again there was the same bustle around the fish flakes and stages and rooms, and the same smell of fish everywhere. Uncle Stan went ashore and found the shopkeeper, Dorman Elliott by name, who came aboard and looked at the meat and bought the remaining three quarters.

Soon we were out of the Tickle into the main run, heading south over light swells in a patter of rain, running down the western side of this long rugged island, so as to have a better chance if the wind picked up. Past Red Rock Cove and Ragged Islands and Smoker Island we went, keeping well off because of the many shoals and sunkers, then easterly to South End. Within two hours we passed Farewell Head and set our course due south on Dog Bay Point. It was just before dark and getting squally when we tied up to our own wharf. For the next three days the northeaster raged. But I made about $25, the most money I'd ever had.

Jim John died at 102 in an old folks' home in Michael's Harbour near Lewisporte. That was around 1975. He was a wonderful man, always in a good humour, full of jokes, very strong in his day, and a superb woodsman. In the *Book of Newfoundland*, Volume One, there's a picture of Jim and me holding a big string of trout taken at Fourth Pond around 1930. I'm proud of that picture.

A Taste of Turr

Around 1922 Father decided to open a small general store, a branch store, in Horwood. Between the Horwood Lumber Company sawmill and the lumberwoods, quite a few people lived and worked there, and he hoped to get some of their business. So he built a small shop, stocked it from the main store in Clarke's Head, and put me in charge. It didn't take long to see we wouldn't make money. True, we were in direct competition with the company store, but that wasn't the real problem. The real problem was that Horwoods paid its workers in what we called scrip, or company money. This money came in eight-sided aluminum coins about the size of a twenty-five cent piece with the words "Horwood Lumber Company Limited" on one side and "Good Only for Trade" on the other. As I recall, it was issued in values of a dollar, fifty cents and twenty-five cents, and since the workers and their families could only spend it at the company store, and had very little ready cash, we didn't get much trade. After a few months we had to give it up for a bad job. But I stuck it out as long as I could.

Late in November Dad wired for the second time to urge me to come home and get the motor boat and pack up everything and close up shop. So I walked the twenty miles to Clarke's Head over the mail route, stopping in at Wings Point on the way to hire Dorman Head to help me. Dorman was older than I, and a good saltwater man. When I left home for Horwood the next morning it was civil with an overcast sky and hardly any lop. The *Matilda* took us there in good time. After a hard morning's work we had moved all the contents of the store, everything from longjohns to molasses to hair tonic, down onto the wharf and stowed it carefully under tarpaulins.

In those days we always carried our shotguns in case we spotted some sea ducks or a bay seal. Seeing as we had all kinds of time we decided to do a little birding at Farewell Head, which was only five miles or so out of our way to the northeast. Farewell was always a wonderful place for birding. From November until April, especially in the spring, gunners travelled there from as far away as Boyd's Cove to the west and Carmanville to the east to hunt the eider ducks and turrs and bullbirds that passed the headland in swarms on their migrations. And most of the gunners returned home with enough fresh meat to feed their families for a month or so.

Some of them came home with sore shoulders too, from the kick of their great long muzzle-loaders which they stuffed with three or four fingers of black powder. They shot the birds from gazes or blinds made of a pile of rocks set up where the birds flew close to shore. There's a story about an oldtimer whose gun, though faithful as the sun, packed such a wallop that she would send him reeling backwards — which is risky when you're perched on a cliff in the wind. So he formed the habit of always leaning forward, and the recoil would always set him up straight again. But one evening after a day of birding on the Point he failed to return. They figured the gun must have failed to go off.

We anchored in Big Farewell Harbour, and before taking the punt to scout for birds, we went below to boil the kettle. While eating our lunch of roasted caplin and bread and bakeapple jam and enjoying the warmth from the stove, we heard a faint rattling overhead. Then we felt the boat gently pitching against her moorings. "Must be breezin' up out there," remarked Dorman. "The anchor chain is scraping in her hawse pipe." Through the cabin porthole the sky looked suddenly very dark. We went on deck just in time to feel the first blast of wind and wet snow out of the northeast. To our surprise, four big schooners had arrived while we were eating. "It's a bad one," said Dorman, "or else they wouldn't be here. Big Farewell's a good anchorage for they in a southeaster — but 'tis no place for the likes o' we."

So saying, he hauled anchor and started the engine and we slipped through a narrow tickle into a perfect haven, Little Farewell Harbour, and hove the grapnel overboard again. "With this anchor to keep her off the rocks and a stern line to the shore, we could ride out a hurricane," he said. And while we were getting her squared away the wind reached gale force. Already the snow was coming so thick you could hardly see the shore. Grabbing a couple of armfuls of driftwood from the beach, we dived for the shelter of our cramped little cabin, barred the hatch, stoked the fire, and got ready for a long night.

We didn't sleep much: the boat rocked and creaked, the wind roared, snow and spray hissed against the portholes. I was enjoying it, but toward morning I woke to the sound of Dorman fighting for breath. Lighting the lantern, I asked him what was the matter. "Throat," he gasped between fits of hard coughing, "...hardly swallow." I got him to open his mouth wide. Even by the dim light in the drafty, lurching cabin I could see that the membranes were an angry red.

It looked like quinsy throat to me. In those days people cured all kinds of things with poultices, especially bread-and-mustard poultices. I had bread, but no mustard. In desperation I took some kerosene from the lantern, mixed it with soap, and spread it on bread. I bound the mixture to his throat with a strip of my shirt-tail. For a time the poor man was in worse misery than ever, for now his throat was sore both inside and out.

But by mid-morning he felt better. Around midday the wind slacked off and the sun broke through rafts of scudding clouds. The islands as we crept out of Little Farewell looked handsome — all patched with blinding white snow, and great big grey seas heaving in from the northeast. It was no day for birding. During a lull we made for home, hugging the lee shore as long as we could, then striking south for Dog Bay Point. Near Stearin Island we saw something big rolling in the waves. At first we fancied it was a whale. On drawing closer we saw that it was the bottom of a capsized bulley boat or small schooner. The blizzard must have caught the crew completely unawares, because her jib, foresail and mainsail were still in sailing order; down in the green water they looked ghostly. And she wasn't in any danger of going on the rocks, for her anchor had fallen clear and caught in the bottom.

But where was the crew? The nearest lighthouse was on South End, Change Islands, over five miles to the northeast. Thinking we should report the mishap to someone, we set out for there. By running in the lee of the three larger Dog Bay Islands we managed to work our way two miles off the lighthouse without shipping too much water. From there we just took in water and bailed. We didn't have much time to look, but all the time we expected to see bodies washed up on the rocks, or someone signalling for help from shore.

As we neared the jetty the lightkeeper, John Elliott, strode down the rocky path to meet us, head down against the wind. "No need for to worry, me sons," he sang out as we tossed up our bow line for him to make fast. "I've been watchin' ye through the spyglass. The crew of that boat reached here yesterday in their rodney before the storm got too fierce." He spat tobacco juice downwind and shifted his quid to the other cheek. "I'm after wirin' Carmanville for a motor boat to come and tow her someplace where they can right her, poor thing. She's a menace lying in the run like that. C'mon up to the house now and have a mugup before you both perish in this wind."

Inside his cozy kitchen we met the crew of the bulley boat — two men and a boy. Mr. Elliott, after pouring us mugs of strong tea laced with rum, related how in the same storm a thirty-ton schooner belonging to Paddy Newman of Boyd's Cove had run on the rocks and become a total loss, and how Newman and his wife and another man had escaped in a punt and spent the night on tiny Smoker Island off Deep Cove, Change Islands. "Carryin' their summer's catch to Fogo they were," he sighed, "and lost pretty near the whole shootin' match. So it's a hard winter they're in for, isn't it? Ye were damned lucky not to get caught out in that one."

It was too late to try for home that day, so we made for Southern Harbour on Dog Bay Islands, having first wired my parents to say we were safe. From there it took us most of the next day to reach Clarke's Head. Even before we reached Wings Point the *Matilda* was sheathed in ice from stem to stern, for the wind had backed into the north and turned bitter cold, sending freezing spray over our starboard gunwale all the way.

Thanks to this birding expedition I delivered my father's stock two days late, and caused some sleepless nights. I wished we could have sweetened things with a meal of birds, but for all our trouble we never got so much as the taste of a turr.

On the Surveys

In the summer of 1922 the talk of Gander Bay was whether the government and the big timber men would build a pulp mill on the River. The Anglo-Newfoundland Development Company had started up in 1909 at Grand Falls on the Exploits, and the Terra Nova Sulphite Company was busy building one at Glovertown. The word was that there would either be one at Corner Brook on the west coast or one on the Gander. When the surveyors came that summer everybody was pretty sure we would be picked. The surveyors set up their tents at First Rattle, just above The Works on the north side. There they built a floating raft to carry a big air-drill powered from shore by a gasoline engine. By stringing a strong cable across the River and hooking the raft to it by a pulley, they were able to position the drill any place they wanted. As soon as it was in position the men on the raft would lower the hollow bit into the water, signal the engine man for power, and start to bore into the bottom, adding lengths of pipe as they went. Then they would lift the core, move the raft, and sink a new hole. At the same time there was a crew of men working a half mile in on the north side, digging pits ten to twelve feet deep in back of the high ridge that comes out between Bread and Cheese Steady and The Works. These pits lined up with the drill holes in the River. I suppose they dug pits on the south side too.

The foreman on this job, which lasted all summer, was Allan Peckford of Clarke's Head. The idea of the drilling, he said, was to find out whether the bottom was suitable for a dam to provide power for the mill. If it was, then a pulp mill would be built at tidewater. If it wasn't — no mill.

A job like that with over a dozen men took a lot of grub and supplies, and these had to be brought up every week. At the same time, the heavy cores had to be carried out and shipped away for analysis. The chief surveyor on this operation was Ewart Hall, a short energetic man whom I was to get to know better the following winter. For that amount of freight he figured a small motor boat would be best, so he went ahead and hired Eli Hillier, with Louis Francis as pilot. Eli's boat was eighteen feet long with a 7½ horsepower Faroe engine. Although First Rattle is not far above tidewater, there just isn't enough depth for that size of boat except at top-high tide. With a full load, it was aground more than it was afloat.

Homemade canoes were being built in Gander Bay then. They were modelled on the Old Town, Maine cedar canoe — pointed at both ends — but made of fir planking on black spruce ribs and a juniper stem and keel. Although too heavy for a spoon paddle, they were ideal for poling and rowing and could carry a good load in as little as eight inches of water. Seeing a chance to earn money carrying freight, I got Ned Francis to build me one. This was my first canoe. With Eli's boat to bring the supplies to The Works and mine to take them the rest of the way, we managed very well. To get the cores down to the Bay we did the same in reverse. Since there was nothing much to do when Eli was away, I often went with him. That summer we went as far as Botwood and Cobb's Arm for supplies, and twice to Lewisporte with core samples. From Eli I learned a good bit about getting around on that side of Notre Dame Bay.

But the upshot of it all was that the surveyors found no good bottom at First Rattle, nothing only gravel to build the dam on. Around the middle of the summer they shifted everything upriver to Big Chute and started in again. Here the motor boat was no use at all, but this was a boon for me because everything had to come and go by way of Glenwood, on the train. Along with two or three fellows from there I was kept pretty busy. It doesn't take a surveyor to know that Big Chute has a solid, cliffy bottom, perfect for a dam. What dealt the final blow to this pulp mill scheme was the lay of the land. Hall, with his transit and level, soon determined that the water could be raised no higher than fifty feet. After that it would spill out of the eastern end of Gander Lake into Gambo waters. Worse still, before it reached that depth it would have flooded not only Glenwood and the railway, but the Northwest and Southwest for ten to fifteen miles up, putting a large expanse of prime pulpwood under water.

Five years later, when I was in New York on the streetcars, the International Power and Paper Company sent a civil engineer from Toronto to have another look at the possibilities, a man called Grant Patterson. He came to the same conclusion. So that was the end of our pulp mill, and with it our chances of becoming a big town like Corner Brook or Grand Falls. Back then I felt disappointed: looking back, I can only be thankful it didn't come to pass. A dam anywhere on the River would have ruined the salmon fishing — and if by good luck or management it didn't, pollution from the mill would have.

In the fall of 1973 Leslie Gillingham, searching the woods back of The Works for a juniper with the right crook for the stem head of a canoe, came across a good-sized apple tree. Surprised to find it there, and pleased to see some fruit on it, he decided to take it home to plant in his front yard. The next day he dug it up and towed it home behind his canoe. Whether it was the long soaking or his planting technique, I don't know, but it died. I feel sure this apple tree started from seeds in a core tossed away by one of Hall's surveyors some fifty years before.

Anyway, we got a good summer's work out of it, and later on Hall was responsible for getting me a job for the winter too. This came about in an odd way. That same summer, while taking some freight to Glenwood, just slowly poling toward Third Pond Island and enjoying the peace and quiet, I had heard something up ahead that sounded like a bunch of men in a barroom brawl. When I saw the cause I could hardly believe my eyes. There on Third Pond Bar were four yellow Banker dories all aground. That they were aground didn't surprise me, for we never use that run except during high water in spring or late fall. What amazed me was the sight of saltwater dories on the Gander. Where had they come from, and what were they doing there? All seemed heavy laden, and a dozen men were out in the water, cursing and swearing, trying to haul and prise them along with ropes and oars.

"Is this the right channel, ol' man?" one of them sung out as I came abreast of them in the other channel.

"No," I bawled back, "I'm afraid you're off course. The run is over here, the South Run we call it." After another spell of scoting at the painters they got clear of the sandbar and rocks and found enough water to float the dories. It turned out the crew were part of a surveying team bound for Gander Bay to renew the boundary lines of the Reid Newfoundland Company's limits on the Southern Neck, between the Bay and Musgrave Harbour. They too were working for Ewart Hall. I piloted them down as far as the upper end of Second Pond, gave them directions for the rest of the way, and resumed my two-day journey upriver. When they reached the Bay they set up camp in on Barry's Brook, a few miles back of George's Point where the Crown land joined the company land, and started in.

For the rest of that fall we never saw much of them, except when Hall and a couple of his men would come across the Bay in a dory to pick up grub and supplies. By then they were in around Weir's Pond, on a southerly course.

Along about the middle of December Hall let the whole crew go home

68

for Christmas. Walking out to the Bay, they hired three horses and sleighs to take them overland to Boyd's Cove and on to Lewisporte, where they took a train. Home was Carbonear; the whole works of them came from there. Before they left for Boyd's Cove, Hall stopped in at our shop for a chat and offered me a job after Christmas. He said they would be working north and east this time, and then south to Benton, and they would need packers to keep ahead of them. The pay was a dollar a day. I accepted. It was to be my first real job for wages.

On January 6, 1922 we started in at Barry's Fourth Pond where they had a storage tent. The party now had fourteen men. Besides Ewart Hall there was Grant Patterson, a young man called Robin Reid who took notes and photographs, and John Long, the cook. The rest of us were compassmen, axemen and packers. Two others I recall were Mark and John Ash, and there was Reg Oake from Fogo. Reg and myself were the only two not from Carbonear. It soon became apparent that the Ash brothers wanted only Carbonear men on the survey.

We stayed under canvas, four to a tent. The first job was to lug in our winter supplies before we got too far inland. As there wasn't much snow yet, we had to do this on our backs and everybody had to pitch in. The packsacks weighed between sixty and eighty pounds. One day Mark, a line-cutter, accused me of shirking — went to Hall and said my pack was underweight. I denied this and we got in a bit of a row. He was a man in his forties and I was eighteen, but I didn't intend to put up with that. To settle the argument Hall got out a set of scales and weighed the two packs. As it happened, mine was slightly heavier than Mark's. After that he had a grudge against me.

Six days a week we lived on snowshoes, surveying, on average, a mile a day. This meant following the old blazes and corner posts with transit and measuring chain, chopping out any brush or trees to make the line about six feet wide, and cutting new blazes and posts. Meanwhile, Reg and myself, with the cook and cookee, would tote everything ahead to a suitable campsite and set up the tents for the night. Once the snow came we carried everything by snowshoe and toboggan, about 150 pounds to a load. The four tents alone — big nine-by-twelve-foot sidewall tents with double thickness against the cold — made two loads. A good spot to camp was one with more or less level ground, and in the lun — out of the wind — behind a thick droke of spruce or fir or a cliff. If there was a small brook nearby, or a pond, so much the better. But we could always get enough water by melting a kettlefull of snow and ice. Every day we set up camp we had to cut and trim out twenty-eight poles to frame up the tents, plus enough firewood for supper, overnight, and breakfast. If it looked like dirty weather we would lay in extra wood. The three tents we lived in had tin stoves, and with a roaring fire they could drive you out, even on the coldest night. But toward morning, unless somebody woke up and stoked the stoves all night, it was just like being outdoors. The fourth tent was never heated. That was our supply tent and all the meat and vegetables had to be kept frozen if possible. If there was a sudden thaw and things started to go soft, we had to eat them first. For vegetables we had the usual — potatoes, turnips, cabbage and carrots. For meat we had salt beef as a standby, and also some salt pork and back bacon.

After we got a good ways in the country it was too far to go out for supplies, but that was all right because the only thing we wanted for was meat and we could get that in the woods. There were rabbits in plenty, which we caught when we had time to tail slips. Caribou we never saw, though there was supposed to be a few still left on the Southern Neck. In fact we came across John Day's Lookout in back of Musgrave Harbour, which the oldtimers used in spotting them years before.

In case we saw a caribou, or anything else for the pot, Hall lent Reg his rifle. This seemed to gall Mark. Reg and me slept in the same tent and one bitter-cold night after we were both gone to sleep he came on the sly and dumped a bucket of ice-cold water over us. It soaked us to the skin, and our blankets too. If we hadn't got a fire going directly we would have had a hard night of it, I can tell you. Nothing was said right then because we weren't sure, but the next day we could tell by Mark's little jokes that he was the culprit. Without letting on to anybody, I watched my chance. One even colder night a couple of weeks later — good and late so the stove would be out — I played the same trick on him.

Well, sir, what a commotion and outcry! He woke the whole camp. And pretty soon Ewart Hall rushed out of his tent with a lantern to see what was going on. By then I was back in my bunk making out nothing had happened. But Mark, as I expected, told on me.

"Is this true what Mark says?" asked Hall, poking his head in through the flaps of our tent. I could see Mark grinning behind him..

"It certainly is," said I, getting up.

"But why? Why in the devil would you do such a thing? I thought you had better sense."

"Because he did it to me first, Sir," I said, "a fortnight ago." He turned to Mark and asked if that was true. Mark looked at the ground. Just then somebody goosed him, so we all had a good laugh and went back to bed.

During the three months I worked on this survey we made our way east to within ten miles of Musgrave Harbour, then southeasterly toward Cape Freels, then southward a few miles in back of Wesleyville and Badger's

Quay. After that we turned straight west and followed along the north boundary of a block owned by the A.N.D. Company behind Indian Bay, then along the south boundary of another, bigger block that took us between Indian Bay Big Pond and Home Pond. About the middle of March month we struck south on the last leg of our work. When we sighted Soulis Pond we knew we were almost to Benton and the railway track, and that meant we would soon be home. All of us were more or less homesick. Except for a scattered trip out to civilization to pick up grub and supplies, we had been in the woods for nearly three months. There was no radio then, and any mail we managed to get was stale.

At Benton we slept in our clothes on benches and tables in the train station. By and by the eastbound arrived, and Reg and I were left waiting for the westbound to Glenwood. During the night a couple of feet of loose snow had fallen, and a wild northwest wind started whipping it into drifts. Heading into it, we could hardly see the trees at times. Twelve miles west of Benton the engine and snowplow struck a drift so deep the plow was derailed. Suddenly the whole train came to a halt, throwing people off their seats and setting off a great clatter of couplings being smashed together.

Within minutes the roadmaster, a burly, red-faced St. John's Irishman named Paddy Walsh, came wading through the cars handing out snow shovels and yelling, "Turn to, now; all hands out and help dig the plow out so's we can get this train back on the rails!" Most of the crowd took one, but I lifted my pack and bedroll down off the baggage rack, picked up my snowshoes, and got ready to leave.

"And where might ye be off to, lad?" said Walsh, eyeing me over the top of his wire-rimmed glasses.

"Home," I said, shrugging into my shoulder straps.

"Home," he said. "And where might that be now?"

"Clarke's Head, Gander Bay," I said, stepping down to a snowbank and starting to tie on my rackets. By now a group of the other passengers were watching. Reg was among them, grinning away.

"Gander Bay? Why lad, that must be fifty or sixty miles from here." He was really worried about me. I told him it was under forty miles and that there was nothing to worry about.

"Through the woods by yourself? With no tent, no map, and no compass? Are ye daft? Suppose another blizzard like last night's comes down on ye all of a sudden? Ye'll go astray for sure and leave your bones to bleach on some bog. No, stay with us, son; they're after sendin' a crane from Bishop's Falls to lift the engine and plow back on the rails. Here, grab a shovel and pitch in." I explained that if I went by train to Glenwood

71

I'd still have to snowshoe thirty miles to get home, and seeing I had been tramping the woods all winter, what did another few miles matter? But it was no use, so I left him then, shaking his head in disbelief, and struck out for home. He was a city man and didn't understand about us Gander Bay men, how we were always beating around in the woods. And after my three months on the survey I felt equal to anything, welcomed it even.

The place where I left the train was near where Gander Airport is today. It was already late in the day, so I made for the west end of Jonathan's Big Pond. The snow had a crust on it with drifts in the hollows, and in the long March twilight I made good time. That night I ate my bread and cheese with tea made in a tin can and slept under a bough whiffet or leanto on the shore of the pond. The next morning bright and early I headed due north, crossed the River at Second Pond Narrows on the ice — I didn't want to chance crossing the Bay ice — and arrived home by dinner time.

That winter my parents were living in a winter house or log cabin on their land in by Clarke's Brook, and they had another servant girl. Now a winter house in those days usually had few partitions, and only pieces of smoky cotton hung in the doorways for privacy. My parents slept in one end and the girl in the other, while I had the couch by the kitchen stove. One night after all hands were turned in and Father was snoring away, I awoke from a dream where someone was calling my name. "Brett, Brett," the voice was saying very softly. The odd thing was, after I woke I could still hear it. Then I realized it was the servant girl calling from her bedroom. It made me think of the night of the Orangeman's dance two years before. This time I wasn't shy.

That spring, catching muskrats on the Northwest with Uncle Stanley for a few weeks and helping to cut our next winter's wood, I took a job cruising timber for the International Pulp and Paper Company. The area we surveyed was on the Northwest Branch of the Gander from Stag Brook down to Big Gull River. There were eight of us in the party. Each morning we would start at the base line, which followed the River, run our line inland two to four miles, then offset a quarter mile and come out on a parallel course. Along each line we mapped the timber conditions on our cruise sheets and drew in any ponds, brooks and bogs. Every ten chains, or 660 feet, we took sample plots, tallying all trees by the type and size. Black spruce, fir, birch, and aps (or aspen) were the main types, with sometimes a few white pine. These pines were usually twice as tall as anything else, but not much good because they were windshook — cracked in the heartwood from having been exposed to the storms after G.L. Phillips logged those stands thirty years before. But the spruce was excellent for pulpwood. One of my tallies showed fifty-three cords per acre. This seemed so high that they had it checked by the party chief, whose tally came out even higher.

I also worked one summer as timekeeper for the A.N.D. Company in Grand Falls with a crew that was installing a new penstock in the hydro dam. It was nice for a change to get clear of the stouts or mooseflies. And it was nice to be earning a bit of cash and seeing more of the world.

The Warden and the Bear

In 1924 I got a summer job with the government as a fisheries warden on the lower Gander, a job I had in later years as well. My patrol was from First Pond to just above Second Pond; another fellow did from there up to Glenwood, and a third from First Pond down to the Bay. So each of us had about ten miles. We made our rounds in canoe, and we paddled and poled everywhere — a nice quiet way to catch poachers. Only trouble was, poachers were scarce as hen's teeth, for there was all kinds of salmon to be had then; you could buy it fresh on the wharf for five or six cents a pound, or get a smoked salmon for a dollar. On top of that, most Gander Bay men were away to work, either on the Exploits main drive if it was in the spring, or a shareman on a codtrap crew down Change Islands way, or in the lumberwoods cutting pulp for the A.N.D. Company. And sport fishing was still in its infancy.

So you might say I had a soft job. There were no luxuries or fringe benefits, though. It was seven days a week in all weathers for $50 a month, and find your own grub, bedding, and boat. For nighttime we had no lanterns, only candles. But oh, you talk about peaceful on the Gander in those days. No outboard motors yet, no highway traffic sounds in the distance, not even an airplane to break the silence; all night long the sound of salmon jumping somewhere, or a faraway loon calling. And in the morning a charm of birds to wake you up. I had no radio; none of us did. We got our weather forecasts from the sun and clouds, from the birds. It was no trouble then to see a dozen baby seals chasing the salmon in a pool while the old ones sunned themselves on the rocks round about, or a fish hank diving for a meal, or a pair of bald eagles nesting in a big pine overlooking the River.

74

Speaking of wildlife, that summer I had my first close encounter with a bear. It was my own fault — I should have known better. I had finished my patrol at Second Pond late in the afternoon and, since it looked like rain before morning, had set up the tent. For supper I fried a small salmon — one of the few fringe benefits a warden was permitted. While it sizzled away I cut fir boughs for my bed and picked up some driftwood for the morning fire. After supper I washed my tin plate and cup in the River, stowed the bread, butter, and molasses in the grub box, and rigged up a fresh candle by looping a narrow strip of birch rind around it and wedging the ends into the split end of an alder rod which I stuck upright in the ground by my bunk. There being several pieces of salmon left in the pan, I set it inside the door of the tent for breakfast. After smoking a pipe I checked the canoe and the sky, blew out the candle and turned in. It was dark as the grave, with no moon.

Sometime later I woke with a start, sure I had heard something in the tent. After listening for several minutes I told myself it must have been a mouse, and dozed off again. The next time I woke there was no mistake. A bear was sniffing loudly along the wall of the tent not four feet away. As I groped for matches in my shirt pocket my scalp prickled. But I wasn't all that worried. All my life I'd heard stories about bears. None of the men I respected ever told of them attacking a person, unless it was a sow bear with cubs. Still, I thought, there's always a first time. When the match flared, all sniffing stopped. I lit the candle and held my breath. Not a sound. He's gone away, I said to myself. Then, just as I went to blow out the candle, the tent wall bulged in and a black paw twice the size of my hand came inching under the canvas. I couldn't take my eyes off that paw. Its claws were long and curved and sharp, and its smooth black coat of hair gleamed in the candlelight. It seemed to have a mind of its own. Like a blind man with a cane, it would halt to feel gently right and left. But it never faltered on its general course — straight for my frypan.

Now, if I'd had the sense I was born with I'd have heaved that frypan out the tent door right then and there. Instead, I froze. The hair on my neck stood up, and goose pimples started marching up and down my spine so fast they were getting in each other's way. I had no gun. My axe was down in the canoe, fifty yards away. Mother had always taught us to pray when we were in trouble, but I couldn't think of a good prayer. All I could think of was my salmon. On the woodpile were several good-sized junks of birch. Without getting out of the bunk I picked one up and with both hands brought it down as hard as I could on that paw. Quick as a flash it disappeared, followed by a lot of bellowing and crashing until the bear got himself pointed in the right direction and took off out of there on his three good feet.

All of a sudden I felt brave as a lion. Sticking my head out through the flaps I sung out at the top of my lungs after him: "Go catch your own salmon, you sleeveen!" Yes, I felt pretty cocky. I blew out the candle then and lay back for a good night's sleep.

In less than an hour he was back. This time it was his growls woke me as he circled the tent, grumbling to himself. With hands shaking I lit the candle again. He kept on growling and circling. It was no trouble to figure out what he meant. There was to be no more foolishness out of me; he was going to have that salmon or else.

This was a bad position for a recently-appointed government official to be in. My pants seemed to take a fortnight to haul on. Several hours were lost groping for one boot. Would he rip the side out of the tent, or would he come in through the flaps? If it was the flaps, I didn't want to meet him on my way out. What I needed was a torch. Yanking my candlestick from the ground and removing the candle, I jammed in a handful of birch rind from the woodpile and set fire to it. The growls were coming faster now. As the oily bark flared I grabbed my bedroll in one hand, waited until he was at the back of the tent, and dived through the doorway. With torch held high and roaring at the top of my lungs I reached the canoe in about three jumps, hove in the bedroll, and shoved off into the dark. I never slacked off paddling until she struck the beach on the other side, a quarter mile away. There I spent the night tending a big fire and wondering how far a hungry bear would swim.

In the morning, very quietly, I paddled back. While still a nice piece from the campsite I could see the tent was still up, though sagging at the front. For all I knew, the bear was still handy. Before the bow touched the strand I stepped out as quietly as I could and crept up to the tent. On the guy rope I saw some hairs he had left while squeezing under it. My heart commenced to pound a little. In the bushes behind the tent I picked up the frypan. It was licked clean. A few feet away was my grub box. Except for my butter and sugar, which were in screw-top pickle bottles, everything edible was gone, including my soap and spare candles. Even the tin of condensed milk was punctured and sucked dry. Finding the rest of my stuff took an hour or more of poking through the alders. In a patch of wet mud I came across his print. Though not quite as big as I'd pictured him in the flickering light of the candle, he was hefty just the same.

The rest of that day I spent paddling ‿even miles in the rain to Clarke's Head for more grub, and then poling back. I also had to replace the leather hinges on my grub box. I had learned what every young backpacker worth his salt knows today — never keep food where you sleep.

Not taking any chances, I cut aspen logs and built two sturdy cabins to stay in for the rest of that summer, one at each end of my circuit.

That was my only close call with a black bear, even though I've seen a good many in tight quarters. I have known them to steal a tub of butter right off the table between us as we slept in our two bunks in a small cabin, and I know of one that jumped through a window, sash and glass and all, when cornered inside a camp. I've shot a few too. Of course I'm not talking about half-tame park bears. That's another story altogether.

Although anglers were a rare sight on the Gander in those days, now and then the government would hire a guide or two and bring some dignitary and his guests down for a holiday. Paddling slowly downstream one sunshiny morning I saw, several yards ahead, lying face-up on a wide flat boulder in mid-stream near Third Pond, a woman sunbathing. As I drew closer it became clear that what I had taken for a skin-coloured bathing suit was in fact not; the woman — young and blond and well-favoured in every way — was wearing nothing but sunglasses. Just for devilment I turned the canoe in her direction and in silence let it drift down upon her. Except to brush a mosquito lazily from her left nipple, she never stirred. When the boat was right alongside the rock I leaned over and said in a low voice, as casually as I could, "Beautiful morning, isn't it?" Well sir, she opened her eyes, screamed, and tumbled into the river. If the water had been deep I'd have been happy to save her, but it was shallow and warm and no harm done. What a lovely sight she made, prancing and splashing ashore like a frightened doe.

Poachers were few and far between, but that summer I had the misfortune of coming in tack with a biologist who was sent out from St. John's to study the habits of the Atlantic salmon. This man, Dr. Blair by name, managed to slaughter more salmon in a week than all the poachers for the previous five years. A thin, sandy-haired fellow with glasses, he doubtless knew a lot about his chosen subject, but when it came to their day-to-day habits he was poorly informed.

His plan was to catch them and tag them with me as his helper. Every fish we released would have a little numbered metal tag in the small back fin next to the tail. Whoever caught the salmon next time was supposed to tell where it was caught and send in the number to the government. We set three nets off Booming Point, each upstream from the other. The lower one had a six-inch mesh, the next was five, and the upper one was four-inch. By dinnertime we had everything ready. That afternoon we sat on the shore in the sun and watched the three lines of cork floats strung out across the calm water, all set to meet the salmon after their six-mile run up from salt water. Booming Point was a good choice because it's their first rest from the current and they would be still strong. Some of them would still be carrying the sea lice — the flat black parasite that drops off after a day or so in fresh water — on their sides.

All that day not a salmon struck our nets. Which only makes sense since salmon mostly rest by day. But at dawn the next morning the nets were so full that all the floats were dragged under. Altogether we counted 367. Counting them was easy because all but a dozen were dead. These live fish the biologist placed in underwater cages for tagging.

Dr. Blair was staggered by the number of fish. He said he never expected so many, nor that they would all come at night. He said he thought we would be able to pick them out a few at a time, tag and release them. Shaking his head, he measured the survivors, clipped his little metal tags to their rubbery black adipose fin, and let each one go. The largest was a fourteen-pound male, almost three feet long. When released, this fine fish charged off up the pond, lashing his tail from side to side with powerful strokes, his dorsal fin slicing the water like a shark's. He did this for a quarter of a mile. Then, slewing around, he came right back to where we stood and ran himself aground and died. That made the biologist and me feel even worse. Gathering up all the dead fish in brin bags, we dumped them in the woods. I didn't even have the heart to cook one for supper. But the bears had the scoff of their lives. The next day Dr. Blair took up his nets and went back to St. John's.

Poor Stan

Poor Stan wasn't his real name. They only called him that after he was drowned — it was a fashion the old people had. His real name was Stanley Gillingham and, as I said earlier, he was one of my mother's three brothers. All the Gillinghams liked the woods, but of the three he turned out to be the one with the greatest liking for it, the one who as a youngster was forever out in canoe, or sneaking off when he shouldn't to try to bag a duck or a goose. Before long he was making a name for himself on the log drives, both those of the Horwood Lumber Company and the A.N.D. Company's Exploits River drive. They said he was just like the cat. And I can vouch for that because when I was a boy I watched him more than once run across a boom of logs for sport on a Sunday evening and never so much as wet his shoes. Dark and wiry, just over middle height, he was a hero to us boys. I suppose he would have been about twenty then.

So when he asked me to go partners with him, muskrat trapping on the Northwest, I jumped at the chance. And that was how I came to be connected with his death. At any rate I've always felt a connection, because it was on a muskrat trapping expedition in April of 1924 that he was drowned, at the age of thirty-two. It was only by chance I wasn't there, for I had gone with him three springs already and trapped with him as a full partner the winter before. The only reason I didn't go with him that spring was that I took a notion to travel up to Toronto and look for a job, to see how I liked city living. When I gave him my muskrat traps that April there was no hard feelings about it. He just laughed in that easy way he had, wished me well, and said he guessed he would have to find another partner.

Life is strange. A few weeks later he was dead. Perhaps if I had been in the bow of that canoe going up Second Narrows she wouldn't have capsized. Perhaps if my cousin Stanley Gillingham had been with him nothing would have happened either. For Uncle Stan had asked him to go too, and my cousin had agreed, and they were only waiting for the River to break out. But my cousin was in the woods cutting pickets one day and chopped his foot pretty bad with the axe. So Uncle Stan asked Herbert Francis — one of Charlie Francis Jr.'s sons and about his own age — to go instead.

But let me go back a bit and tell what it was like muskrat catching, and about my first and only winter trapping with him, and how he saved my life. I think this was the hardest thing about his death, that he had saved mine but I wasn't there to try to save his.

Muskrat trapping season was from October 15 until the end of May. In March of 1924 Uncle Stan had brought home a good catch of winter fur — lynx, otter, and fox — which he sold to Esau Gillingham. He sold him some beaver pelts too. There was no open season on beaver, but Esau used to buy them anyway. Whether he shipped them with the rest of his furs to J.H. Ewing in St. John's, or sold them somewhere else, I don't know. Esau never worried about things like that, and trappers had to make a living. As for me, I was twenty and eager to get up on the Northwest again. We went up in late April by cedar canoe, paddling and poling the seventy-five miles to Big Gull and the six miles from there up to Gull Steadies. Gull Steadies has these long stretches of low mud banks with slack water, the perfect place for muskrats. It took us close to a week to get there, and when we did we found that a bear had visited our wigwam and ripped the side out of it. We cut a few poles, peeled some birch rind, and soon had it shipshape again. Then we cut some fresh fir boughs for our bunks, collected some wood and splits, laid out our gear and we were in business.

Muskrat trapping is easy. The rats had their holes along the banks on either side, just under water, with their dens up in under the overhang. All we had to do was find where they were using a half-sunken log or a rock in the water and set our trap there. We did this up and down both sides of the Steadies. In the mornings we'd collect our catch, and after dinner we would skin them. Some days we would catch two dozen. We didn't stop much, I can tell you. And we smelled of muskrat, that sweetish fatty aroma, the whole time. The meat was good to eat though, as good as duck and certainly better than stale venison.

And it was the nicest time of year. Every fine morning we woke at daylight to a charm of birds — robins, hitch sparrows, whitethroats, chickadees, all kinds of them singing their hearts out. They would keep at that until the sun came up and then slack off. And then again at duckish, if it was a civil evening, you'd hear them, only quieter than in the morning, with a scattered vireo or hermit thrush mixed in. I always enjoyed that. The ice would be almost gone, the snowbanks in the thick woods would be sugary and melting fast, and you could leave your mitts off and even work in your shirt sleeves some days. Best of all, the nippers and black flies weren't out yet. Two or three weeks like this and we would make seventy-five, perhaps a hundred dollars apiece.

One day we had gone different ways to check our traps, and when I came back and was climbing the bank with my load of rats I heard a rustle from inside our camp. Thinking Uncle Stan had got back first, I sung out. No answer. As I started toward the door, out walked a big black bear with a bottle of molasses in his mouth. He looked so comical I burst out laughing. With that he dropped the bottle and bolted. But mostly our days and nights were uneventful; just hard work and eat and sleep and try to get as much fur as we could before the flies got too bad. That year we were finished, had our limit, and were back home before the season closed on May 31.

It was the next winter he saved my life. When he asked me to be his winter trapping partner I felt proud because it meant that, in his eyes, I was a man. So in late November month, when the ice was making hard on the ponds and coves, we loaded our gear and grub for a month on a slide and took off with three dogs for Big Gull. From Clarke's Head, following the River most of the way, it was a seven-day trip behind the dogs. At the mouth of Big Gull, Stanley's half-brother John and Uncle Joe Gillingham and one of the Hodder brothers had a good wigwam that was later burnt. With this for our base camp we trapped a ten-mile strip on either side of the main river, five miles up and five miles down. We also trapped in around Easter' Branch Pond and Frying Pan Brook waters, building small overnight wigwams for sleeping, or sometimes just a bough whiffet. And we had the wigwam at Gull Steadies. Since a two-man wigwam only took two hours or so to put up and a bough whiffet much less, we were never stuck for shelter. Except for Sundays or stormy weather, we never saw each other all week. Wherever we were working, Uncle Stan would take one route and I the other. For instance, he would go thirteen miles up along Big Gull, stay in a wigwam and skin his catch, cut west seven miles across the country, and come out to the main river and down to camp. Meanwhile, I would make a similar circuit.

Our grub was the usual bread and tea and molasses, with turnip and cabbage, salt beef or salt cod, and venison or rabbit. We usually had smoked caplin or beans for a treat. Flapjacks was our standard mid-day meal. For frying them we used fatback pork or caribou lard. You would fry up a batch every morning and carry them with you. And rather than chop a hole in the ice, when you wanted water to mix your batter you dipped your fry pan full of snow — the snow was clean in those days — and melted it. At the base camp we made our own bread — bannock bread we called it — but on the trail we just made flapjacks. Perhaps the bannock wasn't too good because I recall after Christmas we came back with a barrel of home-baked bread. This lasted us till March.

One Saturday evening in February, trudging home to base camp behind the tired dogs, I fell through the ice. It happened just around the turn below the last cliff at Rolling Falls. This was normally a place of strong ice, but the week before there had been heavy rain followed by a freeze, making two layers of ice, one above the other. I was tired and not paying proper attention. One minute I was going along thinking how nice it would be to lie in a proper bunk again and wondering if Uncle Stan was already back, and the next minute I was up to my armpits in broken ice and bitter cold water. The current was strong: I could feel it tugging, and I knew that if I didn't get my arms on solid ice right away I was done for. After a struggle I did, but couldn't haul myself out.

Hearing the commotion the dogs stopped and looked back, then sat on their haunches to wait for me. "Go home!" I yelled to them. Their ears pricked up but they never moved. I called out again and again. Finally Jack, the older dog, got up and tugged at his traces. The thought struck me that, with all my splashing, perhaps the sled runners had frozen fast. Then Spot decided to help and the sled moved. They didn't really want to leave me, but I drove them away with my voice, and finally they stopped glancing back and made off for camp at a good clip.

Where I fell in wasn't more than three miles from our base camp, yet by the time Uncle Stan reached me I was barely conscious. All I recall is the glare of a lantern blinding me, the dogs' warm wet tongues on my face, and the sound of heavy breathing as he dragged me out on the ice, rolled me onto the sled and raced for camp. There he stripped me naked, stoked up a good roaring fire, and made me hobble around the room, back and forth, until the circulation came back to my legs. Afterwards I must have slept for twelve or fourteen hours straight.

We worked hard that winter. Muskrat trapping was nothing compared to it. I had never skinned anything but a muskrat, and now I had to learn to do lynx, otter, fox, and beaver, all different and all calling for different tricks and skills. The slightest slip of the knife in the wrong place could ruin a $50 fur — a $1,000 fur maybe, if it was a silver fox. Uncle Stan patiently watched over my efforts and gradually I learned to do a passable job. Even though he was twelve years older than me, we were more like brothers than uncle and nephew because we both liked trapping so much.

Oh, we had our arguments now and then. I was proud and quick-tempered, and sometimes I felt he wanted me for a lackey, not a partner. One day I said that to him, right out, because he wanted me to lug heavy rocks to sink his beaver traps and I got crooked. He never asked me to do that again. The other thing that got my goat was the way he treated a beaver house. Most trappers coming to trap a new house would move quietly, trying not to disturb the animals inside. Not my uncle; he would make as big a racket as he could, stamping on it, yelling, or beating the water with a big stick. His idea was to drive out the beaver so he could shoot two or three first. After that he would set his traps. I suppose that was the old way.

As the days grew longer and the weather milder we concentrated on otter and beaver, trying to make the most of the time we had before the ice got rotten. Uncle Stan drove himself, skinning late into the night and then getting up at daylight and rooting me out to get on the trail. I began to wish for a blizzard like we had in January when we laid about in the camp, snowbound three days, and he told me stories. He recalled the time the big forest fire of 1912 caught him and his buddies on the Dog Bay drive, and the time on the Northwest when he was a guide for the hunting party of a famous British surgeon, Dr. Seccombe Hett, and Hett sent him back thirty-eight miles to Glenwood to get another case of rum and on the way old Peter John, Billy's father, tried to shoot him for a caribou. I could listen to stories like that all night. But now we had to make the most of the season.

Yet when we finished that spring I was having my doubts about being a trapper. I had been at it for six months out of the last twelve. I needed a rest, something completely different, not just to go home and cut firewood and then turn around and go right back to Gull River on the muskrats again. I was restless. The idea of Toronto came to me. Paddling home I pondered it a lot. Much as I loved every rock and ripple of this River, I needed a change. I had my grade eleven, a good education for those days in Newfoundland; I had lived in St. John's; I had worked on the survey and clerked in a store; I should be able to make it. When I stepped out of the canoe by Father's wharf I had made up my mind to take my trapping money and buy a ticket out of Clarke's Head, perhaps for good.

And that is why Uncle Stanley went with someone else that spring of 1924. The next thing we knew, he was drowned. It was Simon and Edgar Francis brought the news on a Sunday evening. On April 25, a few days after Stanley and Herbert Francis had left for Gull Steadies, Simon and Edgar had also gone to the Northwest to trap muskrats. And just below Little Narrows they saw a knapsack floating, but no sign of the canoe. Alarmed, they went ashore to look around. A light snow had fallen, and to their surprise, between First and Second Narrows, they picked up a man's track heading downstream. Now Billy John had a camp nearby, in back of the River a piece, his father Peter's camp it was. Figuring the man might be headed there, they followed his prints. By now it was just getting duckish. Coming abreast of the camp they sung out. Nobody answered. Yet they could see flankers coming out of the stovepipe. They walked up the path to the log cabin and banged on the door. Still no answer. Inside they found Herbert huddled by the stove, staring. The camp was stifling hot and his clothes were dry. All they could get out of him was that the canoe had upset going up Second Narrows in the morning and that Stanley had drowned. He wouldn't say more. Herbert always was quiet, a man as deep as the ocean. Now he seemed to be in shock as well.

Simon and Edgar spent the night with him. Early in the morning they went looking for the body while Herbert stayed in camp. With the River in spring flood it was hard to see anything in the water. They found a few of his garments, including a suit of underwear that must have washed out of his knapsack. They found the double-ender canoe drove ashore, bottom up. But that was all.

The day they brought the news to Gander Bay we rounded up half a dozen men and had left for the Northwest in three canoes. I went with Nat and Walter George Gillingham. Five days had passed since he drowned. We had to find him or the eels would have him first. Figuring the current would have dragged and floated his body downstream by now, we began our search at Long Angle Island and worked up. The water had dropped some already, so we didn't need to drag with grapnels. We could see bottom nearly everywhere. The procedure was to set one fellow ashore on each side of the river, while the rest of us, poling slowly in the three canoes, did a slow sweep upstream. For two or three hours we found nothing. Then, right below Second Narrows, in the eddy below the cliff on the north side, we saw him. He was half floating, face down. His black hair waved like underwater grass and he still had on his long rubbers and his green mackinaw.

We dragged him ashore and looked for marks, broken bones, any clue as to how he drowned, for his lungs were full of water. The only mark was a small nick on his forehead, not even a bruise, so small that it could have been made by a sharp twig. There was nothing to do but roll his bloated corpse in a tarp and start the long journey home.

On the way I tried to figure out what had happened. The boat must have capsized, but how? They were both good canoe men. The only clue was something Herbert had said about a sail. He claimed that Uncle Stan, against Herbert's wishes, had put up a blanket to make better time. Now it so happens that at the top of Second Narrows you have to cut in close to a rock, but you won't strike it because the current keeps you clear. If a gust hit them just there, and if the canoe started to tip before Uncle Stan had time to slack off the sail rope, then Herbert — being up forward and unable to see what Stan was doing aft — might have panicked and jumped to this rock. If that happened, the boat would have upset instantly.

What I couldn't understand was why my uncle, a strong swimmer and in the prime of life, didn't make it ashore. At the Upper Narrows the River is less than 150 feet wide, and they were close to shore. Even in April, with the water top high, it should have been easy. As I've said, he was on the drive for years. There was a bunch of them used to go all the time, him and Edgar and Simon and Herbert Francis, Maurice Thistle and Fred Hurley, and Willis and Charlie Bauld. They practised log-rolling every chance they got. They said Uncle Stan could jump on a log, stick in his pickpole, run to the other end and stand still just looking at it. They claimed he even dunked Ronald Kelly, the legendary boss of the Badger Drive — the one that's in the song by the same name. The only explanation I can think of is that somehow the blanket or the sail rope got tangled around his head and he couldn't get clear in time. I don't think he struck his head — in April there's fifteen or twenty feet of water at the Narrows — and I doubt that he took a heart attack.

That trip is all a blur to me now. It seemed to take a month. At Glenwood Simon wired Father:

FOUND BODY STOP MAKE A LARGE COFFIN

All I can mind is that when we reached the Bay at last and neared the wharf with the crowd of people waiting, Nat and Walter George started singing "Onward, Christian Soldiers" and the rest of us in the boats joined in, singing and paddling slowly until the canoes, one of them with the body draped with canvas, touched the strand. His widow, Dorothy, and young daughter, Nellie, having agonized for over a week about what happened, came forward, and after them came Father and Mother and her brothers, until we were surrounded.

My uncle had been an Orangeman of the third degree, a Royal Arch man. After the service they carried his coffin in a procession from the Anglican Church down the road a quarter mile to the cemetery. On that dark day in April — the same month and almost the same date his sister Victoria had died fourteen years earlier — their cheerful orange and purple sashes seemed out of place. They buried him near her in the new family plot, behind the white picket fence with the woods all around.

A few days earlier my brother Harold, then fourteen, had a sort of forerunner, or premonition. It was the day Father got the telegram, and as Harold was kneeling by his bed saying his prayers before turning in he heard three distinct taps repeated three times. "Exactly like a tack hammer," was how he described the sound. Thinking it was coming through his open window from somewhere nearby he got up and listened, but heard nothing more. The next night at the same hour — as they tacked on the cloth covering on the coffin lid — he heard the selfsame sound and knew what it meant.

As far as I know Poor Stan was the first Gander Bay man to drown on the River. Though only a young man, he was one of the finest rivermen Gander Bay ever produced. His grave marker has disappeared, but he has a monument nonetheless. Just above The Works there's this stretch of calm water where he and a companion stopped one summer day to boil the kettle. The flies were thick so they decided that rather than go ashore they would have their lunch on a boulder in the stream. To this day we call that place Bread and Cheese Steady and that boulder Bread and Cheese Rock.

PART II

Away

Toronto

After Uncle Stan was drowned, after the funeral and all that, I lost my appetite for Toronto. Getting out of Gander Bay and seeing the world didn't seem to matter any more. All that summer I moped around. I packed shingles in the mill, helped Father in the store, carried a few passengers in and out the River, unloaded freight from the *Clyde* — anything to keep busy. I had long talks with my girlfriend, Winnie Layman, the young postmistress from Fogo. Sometimes I had nightmares. Mother and Aunt Dorothy cried a lot. It was a hard summer on us all.

Finally, in August, I made up my mind to go, hauled up my canoe and said my goodbyes. Someone took me to Glenwood where I boarded the westbound for Port aux Basques. Already the birches were turning yellow on the hills. After the train rumbled across the Exploits River it was night and I fell into a fitful sleep. The next thing I knew the conductor was singing out "Robinson's Station, McKay's, St. Fintan's, Doyles," the sun was streaming through the windows of the coach, and I felt like I was in a different world. After washing and shaving I went looking for breakfast. In the dining car I ate bacon and eggs and watched the Long Range Mountains slide away to the north with streamers of mist hiding their high ridges, and I felt better. On the Gulf a stiff westerly breeze had raised a nice lop. I climbed up forward and watched the waves break in white foam against the bluff bows of the *Kyle* as she plowed along at a good twelve knots. She was faster than the *Clyde* and over sixty feet longer — a dandy ship. By the time she blew her whistle in North Sydney harbour that afternoon, my troubles had taken wing like the seagulls.

The North Sydney train was a surprise. On the mainland I had expected something better than an empty coach, just run-for-run you know, with wooden benches along the sides and a big pot-bellied stove at one

89

end. But that's what they had. Standing around the stove was a bunch of fellows stirring something in an iron pot, and the smell was delicious. I stowed my luggage under a bench and asked if I could have some. "Sure," said one of them with a laugh, "if you'll cook the next batch!" It was mutton stew and some good. As we sat back eating they explained that this was a Harvest Excursion Train that went out West every summer. One fellow asked if I was going as far as the Prairies. He went every year, he said, to work on a farm in Saskatchewan, and for good money too. I told him it sounded tempting, but that I had relatives in Toronto and hoped to find work there. They filled my tin plate a second time. There were mostly Cape Bretoners in that car — fishermen, out-of-work coal miners, a few professional hoboes. Going through the woods of northern New Brunswick that night they got out the mouth organs and fiddles and we sang until the small hours. Here and there the train would stop to take on more men and soon the benches were full. One newcomer joined in and sang all the verses of "The Miramichi Fire" without a pause or any music, just his mournful singsong voice rising and falling while the coach rocked and swayed and some of us fell asleep and others kept time with their feet.

At Lévis the next morning there was such a long wait that four of us got off and went for a stroll. Our coach was well to the rear. On the way forward we passed several cars like ours with their doors slid back, crowded with men, women, and children talking excitedly in a foreign language. Someone said they were Russian immigrants headed for the Prairies. Along the track on one side stood a high, unpainted wooden fence, and from that direction came a tantalizing aroma of freshly-baked bread. Not only that, but the bakery had arranged it so people could buy right over the fence. All you had to do was put your money in a basket which they lowered on a string. Up would go the basket over the fence, and back it would come a minute later with one or two loaves of hot whole wheat bread. We each bought one to munch on as we dodged along, taking in the sights.

We walked all the way up to the station. There must have been fifty cars. While we were watching the people the train whistle tooted a warning. Before we could reach our car she started up. One fellow from our crowd got left behind. and it was only after a hard sprint that we made it back on board ourselves. Walter, the uncle of the man that got stranded, had made a practice of walking back to our car every so often to see how the young fellow was making out. Walter carried a small iron grapnel everywhere he went, the way most men would carry a briefcase or a cane. "Keepsake of Cape Breton in case I get homesick on the damned prairies," he had explained. When we broke the news about his nephew, he went white as a sheet. dropped the anchor on his toe and went hopping away holding his foot and shouting "Stop the train! For Christsake stop the train!"

Toronto was different than I pictured it. I guess I expected more skyscrapers. Still, it was the biggest city I'd ever seen, miles and miles of brick and stone houses all laid out checkerboard fashion with fenced gardens in back and streetcars plying the main streets up from the lake and east and west. I had no sooner got settled than I met this fellow from Burin by the name of George Bartlett, a salesman for the Princess Motor and Battery Company of Toronto. Having convinced himself that the place to sell batteries was Montreal, he was looking for a partner. Soon he convinced me too. So the two of us took the train to Montreal, found a place to board with this French family on Park Avenue, and rented an office at 5 McGill Avenue. The place where we lived was on an extension of Bleury Street, out beyond the last streetcar tracks but still in sight of the cross on Mount Royal. We didn't mind the long walk, but lugging our sample batteries from garage to garage soon got us down. What we needed was a motor car. With the few sales we were getting, this was out of the question. The problem was that all the garage owners and mechanics spoke only French, while we spoke only English — and with two different Newfoundland accents at that. After a few weeks of this we fell behind in our rent. Then Bartlett, although he had a girlfriend in Toronto — an Elliott from Change Islands — took to visiting a whore on St. Catherine Street. I gave up the battery business then and headed back to Toronto. On Front Street near Yonge I found a cheap, clean boarding house; the lakefront in 1925 wasn't developed the way it is now, though it was noisy. Day and night the streetcars rumbled and screeched outside my window, while the wind brought the sound of shunting trains and mournful ships' whistles. For a while I hardly got a wink of sleep.

Every day I combed the papers and walked the streets searching for a job. Most of the ads called for a trade of some sort. When I saw an ad for a course in auto mechanics at the Hemphill Trade School, registration $25, I sent in my name with the money. To my surprise I was accepted right away. I should have smelled a rat then and there, but I was young and green and I had to get a job somehow. Turning up for classes at the appointed time, I found that I was one of six male students apprenticed to a short, red-haired Scotsman who unlocked the door in the morning, pointed out the work to be done, and never showed his face again until suppertime. The school was nothing more than an old shed with a rusty corrugated iron roof and a Model T Ford set up on cement blocks. There was one box of tools for us all. We took the Ford apart bit by bit, then tried to remember how to put her back together. It was the blind leading the blind. After a fortnight I got fed up and quit. The Scot refused to refund my money.

One day this ad appeared in the *Telegram*:

> WANTED Young men and women, fifty of each. Apply to Room 326, King Edward Hotel, 8:30 AM.

The date given was the next day. I arrived early but already the room was half-full. Nobody knew what the job was. In fives and sixes the applicants were called into the next room to be interviewed. Finally, our turn came. The interviewer, a sun-tanned sweaty man in a loose-fitting white suit, slouched at a desk and chewed a cigar as he eyed us. It so happened I was the tallest in our group. "You," he said, pointing the cigar at me, "let's see you with your hat on." I put on my guiff. "Mmm...good," he said. "Own a top hat?" I said no. "A walking stick?" I lied and said yes. "Be here tomorrow morning at eight sharp," he said. "A bus will take you to the Woodbine Racetrack."

At Woodbine the next morning they explained that we were to be extras in a film, that this film had a racing scene in it, and that all we had to do was imagine we were at a horse race with big money riding on the winners. "Just pretend," said the director as the cameras were set up, "that your horse has just won $10,000. Jump up and down, throw your programmes and hats in the air, hug and kiss each other, really show your excitement, OK?" By the time he was through we could almost hear the hooves pounding around the track. We sat in a corner of the bleachers, the only people in the whole stadium, reading and re-reading our programmes, waving and cheering and clapping and raving on cue. The shoot lasted three days and it was a barrel of fun. I never did buy a top hat or cane, but nobody seemed to notice. I got paid six dollars a day and board. It beat muskrat trapping by a long shot. The name of the picture was *Lady Windermere's Fan*, a romantic comedy produced by Ernst Lubitsch from Oscar Wilde's play of the same name. Irene Rich played Lady Windermere. Most of the film was shot in England. Years later I saw it; it was pretty good, but I couldn't even make out my face in the crowd.

In late October I saw an ad for apple pickers. Two of us went to check it out. The orchard was thirty miles north of Toronto and the owner, a thickset farmer chewing a wad of tobacco, asked about experience. I had none, but my friend spoke up and said he would teach me. "All right," said the farmer, "take this ladder and set it up to that there apple tree."

My friend passed the test and we were hired. But when the farmer informed us we'd be bunking in the barn loft over the horses, I told him that although I had nothing against horses I had never slept in a barn before and didn't intend to start. My friend backed me up in demanding proper sleeping accomodations. But the farmer told us to get lost.

After that I tried Eatons and the Robert Simpson Company, who both wanted clerks. At Simpson's I was offered six dollars a week — exactly the price of my board. It was coming on winter, with frost on the backyard fences in the mornings and now and then a bit of snow on the pavement. My shoes were wearing thin like my bank account, which had never recovered from our venture in the battery business. If this kept up I could see myself in the soup kitchen lineup before long, or else riding the boxcars back east.

Then I saw this ad for a clothing salesman. In my boarding house there was a fellow who was a whiz with words, so I got him to put together my letter of application. Another week and I had the job. The man who had placed the ad was Hugo O'Donnell, a farm boy from Orillia who had worked his way up and now owned two clothing stores, one at 368 Yonge Street and another at 338 Parliament, where he and his wife Agnes lived. Agnes ran them both. O'Donnell made his money by buying used garments from a fellow called Rosenburg who collected them free off wealthy people in the swankier parts of Toronto. Wearing a shabby overcoat and battered hat, Rosenburg would trudge from door to door in all weathers, lugging all the garments they gave him in a big grey army blanket slung over his shoulder. People took pity on him and he did well. O'Donnell would go over this stuff and pick out what he wanted. For a man's suit he would pay Rosenburg two or three dollars, send it to the cleaners, have his tailors alter it and sell it for $20, $30, maybe $40. One day a well-dressed man came in and bought one of our most expensive suits for $33. "Why," he exclaimed, "in our store this would cost over $100!" After he left, O'Donnell gave me a wink and whispered: "That, believe it or not, was the manager of Simpson's men's clothing department!"

Hugo O'Donnell was a beefy, pleasant man who always wore a wide-brimmed felt hat and carried his head to one side as if listening to faraway music. I never knew him to lose his temper. Everybody — the tailors, seamstresses, clerks, Rosenburg, the janitor — thought the world of him. Word had it that dozens had applied for my job, so one day I asked him why he had picked me. He looked out the window for a minute. "Because you're from Newfoundland," he said, and walked away. He seemed to connect my background with his own experiences as a poor farm boy.

Certainly he was fascinated with trapping. He was full of questions about it. Now it so happened there was a lot of rats in the cellar of his store on Yonge. If you barged in looking for something it was no trouble to see and hear them scampering for cover. On a quiet evening we could even hear them from upstairs. Perhaps that was why he went about whistling softly, so the customers wouldn't notice. But he never bothered trying to get rid of them. So when he asked me if I would mind catching one, I thought he was going to make me chief exterminator, and told him no thanks. "Oh," he said, "I just want you to show me how a trapper goes about skinning and preparing the pelt. It's something I always wanted to learn." So I set a trap, caught a whopper, skinned it, and tacked it to a spreading board whittled from a piece of packing crate. "So that's how it's done," he said with satisfaction as I put the pelt up to dry. "Same deal for muskrat, mink, raccoon?"

"Pretty much," I said.

When the skin was dry I turned it fur side out and combed it. The thing didn't look half bad. Hugo was so tickled he took it home and hung it up on the wall of his den. I don't know what Agnes thought of this. He probably told her it was genuine mink. A city girl through and through, she wouldn't have known the difference.

With money coming in again, I moved out of my noisy room on Front Street and found a boarding house at 42 Ann Street. An elderly English couple ran it. A perfect business partnership they were: she did all the cooking and cleaning and he did all the shopping. Their lives were quiet and proper and they expected the same of their boarders. That was fine with me, except that my life was almost too quiet and proper. About all I did besides work was go to the movies and write to Winnie and my folks in Gander Bay. One thing I missed that winter was the skating. At home sometimes you could skate for miles. My father in his youth had been an amateur speed skater, and I was pretty good at it too. So when I discovered that the Ossington Avenue Rink offered skating to music every night I started going. It was a far cry from being out on the Bay under a full moon, but circling with hundreds of other skaters to the carousel tunes grew on me. One night a strange thing happened, a coincidence so odd I still wonder at it.

I remember feeling lonely and homesick as I went round and round to the music. Glancing sideways, I saw this pretty girl in a fur coat weaving unsteadily through the faster, surer skaters, then falling. Coming alongside her I helped her up and offered my arm. She smiled and accepted. After we had gone around a few times the music stopped and we sat down on a bench and introduced ourselves. Studying my face closely, she asked where I was from.

"Newfoundland," said I.

"That's interesting," she said, tossing a lock of auburn hair out of her eyes, "I used to write to a fellow in Newfoundland. I forget his name, but I know he was a trapper or something because he sent me a snap of himself by a log cabin with three dogs all jumping up on him."

"Was it through the Maple Leaf Club in the *Family Herald* you got his name?" I asked excitedly.

"Why yes," she said. "How'd you know that?"

"Because I'm the fellow! I don't expect you to believe this, but it's true, I swear it is."

"Well," she said, "you do resemble him, but...." She shook her head in disbelief. While I was trying to think of some way to convince her, the music blared again and we could hardly hear each other talk. Just as we joined the skaters a tall blond man about my age appeared, grabbed the girl by the elbow, and announced he was taking her home. She shook him off and angrily told him that, since he had stood her up for someone who could skate better, she was skating with me. And we left him standing there, glaring after us black as a thundercloud. Walking her home later I thought of a way to prove my identity.

"Hey," I said, "I've got another snap like the one I sent you. Maybe we can go skating again next week and I'll show you." She was curious all right, but I had caught her on the rebound and the blond guy was very much on her mind. We skated at the Ossington one more time, and that was it.

What I missed most in Toronto was the woods. When the city got on my nerves I would pack a lunch and spent a whole Saturday tramping in High Park or up the Humber Valley or in the ravine behind north Yonge — any place with a few trees and the chance of seeing a wild animal. Of course trapping was against the law, but I would see a scattered muskrat or fox and that would help.

Christmastime was the worst. The week before, Hugo and his wife invited us all to a big party. Before it was over we were all drunk. Sometime before daylight I staggered away, leaving O'Donnell and his friends and their wives paralyzed drunk on the floor. After a while I found Ann Street and the boarding house and my room and flopped on the bed — overcoat, hat, shoes, and all. I woke in the dark with a splitting headache. The clock said a quarter after six. I felt relieved at not having overslept, because we still had some pre-Christmas inventory to do at the store. Holding my throbbing head I reeled to the bathroom, washed in cold water and dressed. Downstairs in the dining room I found everybody eating. This puzzled me because most of the boarders skipped early breakfast.

95

"Morning," I said, trying to sit down without bumping the table. They all burst out laughing.

"The morning after the night before, eh?" said one with a smirk.

"Care for some lamb chops and potatoes and lemon pie for breakfast?" said another. Another roar of merriment. Then it dawned on me; I had slept the whole day; it was suppertime.

By the time I reached the store it was after seven, only two hours from closing.

"You're fired," said O'Donnell, not a smile on his face.

"Well," I said, "if I am it's your fault; you gave me too much of that good rum."

"Yes I did, didn't I?" he laughed, slapping me on the back. "I'm glad you had a good time, Brett. You looked pretty down in the mouth."

Among the boarders at Ann Street was a bookkeeper with the Ontario Honey Producers Company Limited, Lawrence Ingster by name. One weekend he was out in his cash and it was driving him up the wall. We worked at a card table in his room all one Sunday trying to find the mistake. Ingster was highstrung anyway, and when it would get too much for him he would jump up and pace up and down and say he was going to be fired. Every so often he'd pause by the window and take out a matchbox and peer inside. This seemed to calm his nerves. At first I figured he was taking snuff or something. "What's in the matchbox, Lawrence?" I said after the third trip. He came over and slid the cover back a fraction.

"See?" he said. "A queen bee." He said it like he was in church. "She teaches me patience." Late that night we found the error. Lawrence couldn't thank me enough. He even offered me his bee.

"You keep her, Ingster," I said, "She makes me nervous." Just the same, she must have been good for him: he later became an executive in the honey business and made a lot of money.

One warm day that spring we all got invited to the wedding of Rosenburg's daughter. Until then I hadn't even known he was married. Not only did Rosenburg have a family, he lived in a mansion. At the reception afterwards the wide lawn overflowed with guests. The food was fine, the wine flowed, and we danced until daylight.

May month in Toronto was hotter than any July I could recall back home. On fine weekends I would escape to Toronto Island or Sunnyside Beach where you could rent a canoe. A big attraction for me at both places was the girls who were always waiting for a boat ride. One Sunday I took a Scottish girl for a spin. Mabel and I liked each other's company so well we spent the whole afternoon and evening together, and before we knew it there was barely time to catch the last ferry back to Toronto at 11:30

96

p.m. There wasn't even time to return the canoe. We just pulled it up on the beach and ran — only to see the stern lights of the ferry fading as she churned away toward the faraway lights of the city.

Trudging back to the canoe, we started paddling to the dock to return it. What to do after that we didn't know. It was a warm summer night with hardly a breath of wind. At that hour there was almost no boat traffic on the harbour. An idea came to me. It was too much for me to resist. "Mabel," I said, "what say we paddle to Toronto?"

Mabel, perhaps thinking I was joking, said "Sure, why not? A grand idea." But when I swung the canoe about and pointed the bow at the cluster of buildings around the foot of Bay Street and began to paddle in earnest, she fell into a panic, said we'd be drowned, even said some prayers. I told her to calm down, that there was no danger as long as she stayed still, and after that she settled into a sullen pout. Within an hour we reached the Bay Street piers. The girl was silent as I helped her up the ladder. I really shouldn't have done it. To make matters worse, I had no painter to tie the canoe on with. After searching around the wharf in vain, I gave the boat a shove and let her drift. The next day the *Globe and Mail* carried a small item which said that an empty canoe had been picked up on Toronto harbour and that the occupant or occupants were "presumed drowned."

In June I decided to go back home. The weather was so hot there were nights on end when sleep was impossible — something I had never experienced in Newfoundland. The River and Uncle Stan were on my mind a great deal too. I told Hugo. "Well, well," he said, "I was hoping you'd stay. Would more money help?" I shook my head. "Well, I tell you what," he said. "You go home, have a good holiday, and then come back in the fall. In fact I'll send you the fare."

A few weeks later I left. Dolly Ford, a friend I met at Sunnyside, took her vacation from the YWCA and came east with me as far as Montreal to visit her parents on Greenshields Avenue. After a pleasant week I kissed Dolly goodbye in Bonaventure Station and boarded the train east. It was after dark when we rolled into Truro, where we had to wait several hours for the North Sydney train. Stiff and weary, I walked through driving rain to a small Chinese restaurant on the Esplanade and bought a meal of chop suey. With not enough money for a hotel and boat fare both, I slept on a bench in the station waiting room.

The next morning I woke to find my wallet gone. All I had left was $1.26 in loose change. I boarded the Maritime Express without breakfast. At North Sydney that afternoon they told me the *Kyle* wasn't leaving for Newfoundland for two days. I went to Grant's Hotel and paid fifty cents for a room. By now I could have eaten a moose raw. At four o'clock I went to a restaurant and ordered fried salmon and potatoes, apple pie and tea. It cost me thirty-five cents. I still needed five dollars for the fare. Today I wouldn't have the gall, but the next morning I walked into Phinney's Store and asked for the manager, told him my story, and tried to borrow the money. It was like trying to squeeze blood from a turnip. "If we lent money to everyone who came in here and asked," he snorted, "we'd have been out of business years ago." Next I hit up the ticket agent at the dock, a Newfoundlander by the name of Shano. He wouldn't even give me the time of day. Finally I found out the name of the local master of the Loyal Orange Lodge, Captain Angus Walters, the dock foreman. When I shook his hand I pressed my thumb on his third knuckle, a secret sign of an Orangeman. To my relief he smiled and did the same. I told him my plight, and why I needed the money. He seemed sympathetic but I couldn't be sure. "Where are you staying?" he asked.

"Grant's Hotel, Sir."

"I'll see you there after supper," he said. And sure enough, he came to my hotel room and gave me the money. The *Kyle* was leaving the next morning early. I woke in good spirits, paid my second night's lodging, bought my ticket from Shano, and went aboard. I still had no money for food or a berth — only enough for a light breakfast on the train. That night in the lounge my stomach was rumbling so badly I couldn't sleep. Around two in the morning, while the other passengers were snoring, I crept into the galley and helped myself to some leftover beef and bread. That was one of the best feeds I ever had.

At Glenwood that evening I was famished again. The coach was hardly stopped when I knocked on Aunt Louise Shea's door. She was overjoyed to see me, gave me a great hug, and took me in and stuffed me, with salt beef, potatoes and cabbage, things I'd hardly tasted since leaving home. The next morning I found somebody going to the Bay. As soon as I got home and told my story Dad wired Captain Walters the five dollars. I was broke, but I was back with Winnie and back with the River.

New York City

"There's plenty of work in the Boston States." That was all the talk in the twenties around Newfoundland. Certainly there wasn't much work on the island in 1926, although things did seem to be improving a bit from the post-war slump — if you lived in Corner Brook or St. John's. Under Prime Minister Walter S. Monroe of the Liberal Conservative Party there was a big new drydock built that year, the Newfoundland Hotel was built the same year, and out on the west coast the giant newsprint mill that was later bought by Bowater was only a year old. As for central Newfoundland, there was talk of a lead or zinc mine up Buchans way, but our fine Gander Bay pulp mill and townsite was gone to Corner Brook. And although the government was building a scattered gravel road, in Clarke's Head there was nothing to do but guide and trap or work in the shop or mill. That's all right if you've never seen anything else. But if you have and you're only twenty-two, it makes you restless. But I didn't want to go back to Toronto. True to his word, Hugo O'Donnell wired asking me to come back, and offered to pay my way; but now I kept thinking about the States.

It was my girlfriend Winnie Layman got me going. Her cousin, Jessica Coombes of Fogo, had a married sister in New York. Jessie had invited Winnie to join a bunch of them that were going there that fall. There were two other girls and Hiram Combden and myself that went. Winnie had been postmistress in Clarke's Head for going on four years and she liked the job. When she resigned, George A. Veitch, Superintendent of Postal Telegraphs, wrote her a good letter of recommendation. In her place they put Paddy Farrell, also from Fogo, a former polio victim who later lived across the sawdust road from us and raised his family there. Paddy was quick-tempered and strong as a bear. One time, in an argument, he reached out through the wicket and grabbed a man by the throat and lifted him clear off the floor. His legs were withered from the polio, but with a special boot and a crutch he could get around very well. I've seen him climb hand-over-hand up a rope with his crutch over one arm to board the SS *Glencoe*.

Anyway, one squally day in November the six of us joined the little coastal steamer *Susu* — she belonged to Crosbie & Sons — bound in for St. John's on her last run of the year. Not long after we cleared Musgrave Harbour our wireless operator picked up an SOS from the three-masted British sailing vessel *Union Jack*, whose captain and crew were stranded on Penguin Island in the Wadhams and wanted to be brought in to Musgrave Harbour. After an hour's steam we could make out the wreck, a pitiful sight to see under the gray sky, with her mizzen cracked off and she on her port side on the rocks, and the lighthouse only a gunshot away. The islanders had rescued all hands. We took aboard the skipper and his crew and brought them in. They told us the *Union Jack* got tangled up in the Wadham Islands when a sudden snow squall came down on them from the southeast as they were beating down to Cape Freels from Seldom Come By with a load of Labrador fish for St. John's. She was a total loss, but her cargo was saved.

In St. John's we booked passage on the SS *Sylvia* — a vessel about three times the size of the *Kyle* — that sailed once a week to New York. The *Sylvia* wasn't as pretty as her name, but she was the biggest ship we had ever been aboard. We had a grand time inspecting her saloon and engine room and whatever else we were allowed to see. The last port of call on the Newfoundland side was St. Pierre, to pick up liquor and cigarettes. The captain didn't even take her in. We just anchored off and the Frenchmen chugged out in their motorized dories and took our orders over the rail. A bottle of rum or a carton of cigarettes was only a dollar. Up would come a bucket with your purchases inside, down it would go with the money. Good old Prohibition! The captain never minded; all he did was sing out to the dorymen now and then to keep clear of the ship's sides. That night the wind breezed up and the *Sylvia* rolled like a cradle, but we had such a party that we hardly noticed.

Five days later the engines stopped and a doctor came aboard to inspect us. He just lined us up and checked our health certificates and let us go ashore. New York City! I forget if it was day or night; there was so much going on, so many people and so much noise. Luckily Jessie's sister Daisy and her husband Gil Crocker were there to meet us or we would have been lost for a week. The Crockers had a big house at Flushing

100

on Long Island and insisted we stay there until we found work. Winnie's five years' experience in Morse telegraphy, plus her letter of recommendation, soon got her a job as assistant wireless operator with the Postal Telegraphy Company at the Biltmore Hotel, next to Grand Central Station. All I had to offer was a few years' experience as a clerk. Gil, a strapping man who worked as a derrick operator on skyscraper jobs, suggested I try the National Bridge Works in Long Island City. He told me a lot of Newfoundlanders were hired there because they were good on the high steel. So I went. The first thing the employment officer asked was if I had experience.

"No, sir, I haven't," said I.

"Sorry," said he. "Next."

That night when I told Gil he laughed and said, "My son, you're too honest. To get ahead in New York City you got to tell a scattered lie." So I waited a week, went back, told them I had experience, and got a job. But it wasn't on the high steel. They put me in the yard sawing timbers, three-foot-square Douglas fir deals eleven or twelve feet long, some longer, laid out with alleyways between the piles and open spaces where pairs of men worked with saw-horses and crosscut saws cutting them into ten-foot lengths for bridge timbers. The first thing I noticed was this strong smell of burning tar and the smoke hanging over everything, enough to make your eyes water. They had fires of railway ties burning in empty oil drums here and there. The weather was bitter cold, and unless you worked hard it was a job to keep warm. And nobody there worked very hard, I could see that — except when the foreman was around. Directly he left, all hands would drop their saws and crowd around these smoky fires, coughing and thumping their arms across their chests and clapping their gloved hands together for warmth. They even had lookouts posted so the boss wouldn't catch them.

My partner was a stocky, middle-aged Pole with a walrus mustache and some fingers missing on his right hand. He didn't talk much. We had a six-foot Simonds crosscut saw that didn't cut worth a damn. The routine was to saw into one face of the piece, turn it over, then finish the cut. Turning them over was no easy matter — they each weighed close to a ton — and getting them onto the woodhorses was even harder. The men helped each other with that, using a sort of peavey. What with the heavy timbers, the dull saw, and all our visits to the oil drum, sawing one piece took us two days.

"Why don't I take this saw down to the tool shop and get her sharpened, Joe?" I said to my partner the fourth day. "If the boss ever finds out how long it's taking us we'll be fired."

101

"Fired?" he chuckled. "Fired? I been workin' like this for seventeen years and haven't been fired yet! That saw's fine the way she is, young fella. If the boss don't know no different, well, that's his problem." The real problem was that I couldn't work fast enough there to keep warm. A couple of weeks of that and I started to look around in my spare time for something else.

There was plenty of construction going on in New York then — hotels, skyscrapers and the like of that. A lot of the familiar skyline of New York wasn't even built then. Like the Empire State Building for instance. I watched them blast out the basement for that. They had a hole down in the bedrock about forty feet, so deep that it was too much trouble to hoist the men to safety when they set off each blast of dynamite. What they did instead was drop a steel cable net over it to catch the flying rock. The Sherry Netherlands Hotel at Central Park and 59th Street was going up at the same time. One night the tower, which was covered with lumber scaffolding, caught fire at the twenty-storey level and they couldn't put the fire out because there wasn't enough water pressure. All the firemen could do was seal off the upper levels and let her burn. Flaming pieces of wood came cartwheeling down into the street; people crowded in so bad that the firemen had to turn their hoses on them. Mayor Jimmy Walker got drenched too.

I decided I wasn't cut out for high steel. Another couple of weeks at National Bridge and I quit and went to work on the streetcars. After some training they made me a motorman on the Sixth Avenue run from Fourth Street to 49th Street.

Winnie meanwhile was enjoying her work at the Biltmore. One day soon after starting she took a very long telegram for a distinguished looking businessman in a top hat. He was so pleased with her accuracy and legibility that he gave her a fat tip. Winnie asked her boss who this gentleman was, and was told that he was none other than Sir Thomas Lipton, the tea baron, and that he had a suite and offices at the Biltmore. Winnie had the knack of working the telegraph key equally well with either hand, so that she seldom slowed down or made mistakes from tiredness as most operators did. And she could receive so fast that she never had to re-copy her messages to make them more legible. This was important with long telegrams. Sometimes in the Gander Bay Post Office people would gather to read the world news summary that came in on the wireless every day from overseas. As soon as she was done it was ready to post. She had tried to teach me telegraphy. I learned to send fairly well, but my receiving was painfully slow. I recall one time when she was sick and I had to take over the Clarke's Head post office. A message came in for

102

Joe Peckford at Gander Stores, something about an order of axe handles. The rest was all gibberish to me, it was coming so fast. Finally I tapped out: "SLOW DOWN REGULAR OPERATOR SICK." After this the other operator took pity on me, and Joe got his telegram by and by.

Right from the start I liked the streetcars. For one thing I could keep warm — the cars were closed in and I had a nice wool uniform — for another there were lots of people to meet. As for running the car, it was simple. All I had to do was work a control lever for "Park" and "Go" and "Stop" and know where to stop for the passengers. When each group had gotten off and the newcomers had boarded, the conductor would walk along the running board and collect the fares. Then he would pull the bell rope twice for "Go"; if he wanted me to stop it was one pull.

Our top speed was twenty-five miles per hour. The power came from a special wheeled shoe running in an electrified centre rail underneath. For better traction in wet or snowy weather we could throw a lever to dump sand on the rails in front of the wheels — quite a rig. I felt like a train engineer. My first morning convinced me there was nothing to driving a streetcar.

But that very afternoon, coming back uptown in light mist and rain, I had an accident near Pennsylvania Station. Out of nowhere a big stake-bodied truck cut in front of me, its driver trying to cross to the opposite lane between the pillars of the Sixth Avenue elevated railway. Unable to stop in time, I pinned it to a pillar. The driver wasn't hurt and his truck was only slightly damaged, but the cars and trucks soon backed up a long ways, furiously tooting their horns. I felt pretty stupid. An inspector came and untangled us. "Your first day?" he said when we were on our way again. I nodded and, while he travelled to the next stop with me, explained what had happened. He was a burly Irishman, a nice fellow. "I wouldn't be worryin' over it, son," he said. "A bad beginning sometimes makes a good ending. Use plenty of sand, the rails are greasy."

One night just before Christmas a pretty blonde girl, getting off the car with her boyfriend, threw her arms around my neck and started kissing me. I told her it was against the rules of the New York Transit Commission, but she was tipsy and paid no heed. I didn't mind. Her boyfriend, embarrassed in front of all the other passengers, kept trying to get her down the steps while she clung to me. Even though her breath reeked of whisky, it was a nice Christmas kiss.

Next thing we knew it was spring, the spring of 1927 when Lindberg's solo flight across the Atlantic was the talk of the town. I'll never forget the excitement when he landed near Paris on May 21. I was at 33rd Street and Penn Station when I heard the newsboys yelling, shouting until they were hoarse: "Lindy in Paris! Read all about it! Lindy lands in Paris!" He had taken off from Roosevelt Field on Long Island the day before at about eight in the morning, and nobody knew if he and his single-engine plane, *The Spirit of St. Louis*, would ever be heard tell of again. I remember when he arrived back there was a huge ticker-tape parade for him, with a model of the plane on a float, and flowers and balloons; and Fifth Avenue was jammed from sidewalk to sidewalk as the parade moved slowly to Central Park, where thousands more were gathered to greet him. I remember too a small plane writing the words "Lucky Lindy" in white smoke against the sky.

That same month, on May 4, Winnie and I got married. Although we often attended divine service at The Little Church Around the Corner — a small Episcopalian church at 1 West 29th Street where a lot of actors went — we got married in the chapel at City Hall. Until we could find something better we rented a bed-sitting room on Seventh Avenue. It was only a block off Broadway and you could hear singing and partying at all hours. The night we were married someone unlocked our door and stole my wallet with over $70 in it from my pants pocket. High on our list of suspects was the landlady, but even though I reported it to the police at the 47th Street Station, and they sent a detective, neither money nor wallet ever turned up. So Winnie and I started married life on a little over a dollar between us — for the wedding dress had taken all she had. After breakfast we had sixty-six cents left. As it happened, her payday was the next day, and mine was the day after. Even so, to pay our board I had to borrow $10 from a policeman I knew on 42nd Street. We moved to an apartment at 346 West 56th Street, a much quieter neighbourhood.

Summer in New York was murder. The nights, so close and sultry compared to Newfoundland's, made it almost impossible to sleep. On the streetcars, even though the wooden window panels were removed in summer and replaced with sliding green blinds, our wool uniforms made us itch and sweat. The city let us work in shirtsleeves and vests, but nothing helped. And Winnie and I began to be homesick. Oh, there were lots of things we liked about New York, all kinds of things to do and places to go. The slow fox trot was all the rage; Babe Ruth was a hero; "Bye, Bye Blackbird" was the song on everyone's lips. We had a good many friends by now, and the company gave us free passes on all the cars. We used to go to the silent films to see Charlie Chaplin. Sometimes we took in a burlesque show or a concert at Shea's Hippodrome, or else we would take the ferry across the Hudson to Palisades Park in New Jersey. There we saw two of the strangest sights of that wonderful and foolish time. We saw a cove white with floating French safes, and we saw the first man shot out of a cannon.

In August month, when it was hot enough to fry eggs on the sidewalks, we booked passage to St. John's on the SS *Nerissa*, a brand new 3,000-ton British steamer that Bowring & Company ran alternately on this route with the SS *Sylvia*. From St. John's the *Susu* took us home to Gander Bay a week later. There we spent our first winter together, snug in a log home belonging to Levi Cull, a friend of Dad's, on a mossy rise under tall fir trees in by Clarke's Brook. For a couple of newlyweds fresh from the noise and heat of New York, it was just what the doctor ordered.

Boston and Buffalo

In May of 1928, as soon as I got home from muskrat trapping, we packed our belongings and took off for the States again, for Boston this time. The summer before, my cousin Doug Sherring, had guided a wealthy young woman, a Mrs. Mitchell, whose husband owned a sugar plantation in the West Indies and whose father had been connected with the Waltham Watch Company of Massachusetts. Doug told me that she promised him a job in the States if ever he wanted one.

That same summer I had guided two brothers from Buffalo. One of them, Hamilton Ward, was a lawyer for Larkin and Company which ran a chain of paint and grocery stores there. His brother was a bishop. I got Doug to write me a letter of recommendation to Mrs. Mitchell. Between Mrs. Mitchell, Mr. Ward, and the bishop, I figured I could land a job for sure.

Again we boarded the *Susu* to St. John's. And if my memory serves me right, the vessel that took us to Boston was the SS *North Star*, an old American ship about the size of the *Nerissa*. At Customs and Immigration in Boston we had a little trouble because Winnie was now five months pregnant. They put her in detention and made me wait so long I got worried. There were so many European immigrants swarming through there, speaking so many languages, lugging all their worldly goods and trailing youngsters of all ages, I could easily imagine losing each other for good. Finally we got clear of Immigration, hailed a cab, and found a hotel.

Mrs. Mitchell's address on the letter Doug gave me was Beverly Farms, Danvers. The next day we took the streetcar out to Pride's Crossing, the end of the line, and walked the mile or so to where the conductor thought she lived. Passing Beverly, he explained how it had been a sort of summer retreat for the Boston big wigs in earlier years, and that the locals still referred to it as "The Gold Coast." He said the Bostonians of that day even had their own private train for commuting back and forth on weekends — and were put out when outsiders nicknamed the place "Beggarly."

Certainly the houses and grounds were finer than any Winnie and I had ever seen. It was a lovely spring day, so we strolled along Hale Street taking in the sights. It was hard to believe we had left our little log house by Clarke's Brook, with snowbanks still lingering in the shade of the trees, only a week before. We passed two- and three-storey mansions behind huge oak and elm trees with big flower beds just coming into bloom, bird baths and lawn statues, ironwork fences with ornate gates and granite or cement gateposts, people playing a game with wooden mallets and balls — we gawked at everything. By asking our way we found Mrs. Mitchell at last. A tall, twenty-two-year-old brunette, she wondered at first who we were. I told her, mentioned the fishing trip, and passed her the letter from Doug. That broke the ice. She introduced us to her mother, a dignified white-haired lady who sent a maid scurrying to make tea and made Winnie sit down and rest.

Meanwhile, Mrs. Mitchell drove me out to her husband's farm. They had bought a fifty-acre estate outside Danvers, she explained, and they planned to build a house and raise horses. My job would be to cut brush, prune old fruit trees and clear away stumps. She also wanted me to make a run for her Irish wolfhound. She would provide tools and materials, and Winnie and I would live in a nearby cottage, next door to a Mrs. Thatcher, the widow of the farm's former owner. Driving back to Beverly Farms in her shiny Packard, I felt pretty lucky. Our first day in Boston and already a job and a place to live.

I might have known it was too good to be true. First off, the tools — axe, shovel, pruning saw — were rusty and had bad handles from being stored in a shed with a leaky roof. After fixing the handles I had to ask Mrs. Thatcher where there was a grindstone and she sent me down the road to a Mr. Barnes. This put me behind in making the run for the dog, and when Mrs. Mitchell drove out after dinner the next day with the roll of wire and the dog, she was annoyed. That was only the beginning. From the start nothing seemed to satisfy her. At least twice a day, sometimes oftener, she would drive out to the farm to check up on me. Each time she would order me to do something different. If I was pruning apple trees she would tell me to climb down and go dig stumps. I'd just start in on the stumps when she would decide to have me clean out the well. She knew next to nothing about how such things were done, but she never hesitated to give her advice anyway. In two weeks I was so fed up I was on the hand of quitting.

One day she arrived during my usual lunch hour. I was home eating dinner when she rapped at the door and accused me of leaving work fifteen minutes early. Noticing there was a difference of some fifteen minutes between our watches, I pointed this out.

"You think you're clever, don't you?" she said. "I don't fall for that old dodge!"

"Well," I said, "in Newfoundland the Waltham watch has a pretty good name, and mine is a Waltham. But if it's off when you check at home tonight, I'll be glad to make up the time tomorrow and to set my watch by yours."

"Nothing doing, you're shirking and you know it," she yelled.

That made me crooked and I said, "What you want here, Mrs. Mitchell, is some Negro slaves like your husband has in the West Indies, someone who will jump when you crack the whip. As for me, I quit."

"Saunders, I give you twenty-four hours to get out of this cottage, and I'll be back at twelve o'clock sharp tomorrow to see that you are!" Brown eyes flashing, she paid me my two weeks' wages and drove off in a cloud of dust.

After she left I went to Mrs. Thatcher and told her the story. Her round face flushed pink with exasperation and she clenched her big hands in anger. "Mr. Saunders," she said, "I still own that cottage, it goes with my house lot, and Her Ladyship will be in for a big surprise if she tries anything like that. You and Mrs. Saunders can stay as long as you like, and you may tell her I said so!"

The next day, at twelve on the dot, Mrs. Mitchell was on the doorstep. Furious at finding us still there, she repeated her demand. I told her to mind her own business and closed the door in her face. When she drove off, gravel from her rear wheels rattled against the walls. That was the last I saw of her, and the last I wanted to.

A few days later we said goodbye to Mrs. Thatcher and took the train to Buffalo where I hoped to find work through Hamilton Ward, the lawyer. If that didn't pan out I planned to look up my father's brother Ned, a skilled carpenter who had moved there from Change Islands years before. In the lingering June dusk we raced westward through the rolling farms and woodlots of upstate New York, crossed the Connecticut and Hudson, and swung up the Mohawk that I had read about in Zane Grey novels. Above the steady clacking of the wheels, the chuffing of the engine, the mournful hooting of the whistle, we could hear the conductor calling the roll of the places along our way: Albany and Amsterdam and Utica,

Syracuse and Newark and Rochester. We slept in our seats and awoke in Buffalo. Neither of us knew the first thing about Buffalo, only that it was near Niagara Falls. I bought a paper, hailed a taxi and, after a few tries, found a place on Ellicott Street to stay for the next day or so. It was a little seedy, but all we could afford.

Erie County Bank Building, said Mr. Ward's business card. The next morning, while Winnie bolted the door and stayed behind to get some rest, I took a cab there. Inside, I saw a door with frosted glass bearing in gold letters the words "WARD, FLYNN, SPRING & TILLOU." As I entered, a secretary glanced up from her typing.

"Yes?" she said.

"I've come to see Mr. Ward. Is he in?"

"You have an appointment?" she asked, reaching for her book. I kicked myself mentally for not calling ahead.

"No, I'm afraid I haven't," I said, "But would you tell him anyway that Brett Saunders from Newfoundland is here to see him?"

"Just a minute, sir," she said, and went into his office, to appear a minute later, smiling. "Mr. Ward will see you now," she said.

I thought to myself as I ventured in, what if he doesn't recognize me? What if he heaves me out for wasting his time? When I got inside the office, hat in hand, he was sitting side-on to me at a wide mahogany desk, rapidly dictating to a woman taking shorthand notes. Although he was dressed now in a three-piece, pinstriped blue suit, he was undoubtedly the same man I had guided the summer before. As he spoke he turned toward me, but made no sign that he remembered me. Looking around at the richly upholstered chairs, the thick green carpet and the wall of law books, I considered bolting.

"...Yours very truly," he concluded. "That'll be all, thank you, Miss White." Quickly the stenographer withdrew. Still without acknowledging me, he swung his chair around, yanked open a bottom drawer of his desk, and drew out a leather-bound red notebook.

"First trout, two and one-half pounds, Joe Batt's Brook, July 15, 1926," he read, grinning mischievously. Then up he bounded from his chair and grabbed me in a bearhug, telling me how glad he was to see me and asking what he could do for me. I told him about Danvers and asked if he remembered his offer of a job in Buffalo if ever I needed it.

"Sure do," he said, and wanted to know what I had in mind and what experience I had. I told him I had clerked in Toronto and in my father's store. He then had his secretary come back in and take two letters of recommendation, one to the president of Larkin and Company, the other to the president of S.W. Flickinger and Company. When he finished he said to her, "And Miss White, will you add this postscript to each: 'If you want to know anything about sport fishing, ask Saunders; he can take you where you can catch two hundred pounds of salmon and trout a day.'" While I waited for the letters to be typed and signed he relived his week on the Gander, talking a mile a minute about how each salmon had fought the rod, how good each fried trout had tasted, how fierce the nippers had been. On learning that I was now married, he invited us to supper the next night, insisted on picking us up, found out where we were staying and urged us to move to a better section of town as soon as we could. The letters being ready, he scrawled his signature on each, folded them into envelopes and said, "Show these to the personnel officer at either place; I'm pretty sure you'll get a job." His telephone had been ringing for some time; we shook hands, I thanked him, he waved, and that was that.

The personnel officer at Larkins' main store only called two stores before he found me an opening as a clerk in their Tonawanda Street branch supermarket. The manager, Mr. Beale, a serious gray-haired man of about fifty-five, told me the pay would be $18 a week and that I could start work right away. The next day Winnie and I found a nice upstairs flat at 74 Edgar Avenue, within walking distance of the store.

And at eight that night Ward came in his touring car to pick us up. On the way to his place, still talking excitedly about fishing, he forgot all about the speed limit. Next thing we knew a police car took after us and forced us over to the curb.

"Do you realize you were doing forty in a twenty-five-mile-per-hour zone?" barked the officer.

"No, officer, I can truthfully say I didn't," replied Ward. "I was reeling in a three-pound trout at Joe Batt's Brook!" The policeman gave him a queer look and wrote out a speeding ticket.

The first thing we smelled on entering his home was salt beef and cabbage. "Steamboat!" he bawled out as he hung up our coats, "Come out here and meet my friends the Saunderses from Newfoundland!" Out came two smiling girls, one about nineteen and big like her dad, the other around fourteen and slender. "My daughters," he said proudly. "They look after me now that my wife has died — or try to." The food was wonderful, he was delighted to hear my news about the job and our move from Ellicott, and we liked Buffalo already.

So I went to work at Larkin's. And on the sixth of September, at the Deaconess Hospital, our first child was born. A Dr. Schultz did the delivery. We named him Evelyn Calvin, the Evelyn coming from my first name. We had a job, a nice place to live, and now a healthy baby boy. Despite the storm that was gathering on Wall Street and around the world, for us it seemed a good life. I applied myself to learn the grocery business. It was a nice clean store to work in — even had a tabby cat to catch mice. All the tinned and packaged goods like condensed milk and bully beef and Kellogg's corn flakes were stacked along the aisles where the customers could pick out what they wanted. Flour and sugar and the like were weighed out at the counter, just like in Father's store. Beale did up the price tags and wrote the specials in white poster paint on the outsides of the windows. When he saw I could letter them almost as fast inside, working backwards, he let me do it for him. After a few months I was looking after all the displays, taking stock, and placing orders. About all I wasn't doing was the books. Meanwhile, Beale was spending less and less time in the store. "Gotta go on another business trip," he would say, and I knew I wouldn't see him for three or four days. Being overworked, I asked for a raise, but he refused. One day that spring, when Mr. Templeton from head office was there, I overheard Beale running me down. I knew I would never get ahead so long as he had any say in it.

Then I remembered how, after our son's birth notice had appeared in the paper the fall before, a couple of men from the Prudential Life Insurance Company had showed up and sold us a policy on the baby. One was a Newfoundlander from Kelligrews, Albert Fagan by name. While filling in the forms he had asked where I worked. As they were leaving, Fagan said, "Why don't you come with the Prudential? How much do Larkins pay you, might I ask?" When I told him they laughed. Fagan punched me goodnaturedly in the shoulder and said, "Ah, b'y, you're wastin' your time with the likes o' them. With us you can up that by $10 a week. Think on it."

That stuck in my mind, and now, with the grocery business turning sour, I thought about it a lot. The way Fagan had described it, all I'd have to do was take a four-block area, collect premiums from all the policyholders once a week, and then in the three or four days left, drum up new business. And for every policy sold I would get a bonus. I could see he was a smooth talker, but felt there was no reason for him to cod a fellow Newfoundlander. In April, when we couldn't afford to buy a new pram for the baby and had to comb the ads for a secondhand one, I decided I'd had enough of being Beale's lackey and I quit.

The territory Prudential gave me was in the Hoyt and Grant Street area, too far to do on foot. We couldn't afford a car, so in May we moved closer, to 191 Hoyt Street, where we had a downstairs flat owned by a childless couple, a Mr. and Mrs. Weller from Alabama. He was thin and jaundiced-looking and kept to himself a lot; she was overweight and moody and when she came out of one of her periodic depressions she would go on a baking spree and bring us down a lovely cake or pie and coo over our son as if he was her own.

My salary at Prudential started at $27 a month plus commissions. So Fagan was right about that. On my five-block beat there were about a hundred of our policyholders, mostly working-class people. Each had a small payment record book which I had to sign. Some paid weekly, some every fortnight, and a few monthly. I must say, they were very faithful about it too, at least the working class people. If they weren't home, or were sick or had a hangover, they would leave the money and record book under the mat in the front porch or some such place. Some of the people I never saw from one month to the next. Generally it took more time trying to collect premiums from my wealthy customers than for all the rest combined. If a customer from elsewhere moved to Buffalo the head office would transfer their records and give us their name and address. One time I turned up only two days after a woman had arrived from Chicago. She opened to my knock and said, "How the hell did you fellas find me so quick?" It was a smart company that way, on their toes. And they wouldn't stand for monkey business of any kind. Now and then we'd hear of one of our salesmen messing around with a woman client. If it was true, he would be fired.

But as times grew worse, welching on premiums became the rule rather than the exception. People just couldn't pay. Fewer and fewer took out new policies. Our commissions dried up. Then the lines of shabby men began to form outside downtown church halls, waiting hours for a bowl of hot soup. Even more pitiful was the sight of dozens of fellows in their best clothes waiting day after day outside some factory in hopes of landing one of the few jobs that might come up. As for Winnie and Calvin and me, we were all right for the time being, although I was getting worried. Maybe, I thought, a car would double my territory and pay for itself. That spring I bought a secondhand Model T coupe for $35. I had never driven before, but I figured it couldn't be much worse than a streetcar. Without bothering to get a licence — in those days automobiles were still scarce and the police lax about such things — I went right to it. The Ford got me around faster all right, but the money just wasn't there. I tried hard for a couple of months, but the handwriting was on the wall. In July I applied for work on the streetcars; there at least I would be sure of a job and good pay.

Because the Buffalo streetcars were one-man affairs where the operator also had to collect fares and issue transfers, I first had to go through three weeks' training. Then, instead of assigning me a regular run like I had in New York, they put me down on what they called the Extra Board, which meant I filled in for anybody who was sick or on holidays in my district. The district was served by fifty or sixty cars, which were housed and serviced in a central barn where all the routes and operators' names were marked on a big blackboard. Each route normally had three or four cars, more in rush hours. The idea was to have a car coming along every five to ten minutes.

It wasn't too bad. True, I had to work all hours, but the pace was slower than in New York. And the summer, thanks to the cool breezes off Lake Erie and down from Canada, was nowhere near so hot. The crosstown run along Fillmore Avenue, a two-hour trip that looped up around McKinley's Monument and took in the stockyards and the working-class districts, was the most interesting. It was a rundown district that smelled of coalsmoke and slaughterhouses, and the garbage wasn't always picked up. But the people were lively and colourful. At one stop we always had sixty or seventy girls from a hairpin factory waiting to get on at noon and suppertime. This meant a three- or four-minute delay. To keep on schedule I always tried to pick up some time beforehand. During rush hour, Italian and Polish workers, most of whom spoke no English, would come up the steps smiling and hand us transfers several days old, and you had to take them because there was no time to argue or explain. Every so often an old woman would get on carrying a live duck or a hen under her arm and holding the fare or transfer in her teeth. Sometimes the bird would leave a momento. Then a shouting match would break out until the next stop. In their noisy goodnaturedness these Europeans reminded me of Newfoundlanders.

One day, who should board the car but Mabel, the girl who crossed Toronto harbour with me in a canoe. She didn't recognize me, and it was just as well. Speaking of canoes, before it turned cold Winnie and I would take Calvin, now a toddler, and spend Sunday afternoon at Delaware Park, paddling around a small pond in a rented canoe.

About this time I had a misfortune with our motor car. The weather turned cold and I had neglected to put in antifreeze. The water froze, expanded, and cracked the block. That finished her. There was nothing to do but get another. We bought a Model A Ford coupe for $150 with a $15 trade-in, and I put antifreeze in right away.

We had another misfortune that was harder to straighten out. One day Albert Fagan, the Prudential salesman, got aboard my trolley. Right away I saw something was wrong. Normally well-groomed and cocky, now he looked morose and his clothes were shabby. He sat up front and as we went along he told me how he had lost his job and hadn't been able to find another. His wife having died several years before, he had been living with his married daughter, but now the daughter, fed up with her husband's drinking, had run off with another man. So Fagan was out on the street. I pitied him — a fellow Newfoundlander out of work — and invited him to stay with us until he could find a job.

It was a mistake. He moved in and made himself right at home, with barely a token effort at job hunting. After a fortnight of this I offered to get him on the streetcars, but he seemed to consider it beneath him. That made me vexed, and I told him to get out. He went without much fuss, but still hung around, turning up for meals now and then and dropping in at odd times. He was on the bottle now too, which frightened Winnie. At last we decided to switch apartments without telling him, and to make the move right after our holiday.

For our holiday we drove first to Niagara Falls, then to the Canadian National Exhibition in Toronto where we stayed with my Aunt Eliza Oake and her husband Harry, a quiet, hard-working couple from Change Islands. When we arrived at their place at 847 Dupont Street they greeted us like their own. Harry worked all his life as a carpenter at Eaton's and died in 1977 at ninety-two. We had a grand time at the Ex, taking in the rides, the horse shows and the exhibits. The show-stopper that year was a man who stood on the wing of an airplane, a thousand feet in the sky, and jumped into Lake Ontario with a parachute. And on the fairgrounds I remember seeing a 160-foot flagpole, brought all the way from British Columbia via the Panama Canal because it was too long for any rail car.

One day while Winnie and Calvin and I were out for a walk the Oake's twelve-year-old son Holton got in the car and somehow managed to work the spark and gas levers on the steering wheel and got her going. The car chugged backwards out onto the street. There was no traffic or pedestrians right then, so no harm was done, but Holton got a fright. The Model A had its reverse gear on a pedal between the brake and the clutch pedals, and maybe he pushed it in thinking it was the brake.

While in Toronto I also went to Hugo O'Donnell's store for a visit, only to find the store under new management. They told me that after his wife died O'Donnell had sold out and gone to live at the Ford Hotel. I went there to see him, but the life had gone out of him.

Back in Buffalo we soon found another apartment. It was on Grant Street, seven or eight blocks over from Hoyt but still within walking distance of work. It wasn't far enough. One cold evening in October we answered a knock and there stood Fagan, with a week-old beard and shivering in a thin raglan.

"How'd you find us?" I said wearily.

"Saw the car," he said, smiling sheepishly. "These days I walk a lot."

We couldn't turn him away. As he came in I could smell the booze on him. In the weeks that followed I got him off the bottle, bought him a suit of clothes and, though it was against the rules, got him a free pass on the streetcars so he would have a better chance of finding a job. On October 29 the stockmarket crashed. If business was sliding before, now there was an avalanche. It was a frightening time: whenever you picked up a paper or magazine it was full of stories about banks failing, factories closing, and businessmen committing suicide. President Hoover went on the radio and told us not to worry, that the good times of the early twenties were "just around the corner." But more stores were being boarded up, more breadlines were forming every day, and more men were standing on street corners trying to sell apples at five cents apiece. As for Fagan, he was having no luck at all. And I noticed more and more empty seats even on the streetcars. Perhaps, if things got bad enough, they too would stop running? Already the trains were having a rough time.

Prohibition only made the Depression worse. Across the Niagara River in Canada you could buy a twenty-six-ouncer of Canadian whiskey for $2.50; in Buffalo the same bottle cost $7. A favourite trick of the bootleggers was to bring it over in motor launches after dark and unload it up through the trapdoors of certain dancehalls and speakeasies built out over the water. The police patrolled the river but they couldn't be everywhere, and besides, the bootleggers kept dreaming up new twists. An American woman who ran an amusement centre at Crystal Beach on the Canadian side rigged up a fake funeral, complete with a horse-drawn hearse and mourners and a procession of cars with headlamps on, and sent it at a dignified pace across the Peace Bridge. On the way she had her henchmen sidetrack it into an alley and unload a coffin full of booze. She organized several such processions before the police caught on.

As the Depression tightened its grip, troubles of all kinds increased. The papers were full of mobster shootouts, robberies, violent family quarrels. One afternoon as I was going down Riverside Drive just after taking over my shift, a bullet shattered the glass above my left shoulder and went out through the wall on the other side. I don't think it was fired at me, it was just a stray bullet from somewhere. Fortunately the car was nearly empty at the time and nobody was hurt.

One night my friend Clarence Ware, a motorman from Canal, Ontario, and I drove over to Crystal Beach to see what was going on. After touring some of the honkytonk joints we headed back. Clarence was driving, and the U.S. Customs officer asked him where he was from.

"Buffalo," said Clarence.

"What's the last letter of the alphabet?" said the officer.

"Zed," said Clarence. Not until he explained that he was born in Canada where almost everybody said "zed" would he let us back across. Even so, we had to drive over a mirror floor so they could check underneath.

The Fagan situation grew steadily worse. He began to drink again. On weekends we would jump in the car and steal a few hours to ourselves to get some relief. So when Clarence invited us to visit his parents in Canal, near Huntsville, we were glad to accept.

Perhaps if we hadn't been so desperate we would have checked the weather more carefully and left on Saturday instead of Friday afternoon. I guess because the Model A could do forty-eight miles an hour I thought nothing could catch us. I figured six or seven hours would put us there, no trouble. Between Barrie and Orillia, however, we struck heavy snow flurries blowing off Georgian Bay. By the time we reached Bracebridge, some twenty-five miles from our goal, we had a full-scale blizzard on our hands. Still, the car had a foot of clearance and narrow wheels, Winnie had the baby all bundled up and we had food and plenty of blankets, so I wasn't worried. By dusk the drifts were starting to slow us down. I had to gun her to plow through some of them. Oftentimes the windshield went completely blank. At one point, thinking we saw lights dead ahead, I slowed to a crawl and came upon a big Packard hopelessly stuck. All we could do was make sure the driver was all right, tramp two tracks around him, and carry on. Another time the radiator went dry on a long upgrade and we had to stop to fill it with snow. While we were doing this a touring car loomed out of the storm, and the driver, leaning out his window, trying to watch the road, saw us too late and skidded into the ditch. We got him out and went on.

It was around midnight when we reached Huntsville. Hardly a light was on. Right smack in the middle of the main street was this sign saying "STEEP HILL." Thinking the sign was more dangerous than the hill, I touched the brake and tried to avoid it. The car went into a spin, hit the sign side on, bounced against the curb, and went down the hill backwards. Later I discovered that the sign was hinged at the base so motorists could run over it without breaking anything — it would bounce back like a rolypoly.

Canal was about five miles farther on. A couple of miles out of Huntsville we came to a hill too steep for the Ford to climb in the snow. While we debated whether to leave the car and walk back to town a farmer with a team of horses came along and pulled us up the hill. From there we raced the deepening drifts to Clarence's parents' farm, only to get stuck

116

in their lane. We went the last few hundred feet on foot, with Calvin sound asleep in my arms. Mr. and Mrs. Ware were overjoyed to see us safe, and soon we were drinking hot cocoa and telling our tale. Samuel Ware himself was a sunburned, thickset farmer in his sixties with a bluff manner that was very likeable, and his wife was pleasant too. We stayed up until all hours talking, only stopping to check on the storm or to stoke the fire. The next morning only the roof of the car was showing.

"Looks like we'll be here all winter, Mr. Ware," I said jokingly. Little did I know.

"Oh, no fear of that," he said. "This won't last long. It better not, I've got a hundred barrels of potatoes to take out of the ground yet!"

That afternoon it rained torrents, and by the time we left on Sunday afternoon there was hardly a peck of snow to be seen. Before we left I took advantage of the thaw to have a look around. I liked what I saw. The farm was surrounded by wild country, all hardwood hills and cedar swamps with lakes, rivers and brooks. The people lived by farming and sawmilling. Samuel's brother ran a general store and lumber business in Canal, much as my father did. In the summertime Clarence's father and mother took in tourists from Toronto and the States, putting them up in one- and two-room cottages in a maple grove near the north end of their farm. The cottages overlooked Fairy Lake, a pleasant body of water joined to a larger one by the canal that gave the village its name, and over which the road passed. Winnie and I went for a long walk among the maples and pines, crunching through the ankle-deep red and yellow leaves, breathing deeply as if it was the last good air we would get, and thinking about Buffalo and Fagan and the Depression. Already our little boy's cheeks glowed with health. Already I was getting muscled up from splitting wood.

When we got back I asked Mr. Ware if he would consider renting us a cottage for the winter. "Well, I've never done that," he said, "and the cottages aren't built for our winters, you know."

"I'm sure they're no colder than the houses my wife and I grew up in," I said.

"Well," he said, "there's a good wood stove and plenty of firewood, if you're willin' to split your own."

So, then and there, it was arranged. I was sure I could make good money trapping those maple hills and cedar hollows. And we'd be rid of the man from Kelligrews who hung around our necks like a millstone.

That Sunday afternoon we left in high spirits, but not before Clarence's father loaded the rumble seat of the Ford with potatoes and carrots and beets and cabbage, and set a box of beautiful red apples in the back seat. The rear end was almost touching the ground. At the border the customs officer frowned, perhaps thinking we had robbed a farmer's market or somebody's garden, but he waved us through anyway. We weren't home two hours before Fagan turned up. For a moment we felt so good about the trip and our plans that we didn't care. Once I served my notice we'd be free.

Well, you talk about snow in Buffalo that fall. I was no sooner back than they put me on snowplow duty, which meant that each time a storm was forecast I had to go on standby. If it came, and it was a bad one, I might be at it twelve or fourteen hours at a stretch; but if the forecast was wrong and the storm bypassed us, all we did was sit around and play forty-fives or pinocle. Either way, we got time-and-a-half, and it was possible to forget the hard times. But it was always there, growing worse. One evening, on my way to take the snowplow out of the carbarn, I heard a window being raised overhead in one of the tenements and a woman's husky voice call out: "Hey, man, bargain night tonight...two fo' a dollah!" I looked up to see a black girl leaning on the windowsill in a negligee, her white teeth flashing a hopeful smile.

Few volunteered for the snowplows. They were just an open flatcar with a heavy wooden plow underneath and a windlass to raise and lower it. The flatcar had no shelter of any kind and, what with tramping around the windlass in the wet snow, it could get pretty slippery. The plow was made of three pieces of foot-square Douglas fir bolted one above the other, with the bottom piece the longest, about twelve feet. To raise and lower it four men turned the windlass chains just like you would an anchor, and there was a smaller windlass to swing the plow in or out. My job was motorman, and watching for obstructions up ahead. Once I got used to it I sort of liked snowplow duty, with the city battened down and hardly a soul stirring — just us against the storm.

By the time I drew my pay in November we had a nice nest-egg for our new venture. I gave Fagan the rest of my free streetcar passes and some pocket money. We paid the landlady, packed our belongings, jumped in the car and headed north to Canada.

Huntsville and Home

Huntsville's economy when we were there was pretty much based on lumbering in the winter — pine, spruce, hemlock and hardwoods — and tourists in the summer. Being in the centre of a group of big lakes near the southwest corner of Algonquin Park made it a good location for both. Canal was a small farming village a few miles outside town, at the point where Lake Vernon emptied into Fairy Lake, which in turn drained into Mary Lake on the north branch of the Muskoka River. The Ware farm was on the north side of Fairy Lake. In the four months we lived there I got very little fur, but we had some good parties, I learned a few things about wolves, and had a like to drown in a beaver pond.

By the time we settled in it was early December and the nights were growing nippy. The cottage, a one-room affair with a wood cookstove, was cold all right. The first thing I did was caulk all the cracks around the windows and doors, and pile fir boughs around the sills outside to catch the snow. There were no storm windows — and no plastic film in those days. I bought and split plenty of wood and piled it on the verandah where Winnie could easily reach it. Then I set out.

Clarence Ware's brother Allan was the lumberman of the family. He knew the country around there, so before winter came in earnest, the two of us took off by car to scout it out for trapping. Driving sixteen miles or so northeast, out beyond Limberlost Lodge, we parked the car, hid the battery, and struck out north on foot toward the East River. We reached it about sunset and camped overnight by the river. The next day we followed the stream down for five miles or so, cut back across country to the car and came home. That gave me a good idea of the lay of the land. There didn't seem to be much sign of fur, but we did come across a well-kept cabin belonging to a Michigan summer fisherman by the name

119

of Walker. It would serve as an emergency shelter if ever I needed one. Still, I felt nervous. It was all new to me: new country, new animals — in Newfoundland we had no bobcat or mink or raccoon, and no wolves — and it meant new techniques to learn. Would a bobcat fall for the same methods I used for lynx back home? Did the Ontario beaver behave the same way? How would I manage without dogs? What if I accidentally trapped on somebody else's territory?

There was nothing to do but start in. I went to Wares' General Store in Canal and bought myself a trapping license, steel traps for fox, raccoon, otter and mink, and a pair of snowshoes. I talked to everyone who might possibly know anything about the subject locally. I wrote home and had Mother send me some things I couldn't buy there, like my awl and tacker for sewing leather and my little Newfoundland tea kettle — what we call a "quick" because it boils water so fast.

I must say Christmas was a jolly time around Canal. As soon as the snow came for good there were sleighrides nearly every week, followed by dances in different homes. Or there would be skating parties on the lake, with lanterns hung from the trees around shore if there was no moon. And afterwards there would be hot chocolate in someone's home. The people, though fun-loving and sociable, were very sober in their habits. There was never any liquor around. A dance was their favourite social activity, and they would go to great lengths to get one going. One night we ended up at a farmer's house where there wasn't really room for a dance. The kitchen was large enough, but there was this big wood range in the way. Well, sir, that was no problem. "Out with the stove!" they shouted, and while one fellow was dousing the fire with a wet rag, two others were dismantling the pipe and lifting the monster off its feet and whisking it outdoors. A few sweeps of the floor and we were all set. Dancing kept that farmhouse warm that evening! The Canal people never stayed up very late either. By one o'clock the stove was back in place and all hands were heading home.

Each week that winter I would snowshoe about twenty-seven miles on a circular route that took me first easterly past Peninsula Lake and as far as Limberlost Lodge, then north toward Bell Lake, then down a brook that ran into the East River, and finally west down the river and south to Fairy Lake. Along the way I had four bough shelters to sleep in, and Friday night I'd be back home. I got to know the country well. But there were no furs worthwhile in the area. I only saw one set of fox tracks all winter. The hardwood forest was too open to support much game: there didn't seem to be enough brushy areas and cutovers. Along the brooks was the only place I found anything, and that was mostly mink and fisher.

By early February all I had taken was half a dozen mink and one fisher. The fisher was so big that he dragged my trap, anchor-log and all, several dozen feet before it brought up. Being so large I thought he would fetch a good price, but when I checked the furbuyer's list from Schubert's in Winnipeg I was disappointed to read that "smaller fisher are preferred because the fur is finer." They paid me $48.

One day, walking on snowshoes around a beaver house on the shore of a large pond, I broke through the ice and went down to my armpits. I should have known better than to walk so close, for the air bubbles from the animals as they swim in and out under the ice keeps it thin. But the weather was so cold I figured the ice would bear me, especially with snowshoes to spread my weight. But now, as I struggled to lift myself out, I could see the snowshoes might drown me. As the ice collapsed I had heaved my axe ashore and grabbed at some alders that leaned out over the pond. Holding on with one hand, I wriggled clear of my heavy pack and shoved it up onto the ice. Still I couldn't get out because my snowshoes kept catching on something. I knew if I kicked them off I would perish for certain in that country of deep snow. Pulling off one mitt at a time with my teeth and stuffing them safely in my top parka pockets, I ran a hand down each leg, which I bent up as far as I could. That's when I discovered what the snowshoes were catching on. There were two layers of ice. One must have frozen early and been flooded. I imagined sliding away between the two and redoubled my efforts to get free. As each hand reached the harness I undid it and threw the snowshoe up on the ice. Then with waning strength I dragged myself out.

What I wanted most was just to lie there, but I knew that with the temperature already twenty below zero and the sun going down it would be all I could do to survive the night. Because of an air space under the ice my chest and shoulders were still dry, but already my clothes were stiffening and my feet were numb. Keep moving, keep moving, that was the thing; get some firewood, anything dry, a dry pine snag, dry spruce branches, dry twigs. Grabbing the axe out of the snow I chopped an armload of wood, then another. With my knife I peeled enough birch bark from a nearby tree to start the wood. My blood was moving again, but my hands still felt scrammed as I dug down into my frozen pocket for the waterproof match container and tried to unscrew the cover. I seemed to take an hour, but I suppose it was only five minutes before I felt the warmth of the blaze and knew I was safe. Off came every stitch of clothes, right down to my long underwear, which I had to wring out and put right back on before the rest could be wrung and dried on sticks around the fire. As soon as my clothes were dry I shucked the longjohns again, put on socks and pants and shirt, and dried the underwear properly. By the time I finished this rigamarole it was time to make camp and cook supper and turn in. After all that I was almost too tired to sleep, and when I did doze off it was to dream of drifting under the ice, looking for someone and never finding them, though I could hear them calling. When this incident happened I was about eight miles from the nearest habitation.

One day I decided to explore beyond the East River a piece. After a few hours of showshoeing I climbed a rocky bluff to look around. From the valley below I saw smoke rising. As I drew nearer two large dogs started barking and ran toward me. I was just on the hand of defending myself with the axe when a hoarse voice called them back. A tall man with a mop of red hair stood in the door of the camp and eyed me suspiciously. I could smell venison cooking and it was closed season.

"Don't worry, ol' man," I called, "I'm not the game warden. But I am pretty damn hungry!" He smiled then, revealing several missing teeth, and waved for me to come in. He was a trapper too, only he lived up in Burk's Falls, about fifteen miles north, and used to travel home every two or three weeks along the railway line with his dogs.

He was a man in his fifties, a widower, and a dab hand at telling stories. By the meager amount of pelts drying on his cabin walls I saw he wasn't doing so well either. "A bad year in these parts," he explained, and blamed it on the weather, the lumbering, and the number of roads opening up.

We chewed the fat until the small hours. In the morning he showed me where he had three quarters of deer meat slung high up in the forks of three beech saplings, and he showed me how you could bend one down, cut off what you wanted, and let it spring up again. "Any time you're over this way," he said, "help yourself."

"Thanks," I said, "but why so high? The bears are all asleep, the crows can get it whenever it thaws anyway, but what else is there?"

"Wolves," he said.

"Wolves?" I said. "Well, I've heard a scattered howl at night, but so far I've never seen hide nor hair of one. I was beginning to have my doubts there was any here."

"Oh, you won't see them," he replied, "but they're around all right."

A fortnight later I had my first experience with wolves. My trapper friend and I had agreed to meet at an old millsite before heading for his camp. When he failed to turn up by half past four I decided to go on ahead without him and put on supper. It was a good four miles to his camp, and rough ground to boot. Pretty soon it got dark, and darker still in the thick woods. All of a sudden, as I trudged along a footpath through this cedar swamp, all hell broke loose to my left. Such a whooping and wailing and yapping was coming from those woods that, so help me, I thought all the dogs in the world were congregated there.

The hair on my neck stood right on end. I broke out in a cold sweat and wanted to run. This is far worse than having a bear around your tent, I thought. At least with a bear you knew what to expect — but wolves were something new. All I had was a single-shot twelve gauge shotgun. I put one shell in the breech and another in my hand and kept walking at the same pace, wishing all the while that my boots didn't squeak so much. For the howling had stopped as suddenly as it had begun, and I was the only sound in those woods now. Pandemonium — and then dead silence. Every minute I expected the first of them to sink its teeth in the back of my leg. And me with snowshoes on so I couldn't run if I had to, and the snow was too deep to run without them. As if on signal, the howling started again. It kept up the rest of the way to camp, sometimes the whole pack — it seemed like at least a dozen — sometimes just one or two, and always at the same distance. It was with trembling hands that I finally lifted the latch and got inside the camp. The wolves were still howling. Closing the door, I breathed a sigh of relief. And do you know what I wanted then? I wanted a cup of tea. Yes, I would light a fire and boil the kettle and say to hell with them. Trouble was, there was no water in the kettle. It took all my courage, I can tell you, to open that door again amid that howling and walk down to the brook, even with the lantern. And then, worst of all, to bend over helpless and fill that kettle. A short while afterwards my friend arrived, walking through those same woods without even a gun. When I told my tale he just slapped me on the back and laughed and said, "You Newfies will risk your life for a cup of tea!"

When Mr. Ware heard my story he said, "Why, there hasn't been anybody killed by wolves in these parts for nigh on thirty years." Small comfort, I thought. "It was the mailman," he continued, "on the Huntsville to North Bay route and it happened in 1902 or 1903, I believe. The country was pretty empty then, you know, and wild. The story I heard was they were after his horse, not so much him. And that when he tried to beat them off, they pulled him down too...." Samuel Ware was a very sober man, and though I looked for a twinkle in his eye, he seemed to be the telling the truth. I must have looked worried, for he took pains to reassure me that the case was considered exceptional. I resolved to treat wolves with respect but without fear.

A few days later I had a chance to test my resolution. I had stopped for the night at one of my lean-tos along the trail. The place being close to a fir thicket with good rabbit sign, I had tailed some slips. On a previous trip I had done the same thing, only to find the two or three I had caught all torn up by owls or something. This night, just as I was pulling off my pants to turn in, I heard the high-pitched scream of a rabbit in a snare. Hoping to beat the owls to the meat, I hauled my pants and boots back on and ran to the thicket. What I heard was certainly no owl, but the growling and scuffling of wolves. I got out of there fast. So much for courage. The next morning I found bits of rabbit fur strewn a dozen feet in all directions, the snow and moss all torn up, and not a trace of meat. Following their tracks, I saw where four wolves, travelling down the river, had changed course toward the screams. And a week later I saw where a group of wolves, perhaps the same ones, had ambushed and killed a deer out on the ice. The tracks told the tale: three cut it off and drove it into the open while the fourth waited. Then all four dragged it down. I figured it was a family group, likely a mother and three pups from the summer before. They seemed to hunt the same territory all the time.

One thing for sure, they were doing better than I was. Late in February I gave up on trapping and went with Allan Ware hauling hemlock logs out to the town of Dwight. Dwight is on a northerly arm of Lake of Bays. From there they would be towed to a tannery and the logs sawn into lumber. As the sun began to warm up and the snow to pack down, the haul road became a sheet of ice. Going downhill we had to wind drag chains around the bobsled runners so the load wouldn't overtake the two horses — a mishap they called "sluicing" the load. Some of those hemlock logs were over two feet in the butt, but compared to some of the white pine stumps we saw here and there from the old pine logging days of the late 1800s, they were nothing. Allan showed me where the government had gotten Henry Ford to build a quarter mile of trolley track to get logs across from one lake to another for the spring drive. If I recall rightly, it was from the northwest tip of Lake of Bays north into Peninsula Lake.

As the winter drew to a close we saw more skiers trying to catch the last of the good snow. There was one tourist operator used to fly them in to Limberlost Lodge with his own ski plane. One time I met a group of them in the woods completely lost, heading directly away from the Lodge and convinced they were headed right. It took me a good half hour to persuade them to turn around. Another time three stunt skiers stopped in Canal overnight. Everybody was talking about them because they were travelling from North Bay to Toronto on one pair of skis. With skiing such a big thing around there, Winnie and I each got a pair and learned to get around fairly well. I used to carry Calvin on my back.

By the middle of March we had landed seven hundred logs on the ice and hauled home fifteen cords of firewood. Allan wanted me to help him take the logs to the tannery after the spring breakup and I was very tempted to stay; but Winnie was against it. For her, living alone for a week or ten days at a stretch with a little boy to look after, in a drafty cottage without plumbing, where the stove needed constant tending and the chamber pot was frozen solid every morning, it had been a tough winter. The cold was far worse than in Newfoundland and often went on for weeks without a thaw. The nearest house, the Ware's, was almost a mile away and although Mr. Ware made regular trips to check how everything was, the nights were long without a single light in view. The fact was, we had come to Canal in a desperate bid to escape Fagan, not to settle down and become farmers or hermits. Spring was coming on. People were hurrying to get their wood hauled and split. On Fairy Lake men were sawing and lifting out blocks of clear blue ice and hauling them with horses to icehouses. The skating parties were over.

The worst of it was my winter's trapping had been a flop. That was hard on my ego. As I saw it now, the only choices I had were to go back on the streetcars or go home. We both had strong ties in Newfoundland still. Winnie's mother had died of a brain tumor the year before and, being the oldest, she felt she should be closer to help her father and her brothers and sisters. I had three younger brothers and a sister, and my parents were in their fifties. After a week of talking about it we decided to leave for home as soon as we could sell the Model A. In Gander Bay we wouldn't need it.

Selling it was no trouble; I got $75. We packed, bought a ticket for North Sydney, and said our goodbyes. The journey took two days and a night. In Montreal we had to wake up and change to the Halifax train. Blinking in the crowded, high-ceilinged station, taking turns holding Calvin, we waited our turn to go down the drafty caverns where the trains were. Like most of the passengers we couldn't afford a compartment, and slept in our seats. For hours we stared out the window. The Depression was everywhere, but especially in the towns. We saw stubble-faced men in shabby coats huddled in sunny doorways; factories with windows boarded up and no smoke coming from their stacks; school kids with patched clothing; railroad bulls keeping a sharp lookout at the station for hoboes around the cars. Things looked much worse than five years before when I had made the same trip home from Toronto.

At Truro we changed trains again, this time to the Maritime Express. Sydney and North Sydney always were grubby-looking towns, and nothing had changed. That night, after a gloomy afternoon under a threatening sky, we boarded the SS *Kyle*. The normal time to Port aux Basques was seven or eight hours; this time it took thirteen. A sixty-mile-per-hour northeast wind came up before we got halfway, churning up twenty-foot waves that rolled the ship like a barrel all night and all the next morning. At dinnertime only Captain Tavenor and the purser and a few of us passengers could eat. The rest hung onto the bunks and wished to die. I did what I could for Winnie and Calvin, but the stench below decks was enough to turn the strongest stomach. I spent most of the time in the smoking saloon. Sometimes she would roll over so far that the green water would come in over the rail and you could see it race by the windows a foot deep. Then thick wet snow plastered the upper decks. Luckily it was mild enough that her rigging didn't ice up. For something to do I went up to the bridge and asked if I could watch. It was wonderful to see her plow into a huge wave and to feel her whole frame shudder under your feet. But she was a stout ship — they called her 'The Bulldog of the North' from her years on the Labrador — and a credit to the Alphabet Fleet that served our coasts so well. We were soon safe in harbour at Port aux Basques.

But the effects of the storm were still with us, for it had dumped so much snow and blown it around so much that in the Topsails, just beyond Kitty's Brook, our train got stuck in a drift. Even with the rotary plow they could not break through. The conductor, a man by the name of Forsey, came through each car and announced that we would have to stay the night until another plow could come west from Millertown Junction. Later that evening they gave out blankets and moved us all to the first class cars to save heat. As night fell and the wind shifted into the north it got cold and the drifts piled higher. Soon the mouth organs and accordians came out in every car, everyone was cracking jokes, there was plenty of hot tea and cocoa, and the night passed quickly. For sure, it was nothing like the times when trains have been snowbound on the Topsails for two and three days — on one occasion a baby was even born aboard a passenger car up there, waiting for the plow — but it was no laughing matter.

The next day dawned clear and bright, with a light northwest breeze. When Mr. Forsey said the plow wouldn't be along until after dinner, I got out my snowshoes and went for a walk across the barrens and down along a brook. In a droke of spruce I came upon a little log cabin — about eight by ten was all it was — and scraping the snow off its single pane of glass I could make out something wrapped in blankets. My first thought was that it was the frozen body of a dead person. With a snowshoe I cleared a hole and crawled in the door. Inside, the air was almost warm. And there was a familiar smell, like bread rising. Gingerly I peeled off the layers of ragged blankets, two khaki and one red, to reveal a wooden keg full of water, molasses and yeast — a batch of moonshine in the making. In the corner was a small stove like fishermen use in their boats. I lifted the cover. The fire was out but there was life in the brands and fresh coal in a scuttle nearby — railway coal, no doubt. There was no sign of distilling equipment, but it was probably hidden nearby. I refilled the stove, replaced the blankets, carefully latched the door and left.

Around one o'clock our plow came. Meanwhile, we had pitched in and dug out the engine. The going that day was slow and we didn't arrive in Notre Dame Junction for six more hours. Then we had to wait three more for the branch train to take us down to Lewisporte, twelve miles away. In those days people had a joke about that train. A census taker in the area asked a young man where his home was. "Well," he said, "I was born in Lewisporte, Sir, but I was raised in Notre Dame Junction waitin' for the train." Sometime that evening it finally came. After thirty hours on the go, Ella Manuel's hotel in Lewisporte seemed like heaven.

But there was no sleeping in, for I had wired ahead to Father, and our horse and driver would be leaving Lewisporte at nine o'clock for Boyd's Cove, where we would meet my first cousin Doff Gillingham the next day for the last leg home. A sixty-mile journey in all. Bundled in bearskin and caribou rugs against a chilly onshore wind, we set off along the well-trodden mail route — the shore ice was too rough — up around Michael's Harbour, across the neck to Campbelltown, across another neck to Loon Bay, and on to Birchy Bay. The horse was no good to trot, so instead of trying to make Boyd's Cove that day we decided to stay there for the night. The place we stayed was a boarding house run by a Mr. Simmonds. That day, seals were all the talk for they had just struck in around Comfort Cove and Newstead and the landsmen were out after them with guns. In fact, we were just in time for flipper pie baked with pastry and served with potatoes and carrots — our first Newfoundland meal since the time we had salt beef and cabbage at Hamilton Ward's in Buffalo. After the supper dishes were cleared we passed a very pleasant evening in conversation around the cherry-red *Maid of Avalon* stove, we telling of our travels and Mr. Simmonds and his boarders catching us up on the Newfoundland news.

Before turning in I went outside to make a drop of water. The night was still and clear, clear and starry. From the stovepipe I could hear the sounds of the fire. Every time a junk turned, bright yellow flankers would dance among the stars, rising like fireworks until they winked out against the sky.

Boyd's Cove was but a short jaunt up along The Reach the next morning, and there was Doff waiting for us by the post office with our trotting horse, Queen. Queen's ears pricked up and she whinnied as soon as I spoke to her, but whether she remembered me after so long it's hard to say. Two hours later we were across Dog Bay Neck and out on the ice of Charles Cove. A fast trot on the smooth ice — what a difference from the day before — and we were soon passing Rodgers Cove, then Victoria Cove, then up over the winter road through the woods to Tibby's Cove and back on the ice past Wing's Point, and we were home. Whereas at Birchy Bay the ice had been packed in solid against the land, here there was open water. Already the Gander River had worn a black channel down the centre.

The whole family — Mother and Dad, Harold, Aubrey, Marion, and nine-year-old Donald — were out to meet us. It seemed like we had been away ten years. It would be longer than that before we left again.

The original Hodder family home on Salt Island, Gander Bay as it looked in 1984 before it burned. In the early 1800s William Hodder Sr. fished salmon here under a lease probably bought from Garland's of Fogo. In the late 1700s my ancestor Robert Gillingham Sr. and others carried on a river fishery using this island as a base. Descendants of both families are buried here.

At tidewater on the Gander River is this place called "The Works." During low water like this you can see traces of a "rakeworks" or rock barrier built from shore to shore with a gap through which the migrating salmon passed. It is likely the Beothuk constructed it for a spearing place. The settlers took it over and added a pound and gate so they could dipnet the fish into their punts. One day while doing this Robert Gillingham Sr. and his men were ambushed by the Beothuk and one of the crew was beheaded.

In 1890 J.W. Phillips' new steam sawmill at the mouth of the Gander River was one of Newfoundland's largest and most modern. *(Top)* Naming the mill site George's Point after his youngest son, who he put in charge, J.W. added a post office, general store, stables, blacksmith shop, etc. *(Center)* They even had electric lights, run off a steam generator fed by waste wood. Pine lumber was shipped from this wharf. *(Bottom)* Pine deals were rafted by two steam tugs -- note the stack and mast of one at far left -- to square-rigged ships moored five miles away, off Tibby's Island. As tallyman and timekeeper, my Uncle Hezekiah Gillingham is likely in the lower group of men; the bearded one on the far right is Skipper Billy Blake.

(Left) The bearded man with the fiddle and sealskin boots is Gander Bay's first school teacher, James Rowsell from Poole, England. The one on his left with the muzzle loader is my first teacher, Nelson Shave from Fogo. On his right is Bobby Walsh, barn tender for the Horwood Lumber Company. The woman is probably Agnes Gillingham, Mr. Rowsell's housekeeper.

(Bottom) The class of 1910, Clarke's Head, with our teacher Nelson Shave. The face peeking around Mr. Shave's in the second row is Walter Gillingham's. The tallest boy in the second row is Howard Thistle's brother Francis, who was killed in the First World War at 16½ years. The two girls in the front row are Effie Gillingham on the outside and Dorcas Downer beside her. The boy whose face shows right above Dorcas' is Arthur Hoff, and right behind the girls is Levi Harbin. I'm second from the left in the front row, wearing the woolly astrakhan cap. To my left is my cousin Hezekiah Gillingham, and next to him is Howard Thistle.

My father's general store, built in 1919 at Clarke's Head to replace the one he launched from Gander Bay South around 1900. That's Patsy, Aubrey's oldest daughter, about 1945.

Our family home at Clarke's Head, where I was born on February 15, 1904, eldest of five children who lived.

My parents in their front garden around 1953, after the old shop burned. The new one can be seen on the right. Dad died in 1954 at 78, Mother was 97 when she died in 1979.

(Top) In the spring of 1922 I was graduated with my Grade XI and Junior Association from Bishop Feild College in St. John's. Here I'm celebrating with two of my classmates outside Feild Hall. (I'm on the right.)

(Left) That's me the summer I was 16. I'm supposed to be painting the house, but you can tell I'm right full of devilment.

Clarke's Head in the early 1940s, looking northwest from our wharf. At the far left is Allan Peckford's house by Clarke's Brook. To the immediate right of the Anglican church is the two-room school which Calvin and Gary attended. The two long buildings on Burnt Point are Gander Stores *(right)* and the horse barn of the Horwood Lumber Company. Burnt Point used to be Bursey's Point, and John Bursey (1802-91) and his wife Elizabeth (1826-76) are buried there in a little cemetery by the pine tree.

The winter of 1922 my cousin Stanley Gillingham and I were catching and canning rabbits at Fourth Pond. He took this snap of me with our three dogs. To the right you can see a skinned rabbit, ready for the pot. On the wall behind there's two weasel pelts. And on the eave is our skates. We caught 1,100 rabbits that winter.

My Uncle Stanley Gillingham who drowned on the Northwest Gander in 1924. In my teens I trapped with him several springs and one winter. He's wearing the orange and purple sash, Royal Arch Degree, of the Orange Lodge.

That's me in Toronto when I was 20.

The clothing store at 368 Yonge Street where I worked in Toronto, 1924-25.

In May of 1927 Winnie and I went to New York's Central Park with the crowds to celebrate Charles Lindberg's arrival from Paris after his trans-Atlantic flight.

This is where I worked in Buffalo in 1927-28, the Larkin & Company supermarket at 780 Tonawanda Street. That's Mr. Beale the manager behind the counter.

In the late 1930s and early 1940s I guided a group of hunters from Twillingate led by Dr. John Olds, Chief Surgeon at the hospital there. We used to go up the Northwest in November month, and they were some of the best trips I ever had. *(Photo courtesy B.J. Abbott)*

On one of Dr. Olds' first trips Billy John *(Center)* guided him to this fine caribou stag, shot on the Harvest Fields near Mount Peyton. Dr. Olds is on the right. The third man is my friend and trapping partner, Howard Thistle. *(Photo courtesy Dr. John Olds)*

That's Jim John, the Micmac guide from Glenwood, and me holding a string of trout caught at Fourth Pond, Gander River in the early 1930s. *(From p. 116, Vol. 1, **Book of Newfoundland**, 1st. ed., used by permission.)*

(Left) My son Calvin, on his way to school in 1942, pauses to say goodbye to Spot. As soon as I fetch and harness the older dog, I'll be off on the 70-mile trek to the Northwest Gander to trap. *(Right)* That's me looking out the door of our wigwam at Eastern Pond, on a tributary of Big Gull River, in 1942. We used wigwams like this for overnight stops away from our headquarters camp.

Today's Gander Bay Boat *(front cover)* is a cross between a fisherman's punt and a cedar canoe. The first models were home-built "double-enders" like this one being paddled by my brother Harold *(in the bow)* and Gerald S. Doyle in the summer of 1927 or 1928. Mr. Doyle would make the rounds in his yacht **Miss Newfoundland** each year promoting his line of patent medicines, and we'd take him up the River for a spell of salmon fishing.

When we got the outboard motor in 1927 we needed a square stern or counter to clamp it to. Harold's father-in-law William John Torraville built this early version. That's my father Frank Saunders with the oar.

(Left) One of the oddest pieces of freight ever brought out the River by canoe was this fuselage of a **Hurricane** fighter plane that crashed near Third Pond one winter during the War. To carry it we lashed two canoes together. That's Sergeant King of the RCAF, and my dog Sprig in the foreground. *(Right)* In 1945 a **Norseman** bush plane went through the ice in Gander Bay. I took the contract to salvage her, and this is the scaffold we built for to hoist the plane clear. Her engine is under the ice to the left, that's her left wing in the foreground.

This is the **Fox Moth** --VO-ADE-- in which Joe Gilmore, Chief Engineer for Ferry Command at Gander, came to Clarke's Head several times while working on the **Norseman**, and which had the accident. *(Photo courtesy Edgar Baird, taken Bay d'Espoir, 1935.)*

(Top) In 1947 I guided Ben Wright, editor of **Feild & Stream.** He urged me to go into the fishing and hunting business for myself.

(Left) In the 1940s, I used to earn a few dollars guiding salmon and trout fishermen every summer. This is Dr. Bruce Finnigan.

The reels are just over four inches in diameter.

Winnie and me at the lodge in August, 1962 with a
3½ pound brook trout she caught. She was so proud
of it I had it mounted and it's on our mantlepiece.

My youngest brother Don, early
1950s. After he came back from
overseas the River was still in his
blood, so we became partners in a
fishing and hunting business.

Our fishing lodge as it looked in the mid-1950s. Located on Cleaves Island just above Third
Pond on the Gander River, it operated every summer from 1948 until 1966, when we sold it to
the Buchans Mining Company.

(Top) On the open bog and barren country of the Gander's headwaters it can take several hours to get within range of caribou. Here I'm guiding Ebb Warren of Colorado Springs at Big Gull Lake in 1950.

(Middle) Ebb thoughtfully regards his trophy, a 450-pound stag with 26 points.

(Bottom Left) Orlendo ("Lindo") Gillingham with the world record stag he found for George Lesser of Johnstown, New York at Robinson's Bog on the Northwest Gander, September 22, 1951.

In to Bellman's Pond one time I sneaked up on this gray jay pecking at a piece of hide by our camp, and caught him. Then I let him go.

In 1973 the CBC filmed me. Here two of my grandchildren, out in canoe on First Pond, are asking me questions about caribou and moose as we steam along. The show was aired on "Land & Sea" in Newfoundland and later on "This Land" nationally, several times.

PART III

A Dollar Here, A Dollar There

Dole Days

Toronto, New York, Boston, Buffalo, Huntsville — a lot of rambling in
a few years. But now we felt we were back home for good. I can't say
it was the Depression drove us home though; we might have weathered
it just as well somewhere else, I know Winnie could have anyway. It was
me who kept dragging us back. I just couldn't be content away from the
River and the woods. Winnie was just the opposite. Being a Fogo girl,
she had no great love for the woods. And she liked the convenience of
the city, and above all the idea of having a doctor handy. In Newfoundland,
TB and diptheria were rampant, especially TB. In those days if you were
unlucky enough to get it in your lungs it was almost a death sentence.
TB struck my brother Aubrey in his early twenties, but with lots of rest,
fresh air, blackstrap molasses and milk he recovered. Winnie caught it
later, but did not know it until she was in her fifties, when an X-ray showed
a dark spot on her lung that had healed long before. Our nearest doctor
was at Twillingate hospital, an overnight trip by motorboat in the summer,
and a longer trek — about fifty miles — by horse and sleigh over land
and sea-ice in the wintertime. Aside from that, the only doctor or nurse
we ever saw in the thirties and forties was when the hospital boat, the
Bonnie Nell, came on her rounds once a year, taking X-rays and pulling
teeth. It wasn't until the forties that we got the mercy flights from Gander
hospital.

The one good thing about living in Gander Bay was that it didn't
matter whether there was a depression going on or not. Nobody had much
of this world's goods, and cash was rare. But so long as a person was able-
bodied and energetic enough to hunt and fish and tend a garden and cut
firewood, they could get by. Our family was better off than most. Pop
still had the store, the passenger boat, and the green skiff. Though never

131

rich — he gave out too much credit for that — they always had a big garden, and usually a cow, a horse and a pig.

As for myself, I did everything to make a dollar in those years. I carried freight and passengers, canned rabbits and salmon, guided, helped in the store and on the wharf, sold stoves, trapped, went on the log drive. Later on I worked in the mill and in the woods, brewed and sold beer, bought and sold fur, salvaged two airplanes and even did some prospecting. And like everyone else, I cut my own wood, picked berries in the fall, hunted venison for the winter, and shot a scattered eider and turr. Most summers we would go out to Fogo to spend a week or so with Winnie's people and I would jig a few meals of fresh cod and bring back a bag of smoked caplin and salted rounders or leggies to enjoy in the winter. When the squid came in good we would jig them and pick them up and dry them for dog food. Summertime it was the youngsters' job to stab enough flatfish with the hay prong to feed the dogs. Every six or seven years the pothead or pilot whales would appear, mostly on an easterly gale in late fall, and then a good many would be out in boats trying to shoot and spear enough dogfood for the whole winter — or else doing it for the sport.

It wasn't a bad life if you took your time and never got hurt. People in the Bay had lived like that since the early 1700s. I can see old Uncle Dick Gillingham now, dodging out the Portage Road in March month with two or three logs on his handslide, dressed in his homespun gray wool sweater and mitts, with khaki breeks and skin boots, a crumpled felt hat on his head and a short little pipe in his teeth. What work those people did, often on nothing but bread and tea!

My first job that spring was to cut next winter's wood while the hauling was still good. That took the rest of March. Then we had to fix up a place of our own. Father had a two-story building from his fox-farming venture that was being used for storage. I launched that across the road to a piece of our meadow, and built on a porch. Sometimes in muggy weather we fancied we could smell fox, but we had our first home. To get soft water for washing I rigged up running water from a rainbarrel that caught the water off the roof. To keep the drinking water from freezing in the porch, I insulated the walls with sawdust. I built a woodhouse, a root cellar, and a place for our goats and hens. Winnie insisted on getting two goats for the milk; it was good for youngsters and it didn't harbour TB germs like cows' milk sometimes did.

By 1931 we were settled in. Then I began to think about trapping again, and to collect the gear I would need when the time came. I didn't even own a canoe or a sled or a dog, let alone traps and other gear. For a time in 1936 or 1937 I tried selling kitchen ranges. I had seen this ad in the *Family Herald and Weekly Star* and wrote away for particulars. The *Bridgewall* was supposed to be popular with housewives, at least in Peterborough, Ontario, where it was made. It had a baking oven, a hot water reservoir, a warming oven, and plenty of nickel to polish. They said they would give me ten dollars commission for each stove I sold. I sold one to my brother-in-law Tom Layman in Fogo and a few others, and bought one for ourselves. One thing it could do was hold a fire overnight — which our old *Waterloo* stoves could never do.

When I got squared away with the house, helping Father in the store — we always called it The Shop — took most of my time over the next couple of years. The Shop was a two-storey building about thirty feet by fifty feet that stood directly across the road from our family home, with its front to the road and its back on pilings out over the water. Uncle Harry Saunders built it in 1919 after he came home from the War. Facing the road it had two large four-paned windows, one on either side of the door. Inside, the dry goods counter and shelves were on the right and the tinned goods and other foodstuffs were on the left. The shelves went to the high, wainscoted ceilings. In the centre was a stout pot-bellied stove with an empty tin on top for tobacco chewers. To the left at the rear Father had his office, and next to it was the crockery room. Off to the left were kept the barrels of salt beef and pork, the saltfish, bologna, and so on. Upstairs he had more storage space for dry goods, candy, et cetera. He also kept a tea box up there in which he saved nearly every stamp on every letter he ever got. On the northeast side there was a small shed used for canning rabbits, and by law this was divided into a skinning room and a cooking room — you had to do that to get a cannery license. In those years Father canned both rabbits and salmon in season.

Gasoline and kerosene were kept in the oil store up on the wharf, molasses and flour and feed in the Number Five Store where the wharf joined on to the road. This meant we didn't have far to move them once they were unloaded from the scow. Diagonally across from the Number Five Store was Father's original shop. We labelled it the Number Four Store and used it for general storage. It also contained the big boiler used for cooking salmon.

Anything we couldn't bring down the River was landed from the coastal steamer in the green skiff which sometimes towed the big black scow if there was a lot of freight. The steamer came every two weeks, from May until freezeup, and after passing Mann Point and blowing her whistle once or twice in the Bight, would anchor a little east of Burnt Point where the channel was about twenty feet deep. These coastal steamers were mostly under a thousand tons, but our bottom was muddy and they took no chances. The *Kyle* once had a mishap in the Bay: she didn't exactly run aground, but being an ice-breaker her water intake was deep, and she sucked up mud from the bottom and fouled her engine.

Near the head of the wharf we had a swinging boom with a block and tackle rigged for hoisting freight, which was then loaded on a small trolley and rolled along a set of tracks that went past the door of each storage shed. I believe this trolley came originally from the lumber yard of Phillips' mill. The new shop was less conveniently located because everything had to be moved from these stores down the road 150 yards or so. The barrels of beef and pork we rolled, and the rest we took by wheelbarrow or handbar. Once when I was vexed over something — Pop and I didn't always see eye-to-eye over business — I carried four bags of flour from the wharf to the shop myself, one on each shoulder and one under each arm, each bag a hundred pounds.

In those times, when everything was Depression days, the worst thing about working in a store was the look on the faces of the people on the Dole. The government had a small allowance for widows and orphans, but until 1935 there was nothing much organized for the sick or the able-bodied unemployed. All they had to fall back on were their relatives or neighbours. Rather than beg, they would buy on credit, hoping something would come along. If the merchant wouldn't give credit, tempers might flare. The only general stores in Clarke's Head at that time were Horwood's and ours. Andrew Burden managed the company store. One time Alan Harbin, recently laid off by Horwoods, came and asked for some flour on credit. Burden refused him.

"All right then, I'll have to get it myself," said Alan.

"That's what you won't," said Burden, moving to block the door to the storage room.

"You just try and stop me," said Harbin, shoving him aside and striding into the back store. A few minutes later he came out rolling a barrel of flour. Out the door he went with it, and on down the road. A bunch of men were standing around, but nobody said a word to stop him.

Sometimes a man would leave one store and get credit from a rival merchant. This happened between Horwoods and us, and it caused hard feelings. Pop figured Burden always had it in for him anyway; there was no love lost between them. We had a boom of long timber and one night on a strong southwest wind and top-high tide somebody cut the boom and our logs drove away, a big loss which Father always blamed on Burden, though he never could prove it.

In 1932 the government set up able-bodied pauper relief — the Dole.

The next year the new Commission of Government added sick persons to those eligible. In 1935 they called tenders for storekeepers who would undertake for a fee to supply certain items to deserving persons who carried special coupons. The assistance was not to be in cash but in kind, and people could get it by applying to a relieving officer appointed by the government. John Oake of Victoria Cove became the officer for Gander Bay and my father got a contract. At the first going off the coupons were only for food — flour, sugar, molasses, yeast, rolled oats, tea, pork or beef, and baking soda. In 1937 they added an allowance for fuel, urgent travel, and milk for infants. As I recall, the amounts for pauper relief were $1.80 per month for a single person; $3.85 for two; $5.85 for three; $7.70 for four; and $9.00 for five. In St. John's it was higher. This system lasted until 1942 when they changed it to cash payments. By 1946 the outport rate for a family of five had risen to $25 a month.

Still, it wasn't enough to live on. The going wage for a man working in the lumberwoods was about a dollar a day and found for a twenty-six-day month. So if it hadn't been for catching rabbits and growing a few vegetables and keeping hens, lots of people would have starved. Dr. John Olds of Twillingate calculated that the diet of most people on relief came to not more than 1,200 calories a day, with very few vitamins. A starvation diet, he called it, and blamed it for the high rate of beri beri and malnutrition in the outports. Beri beri paralyses the legs. Dr. Olds told me once of visiting a home on Twillingate Island where four of the five family members could no longer walk. Noticing that a teenaged daughter still could, he asked her in private about it. She confessed that she used to get so hungry that she would go out back of the house and eat the potato peels her mother threw out. "That's what saved her," he said. "From those peelings she got the Vitamin B she needed." To cure a beri beri patient in those days took up to eighteen months of rest. Since only the hospital could provide the proper diet, this tied up a lot of beds. Many people were already incurable when they arrived; others refused to eat the food prescribed. "You wouldn't believe how many barrels of tomato juice we had to dump," he told me. " 'Don't like it, Doctor,' they would say, and that would be that."

For this reason Dr. Olds and others came up with the idea of mixing whole wheat flour with white. Everybody ate bread, they figured, and in this way everybody would get their Vitamin B. But people didn't like that either. Some fired it out and others cursed it. Yet slowly it caught on. That was the original enriched flour which today we take for granted.

It was the poor little children who often got the worst of it. A good many died in infancy; those who survived from the down-and-out families always looked wan and hollow-cheeked and small for their age. It was no trouble to see school children going around in the coldest months with only half enough clothes on. On the clotheslines you would see bed sheets and underwear made from bleached flour bag and sugar bag material, with the newer garments still showing faded brand names. So if your underwear was of a better quality, you could perhaps afford to laugh at the joke about the young woman whose flour bag bloomers bore the word "Purity" across the back and, on the front, "Fit for a Prince." Perhaps that was a made-up story based on Purity flour's advertising slogan, but the people's shame was real. Until hard scrubbing on the galvanized or glass washboard erased the letters, a boy or girl would rather shiver in wet clothes than take off their outer garments.

Widows and orphans got free medical care through the relieving officers, but there was no such thing for the general public. The only medicine they could buy was what the patent variety storekeepers carried. Among the most popular that I recall were Carter's Little Liver Pills, Dodd's Kidney Pills, and Dr. Chase's Nerve Food. For colic in babies we sold Baby's Own Tablets, and for sore throats and coughs Smith Brothers' Cough Syrup and Buckley's Mixture. There was no aspirin as such, but you could "take a powder" — a small package, wrapped in paper like a stick of chewing gum, that contained the equivalent in powder form. For aches and sprains we had a lot of call for liniment — Sloan's and Minard's in particular. These were rubbed on people and horses alike. A drop or two of Sloan's put into a new boil would often stop it from rising. Eye infections got treated with a weak solution of boric acid powder in lukewarm water. This was put on with an eyecup, a little thing made of thick, blue-coloured glass that you held over the open bad eye as you tossed your head back. Constipation called for a dose of Epsom salts or the dreaded castor oil. In later years we stocked the much milder licorice-flavoured Castoria which children actually liked, and chocolate-flavoured Tru-Lax tablets. Burns received a soothing coat of Mecca Ointment. Cuts got a daub of iodine or, if the bleeding was troublesome, some sticky brown Friar's Balsam which smelled pleasant. Before that the old people used myrrh from the fir tree or even a mess of cobwebs. If a finger got infected and a poultice wouldn't work they might use a piece of fousty or moldy bread, or — as a last resort — a finger stall with a few dozen newly-hatched fishfly maggots inside. The latter would feed on the pus and proud flesh until the wound was pink and clean.

For poultices the only commercial remedy we had was a salve called Antiflogistine that came in a small aluminum tin and was smeared onto a cloth and bound to the affected part. A poultice was more the speciality of the home remedy expert. Some favourites were the hot bread poultice, the mustard and flannel plaster, and the molasses and flour poultice. One or the other was supposed to draw out the worst of infections — from a rising finger, a boil, or whatever. For dogbite the recommended treatment was the mulched inner bark of the juniper or tamarack tree.

In skilled hands these remedies usually did work. I know that more than once when I was half-dead with a chest cold Mother's thick red flannel poultice cleared my passageways and got me on the mend. She never had much use for sulphur and molasses, though. This, along with kerosene and molasses, was for many years the standard spring purgative around the outports, and in Gander Bay it was no different. In later times the government distributed free cod-liver oil and Cocomalt for the children. Grown-ups swore by bottled tonics like Beef, Iron & Wine, Wampole's, and Brick's Tasteless. Other home remedies included charms or special recitations to drive out toothache and cure styes on the eye and warts. A favourite for warts was to count them and chalk that many marks on the back of the stove. As the marks burned off the warts were supposed to disappear.

To my recollection there was no pain killer except the headache powder sold over the counter. If someone cut off their fingers or had to have a tooth out, brandy was all there was.

In the 1930s we still sold a good bit of Gillett's Lye to women who wanted a good strong soap for washing floors and blankets and the like of that and who made their own. For the fat they used mostly the trimmings from salt beef, and sometimes caribou fat, and the lye did away with the job of soaking wood ashes and straining off the water. (For this the old people used to say that aps or aspen made the best lye.) Winnie made her own soap for years, boiling the fat and lye, letting it cool, and cutting it into cakes. For face soap and dishes the most popular brand was Sunlight Soap. Worn down bits were saved in a wire "soap saver" and used for washing dishes. Liquid and powdered detergents were unknown, and coloured face soap was considered a luxury. The standard disinfectant was Jeye's Fluid, an ammonia compound that you mixed with water.

For biting flies there was Tar, Oil & Pennyroyal which worked well but gave you an instant tan. There was no toilet paper. People used either the *Family Herald* or Eaton's catalogues, old copies of which were hung by a string in most outhouses. The *Family Herald* and other newspapers also came in handy for cleaning sooty lamp chimneys.

Even in those days the power of advertising was taking effect. Those few who had battery radios shared them with others, and between programmes and news they were soon hearing that this or that patent

137

medicine would cure them. Several of the products we carried in The Shop were promoted on the "Gerald S. Doyle News," and Mr. Doyle himself would make a summer visit in his yacht, the *Miss Newfoundland*, taking orders and drumming up interest in some new product line by leaving free samples. One time in Fogo he threw a handful of Tru-Lax packets to a crowd on the wharf and the next day most of them had to stay home with "the runs" — strong advertising indeed. We still have in the family an excellent wool blanket which he gave us. Another advertising medium that people looked to was *Dr. Chase's Almanac*, a small booklet printed on newsprint with a coloured cover. Mailed free to householders, it contained not only advice on everything from marriage to farming, but predicted the weather a year ahead. *Dodd's Almanac* was the same idea.

A clerk in a general store in those days had to be versatile. Measuring out flour and sugar, slicing bologna and cheese, weighing pieces of salt beef or pork (and trying not to get the brine in the cut on your finger), wrapping parcels big and small and tying them with twine, shaking out a few peppermints or common candy from the metal scoop into a small brown bag for some waiting youngster, going up the road to pump gas by hand or to pour kerosene into a can that had a potato to cover the spout, measuring molasses (a tedious job on a cold day), unloading freight from the steamer in the dead of night and then bringing it ashore — all these jobs I did in the first few years after we came home. At times I worked like a dog. My father was over fifty; he worried a lot about the poorer families and kept extending credit to people he knew could never pay. He also worked hard, rising at 5:30 a.m., eating a snack of tea and bread, and toiling over his books until 7:30 a.m., when he had a second breakfast with Mother. Sometimes after supper he would fall asleep at his ledger. With his church work and other community concerns he was kept busy, and he was obviously glad to have my help. From time to time he talked of setting up a new sawmill for his sons.

But looking ahead I saw little future in the family business for Pop and me. I doubted if I could work under him for very long. Although he was the kindest of men — he used to make up boxes of apples and grapes and take them around to needy families at Christmas — I knew we would never see eye-to-eye. In any case, I was likely too independent to work for anybody but myself. So I made up my mind to go trapping. The fur was up there for the taking, and I knew how to catch it. It wouldn't please either Father or Mother for me to follow the Gillingham ways of trapping, hunting and fishing, but I knew that by using my head and picking up what other jobs I could find I would do all right. And I felt sure that Harold or Aubrey would be much better for the shop or mill than me. Even so, I always liked meeting customers. And now and then something comical would happen to brighten the hard times.

Andrew Francis was awful hard of hearing and often got things jumbled up. One day when he came into The Shop for a plug of Beaver tobacco I asked him how he was getting on. "Gone to Dog Bay, you," he replied. " 'E went dis marnin'."

Skipper Johnny Squires was a fine old gentleman who lived at Squire's Point and still built a scattered boat. One day he came with a small gimlet in his mouth, the kind carpenters used in those days for boring small holes to put nails or screws into hardwood. He had it between his teeth like a pipe and I thought nothing of it until he said: "Brett b'y, I lost me smallest gimlet in the shavings and I 'lows I'll have to buy another one."

"But Skipper," I said, "Isn't that your gimlet in your mouth?" And I reached out and touched it.

He took it out of his mouth then and frowned at it, cleared his throat to say something but couldn't think of anything, said "Well!" and hurried out the door and down the road.

In the middle of the shop floor we had a hatch over the cellar where we stored vegetables and whatever else we had to be kept cool. When the cannery was operating in the winter this was also a good place to keep rabbits. Anyone working in the woods at that time would have a few rabbit slips tailed, and when they came to The Shop for anything they would bring their catch. So would the fulltime trappers. Generally these rabbits would come in frozen stiff, so the cellar was also a good place to thaw them out before skinning them next day. A lighted lantern left burning was all it took to do this. So there was generally a fair-sized pile of rabbits right under the hatch. One evening, just before dark, somebody brought some more, and then wanted something at the counter. Leaving the hatch open, Pop went behind the counter to serve him. Meanwhile, Joe Forsey came in the store. There was no lamp lit yet, and without looking where he was going, Joe stepped right in the open hatch and disappeared. He landed on the soft pile of rabbits — but he got quite a fright.

When packaged dry cereal came on the market we brought in a few cases of Kellogg's Corn Flakes to see how they would sell. After a few venturesome customers bought packages we awaited their comments with interest. Sure enough, within two days one of the more outspoken housewives of the community marched into the shop with a box of our corn flakes under her arm. Banging it down on the counter in front of me she demanded a refund — no ifs, ands, or buts. I asked her why. "Because," said she, "this stuff has been on the shelf so long 'tis all dried

139

up!" It was no use trying to explain about dry cereal to her that day; I gave her the refund.

It put me in mind of something that happened when we started selling ice cream years before. Pop had bought a small hand-cranked freezer in St. John's and it was my job to fetch a block of ice from the icehouse, break it up, sprinkle in the coarse salt, then crank Mother's mixture until it was stiff. And, having done that, any money I made on it was mine to keep. One hot day old Aunt Martha came in with her middle-aged daughter, Agnes. Both were mopping the sweat off their foreheads, so I gave them both a cone to try. Aunt Martha smiled, opened her mouth wide, and took a big bite. Immediately she spat it out saying, "I can't eat that, my child, 'tis too cold!"

Yes, we had our lighter moments, but not very many. During those years we were ruled by a Commission of Government consisting of three Newfoundland members and three members appointed by the British government. It is interesting to note that at the end of their term of office, during which hundreds of our children had to wear clothes made from empty flour sacks and thousands of our people suffered from malnutrition, Newfoundland's treasury held a surplus of twenty-nine million dollars.

Furring

I was never so contented as when I was trapping. Fishing is fine, hunting is fine, but there's nothing in the world like being on the trail for weeks at a time with a good partner and some good dogs in February or March where the fur is plentiful. There is no boss telling you when to come or go except the weather; no clock to regulate your hours except the sun. Sometimes you work like a dog, day and night; other times you lie on the bunk waiting for a blizzard to let up. And at the end of the season, if you're any good, you've made more money than if you punched a clock or swung a bucksaw all winter. All my life I've trapped, off and on.

It was my Uncle Stan first showed me how. He started me in on muskrats at Big Gull Steadies on the Northwest when I was seventeen or eighteen. Several springs I went there with him. After that we trapped weasel, fox and lynx one winter, and sometimes otter and beaver. He was a good teacher. Like Jim John, he taught me that to catch an animal you have to think like that animal, study its ways, know its habits and weaknesses, be able to outsmart it on its own ground. He showed me where to look for fresh muskrat droppings like dabs of black grease on half-submerged logs, and how to lay a trap so the rat will drown before it gets a chance to chew off its paw; how to tell if a beaver house is occupied in winter in by checking for ice crystals around the breathing hole in the snow on the roof, and how to rig a beaver snare under water to catch them as they swim out to feed on sticks of alder or maple that you've shoved down under the ice for bait; how to entice a lynx or a weasel into your trap by building a little V-shaped cat-house of logs with a birch rind roof to keep out the rain and snow and some rotten meat or fish in back of the trap; how to fool an otter by building a little overfall of rocks in

141

a brook where he travels and setting your trap in the water just downstream.

When things got bad in the thirties and forties, and there was no other way to keep body and soul together through the winter months, this knowledge came in handy. It was either that or go to the lumberwoods for three or four months at a stretch and work like a dog for starvation wages. The Gillinghams and other Gander Bay men had gone furring above Gander Lake for generations, travelling fifty to eighty miles upriver by canoe in the fall, returning before freezup. The rest of the winter they trapped handier home. It was my generation that started going back on the Northwest and Southwest by dogteam after Christmas. The season for everything but muskrat was October 15 to March 15: why not make the most of it? Besides, there were too many trapping around Gander Bay and the lower Gander.

As soon as I had a roof over our heads and a few dollars ahead, I bought some traps to add to my Huntsville gear and made myself a dogsled and two sets of harness and a pair of rackets. As for a canoe, I needed a new one but would have one built in the spring. At that time you could get one made for less than $50. We still had two good dogs, Jack and Spot. Add to that a gun, a portable tin stove, an axe, a cookpot, kettle and frypan, a handful of candles or maybe a kerosene lamp and some fuel, a fork, knife and spoon, a knapsack, and I was ready for the trapline.

In Depression days we never had anything but our bedrolls for sleeping on the trail. It was World War II brought us sleeping bags. Before that it was all blankets and sleep in your clothes with a bearskin or caribou rug under you. Daytime we wore long woollen underwear, Stanfields or Penman's; two or three pairs of homespun wool socks, the outside pair closed with a drawstring in the top to keep the snow out; a heavy mackinaw shirt under a homeknit sweater, and heavy woollen pants or else Army breeks (breeches), World War I style. On our hands we wore doubleknit cuffs, or mitts, with a finger on them so you could tail slips or shoot a gun without taking them off. For footgear we had either sealskin boots greased with cod oil or the newer rubber boots with leather tops, which we called logans. On our heads we wore anything from a stocking cap to a felt hat. One man, Fred Hurley, wore an ordinary felt hat winter and summer, no ear flaps or anything. But the favourite of all was the aviator cap that appeared during the War. This was sheepskin-lined, with a visor and thick ear flaps that could be tied down under the chin or over your head when not in use. For an outer coat I always wore a sheepskin-lined leather jacket. Many's the time I slept outdoors in that and no other covering in the wintertime.

When you had all your gear packed and a month's grub on board and all the last-minute jobs attended to, it was say goodbye to the wife and youngsters and off you went. The dogs, after being tied up all summer and fall on account of the sheep and lambs, would be all in a tear to go. Meeting up with your partner's team would make them even wilder. But soon they would all settle down to a steady jog with the two of you dodging along behind, helping them on the uphill stretches and taking a free ride on the back runners on the downhills. If the Bay ice was strong enough you would take the direct route across The Gut and on up the River; if it wasn't, through the woods you'd have to go. Either way, there was usually a beaten path. If you were the first after a heavy snow you would have to take turns breaking trail with snowshoes for the dogs and their heavy loads.

A man is foolish to trap alone any distance from home. The camp I used was a good seventy miles up in the country. If anything happened that meant an overnight trip by canoe to get help, or a week's walk if it was winter. The time I shot myself at Big Gull, moose hunting with Howard Thistle, it took him two days to get me to the Bay and it was another before I reached Twillingate hospital by motor boat. Without Howard I would have died up there. A good many times I've fallen through the ice. I've been capsized, threatened by bears and moose, stranded without food and stormbound.

Most fellows need company in the woods anyway. After two or three months alone a man will be talking to himself — or to the trees. As a rule, though, I never craved company. One time I went nearly three months and hardly saw another soul. All that time I was never lonely or afraid. Even with a partner we would be alone most of the week, only returning to the base camp for the weekend. Some fellows couldn't stand to be alone in the woods at all. I knew one — and he was part Indian, too — who was so frightened after dark that he kept a loaded rifle by his bunk all the time. Unless a visitor whistled or sang out to let Ralph know he was coming, he was liable to be shot for a bear. When this man left his boat to go in the woods he would sometimes fire off a shot or two to scare off whatever might be there. But he wasn't a real trapper. Most years I did have a partner. Billy John was one, Howard Thistle another. And for several years my cousin Stanley Gillingham and I went furring together.

The trapper's life was hard on wives and children. They were alone so much of the time, waiting and wondering. I know Winnie was never fussy about it. About the only thing a wife was sure of was that if her man came back he would bring her plenty of washing and darning and smoky clothes, and smell up the house with fresh pelts. Still, we did get some news back and forth by other trappers, who would carry letters or perhaps a piece of fresh meat or a new pair of cuffs.

Every serious trapper had his own trapping ground. This was more or less family tradition, handed down to whoever among the sons wanted to trap. Not many did. In our family of four boys, I was the only one. So I inherited Uncle Stan's territory around the mouth of the Big Gull River on the Northwest. Every trapper knew his own grounds even though they weren't marked in any way. It was just a matter of knowing the country. To a stranger this was hard to fathom.

Concerning this, a queer thing happened once when I was trapping with Billy John during World War II. It was north of Long Angle Island at the mouth of the Northwest, where Billy had a camp. Billy was a full-blooded Micmac Indian, dark and stocky and a superb woodsman. We were after lynx and fox. Although Uncle Stan first took me furring, it was Billy who sold me on the trapper's life. Many's the morning we'd be on the trail before daylight, the moon shining down and Billy dodging on ahead, and he'd say over his shoulder — I can hear him now — "Tail a fox slip in that lead there." And I couldn't even see the lead. So he would show me, and the next week he'd know right where that snare was even if it was buried in snow. Well, we were heading back to camp this drizzly evening in November when all of a sudden Billy stopped.

"What is it?" I asked, nearly bumping into him.

"The bastard," he said, pointing his axe helf at a fresh blaze on a spruce beside the trail. We never used blazes to mark our traps and snares. The most I ever saw Billy do was bend over little twigs here and there for markers. It was something like a youngster would do. We figured it must be the work of some serviceman on leave from the air base at Gander.

Without another word he went over to that tree and started in chopping. It was a black spruce three inches in the butt; he chopped it right tight to the ground. Then he stowed the tree away into a thick droke of spruce, came back, picked up every chip and covered them and the stump with handfuls of moss. It came on a cold rain, but he never slacked. Finding another blazed tree, he did the exact same thing. He also found two fox slips and took them up. When he was done you would never know those two trees or snares had been there. And as darkness closed in he went a couple of hundred yards off our trail and blazed a matching pair of trees the same distance apart. By now I was getting wet and cold and fed up, but he came back chuckling to himself. "That should learn 'em to trap another man's ground," he said. And we went on to our camp.

Another time, so they say, he found where somebody had tailed a fox slip over a log that crossed a brook on his trapline. He took up the snare, they said, and the next time he was there he poured kerosene oil on the log so no fox would go near it for a long, long time.

In the country we had two kinds of accomodation: the base camp and the trail or overnight camp. The base camp or headquarters was built of logs chinched with moss, with a roof of poles covered with birch rind or tar paper. Most often it had a tin stove in the front and a small window opposite the door. On either side there was a bunk, filled with boughs or a straw-filled mattress, and in between there would be a narrow plank table with a shelf or two overhead. As the logs dried, cracks and seams would appear in the walls, so before the snow came we always picked an extra bag or two of moss to fill them with. For chinching we used a blunt wooden chisel and a wooden mallet, both homemade. The stove was homemade too, from lightweight steel. With three or four lengths of stovepipe inside, it was easily carried on a slide or in a boat. In the camp it sat in a sand-filled frame or up on some flat rocks, and you stoked it through a small hinged door in front.

Ron Francis, a small man who found such a stove too heavy for comfort, decided to invent a lightweight model he could carry anywhere. This was before the Coleman and Primus stoves reached Gander Bay. At a plane crash site he had come across a really lightweight, strong metal. This solved his first problem; his next was how to get the stove inside an ordinary knapsack. This he solved by telescoping the stovepipes. At last his invention was all crimped and rivetted together and ready to test. It was light as a feather. "But would it give off a good heat?" he wondered as he set up the shiny box and its ingenious stovepipe and stuffed in the birch rind and splits. It gave off a good heat all right. No sooner had he touched the match to the tinder than the whole works, stove and pipe and all, went into a white-hot blaze, singeing Ron's eyebrows and damned near burning his camp down. It was no wonder. The white metal was magnesium — the stuff they make flashbulbs out of nowadays. I don't think it was this experience that drove Ron to be a hermit — they say he was jilted by a woman in his younger days — but it might have helped.

Away from the base camp we used either a bough whiffet or a wigwam. The bough whiffet was mostly for scouting new territory or if we got caught by a storm. The wigwam was a more permanent shelter on a regular trapline. With a whiffet or tilt you just had a sloping frame of small poles covered with overlapping boughs against the weather. You made your bunk in a hollow filled with fresh, small boughs, fir if possible. With a nice fire in front and the dogs at your back it wasn't too bad. Of course you had to wake every hour or two to chuck more wood on the fire, a chore you got used to. And I had a caribou rug that was wonderful for keeping the frost out underneath. Even so, if it looked to be a bitter cold night I might melt the snow and warm the ground with two or three fires before laying down the boughs. Or I might heat flat rocks to poke under the boughs before I turned in. The main thing was to knock off early enough in the day to cut a good big pile of dry wood and to build your shelter. But for a mild night I might not even bother with a fire. Then if it snowed with no wind I might wake up covered in white, and the dogs the same. To see their heads pop up out of the snow when I called them was comical, I can tell you. Perhaps I've got more aches and pains today because of sleeping that way; I don't know — I'd probably have them anyway.

If we were sure an area had fur in plenty we'd build a wigwam. There's nothing like a wigwam for comfort on the trail. The big thing is you don't need a stove. You've got your cozy open fire and a roof over your head, and two fellows can build it in less than two hours with nothing but an axe and the stuff you can find on the spot. Birch rind — I mean big sheets of birch rind, now, the kind you get off a white birch you can just get your arms around — was all we ever used. We would collect that wherever and whenever we found it along the River and ballast it down under flat rocks to flatten it, then bring it with us to where the wigwam was going to be. We would build it in the summertime or in the fall when the moss and roots were easy to dig and it was no trouble to plant your poles in solid ground instead of on the ice or snow.

Most Indian wigwams were built on a circular plan; we made ours square to give more room for the bunks. We would cut four corner poles, nice tant spruce about fifteen feet long, and we would leave a few short branches at the top to hook them together. That would make a frame eight or ten feet square on the ground. Then, three or four feet down from the peak we would tie a short cross-piece on each side using spruce roots or wire. This formed the smokehole. From the crosspieces to the ground we stuck shorter poles on each side, all cut to length, and leaving a wider space for the door on the most sheltered side. So this made a pyramid, a framework to lay the birch rind over.

The Red Indians, or Beothuk, used to sew the strips of birch bark together, they say, and caulk the seams with myrrh from the fir trees. That was because they lived in their wigwams or mamateeks all winter. We just overlapped the sheets enough to shed the rain and snow, starting at the ground and working up to the smokehole and holding them in place on the frame with short sticks and then longer ones, all leaning in against the walls. Then we banked the base with moss to keep out drafts and give some insulation. Later, using our snowshoes for shovels, we would pile snow all around to make it even warmer. The door was made with birch rind too, but covered on both sides with small fir boughs to give it some weight so it wouldn't blow down. It was a sandwich affair held together by two saplings tied top and bottom with roots or a bit of twine.

Smoke was the chief drawback in a wigwam. On logy days with no wind it hung at shoulder level when you stood up, enough to sting your eyes and make you cough. But on a cold clear night or a windy day the fire would draw like a charm, no smoke at all inside. And by moving the door a little you could adjust the draft any way you wanted it, just like the damper on a stove. If it was a real cold night we kept the fire going. To make sure we wouldn't be burned in our sleep we put green billets around the hearth; these kept live brands from tumbling out and catching our bough beds. Even in the daytime we never burned anything but birch for fear of sparks, and before turning in we always peeled a supply for the night. With those precautions you could sleep easy. And there is no sleep like wigwam sleep on a wild night in the woods, guaranteed. When you've got everything shipshape the howl of the blizzard in the trees, the creaking of branches, the hiss of the snow against the walls, are music to the ears.

Our cooking was simple: flapjacks and tea for breakfast, meat and vegetables for supper. Lunch was bread and tea and some dried caplin or a rounder on the trail. We usually brought enough bread from home to last the trip so we seldom baked anything. For pancakes it was go out and dip your frypan in the snow to get some water for the batter, then fry them in caribou fat which is clean and white — the finest kind of lard — and gives a delicious flavour. We nearly always had caribou. A diet of rabbit meat gets you down after a while. Although we never took more venison than we could eat, we nearly always had fresh meat on hand. Beans and fatback pork was another staple. Canned goods weren't too plentiful in those days: anyway, they were too heavy to lug that far.

I'll never forget the time I was hunting in to the Harvest Fields near Mount Peyton in the early thirties with Billy John and we got a nice doe caribou. After deboning the meat, he took half of it and tied it up in a woven wool strap about three inches wide and twelve feet long which he called the "Indian String." This string, after he had the meat securely tied into a neat bundle, was long enough to make a pair of shoulder straps that worked just like a knapsack. But that wasn't the most memorable thing. With his venison Billy also brought out the head. Since we weren't trophy hunting, I asked why. Billy just grinned and said, "Best part of the deer." When we got to the camp he carefully skinned the head, strung a long piece of snare wire from a rafter, and hung it right in front of the door of the tin stove. Opening the door, he poked up a good fire of coals and commenced twisting the head until the wire would unwind by itself, then wind up again, over and over — a perfect roasting spit. And Billy spent most of the night tending the head and the fire, contented as could be. The next morning we had the best meal of caribou cheek and tongue I ever tasted. Another time Billy and me and his son Lawrence were hunting and we had no pot, so he cooked our supper of caribou heart and pork and onions in a caribou stomach, roasting it in the exact same way. And I remember seeing him another time, years later, sitting in the pouring rain in his oilskins all one afternoon at First Pond, cooking something in this fashion. Rain or snow was nothing to Billy, nothing at all.

Once the snow was on the ground and enough of it, a trapper would let the dogs do most of the hauling. On the downhill, like I said, we would hop on for short distances, and on the level stretches we might have one foot on the back of the runner and push with the other. We never went in for fancy breeds of dogs: ours were mostly mongrels picked for intelligence, strength and good temper. Two or three to a sled was the rule, male or female didn't matter, although I always preferred a bitch myself for lead dog. They all had to be trained to the harness, which we made from a simple leather collar or a chest strap and belly band going back on either side to a wooden spreader. From the middle of the spreader a trace six or eight feet long joined on to the sled. All we did to train a new dog was attach it by a short line to the lead dog's harness and start them off. At first it wouldn't know what it was supposed to do, but when the other dogs started to drag it along, pretty soon it figured out that running was easier — unless it was stunned. If it had the makings of a good sled dog, in no time at all it would be pulling its share. In my time I've had some fine dogs: Gelert that Jim John gave me the winter I canned rabbits with my cousin Stanley, old Jack that speared himself on a fence rail, and Spot and Sprig that were my faithful companions all through the late thirties and early forties.

It doesn't pay to borrow sled dogs. I found that out one winter when I suddenly found myself in need of two replacements. The worst of it was, it was one of the best winters a trapper ever had for travelling. You could skate almost anywhere, keep up with the dogs no trouble. Since most of our traps were along the banks of streams and ponds or along both sides of the main river, this meant we could cover a lot more territory in less time, and check our traps more often. In the midst of this my two dogs took sick with something or other. There was nothing to do but take them home and try to find two more right away.

My father-in-law, Harry Layman, Sr., offered me two he didn't need

148

anymore. That year the bay was frozen as far out as Gander Bay Island and there was good ice between Carmanville and Seldom-Come-By. I stuck some caplin and hard tack in my pocket, strapped on my stock skates, and skated to Stag Harbour and walked from there and got the dogs the same day. In Fogo they were used off and on to haul water. When I harnessed them to the empty sled at home they ran like the wind and I was happy. Not until I got back to the Northwest and tried them on a loaded sled did I find out they weren't worth a damn to me. They just lay down in the trail. At feeding time they were full of piss and vinegar, but that was the only time. It seemed like they were scared of the woods or homesick or something. This went on for several days. I couldn't stand for that. The only cure was to make away with them then and there. One evening, after one last try, I took them out of harness, led them some distance from camp, and shot them. For the rest of that trip I hauled the sled myself. If you've ever pulled a sled or toboggan carrying a couple hundred pounds, you'll know what I went through.

The most important lesson a sled dog has to learn is to stay clear of traps and snares. Our dogs were always hungry in the daytime because if they're fed in the morning it spoils them for running. We always fed them one good meal a day, at night. So a piece of meat or fish in a lynx house or a fox set smelled pretty good to a dog. Some fellows cured this by beating them. A better way, I found, was to set a harmless baited weasel trap handy to camp where the dog couldn't miss it. It wouldn't be long before I'd hear him yelping and howling, and sure enough, he'd have the little trap on his paw or his nose. I would take it off, give the dog a few cuts across the hind quarters with a birch switch, and reset the trap. Two or three mistakes like this and he would steer clear of a baited trap no matter how hungry he was. That's how I taught my dogs to leave traps alone. It was an important lesson because a lynx trap can break a dog's paw.

Although my dogs would avoid traps, they would sometimes chase rabbits or other game. Billy had a very intelligent dog named Peggy who would stay wherever he told her. The first time he told me this I wouldn't believe him; I just laughed. To prove it, he picked a spot on our way home one evening and told her to stay there. We dodged on to the camp, but no Peggy. After supper she still hadn't come. The next morning we went back and she was right where he left her. It was a cold night, too. She almost wagged her tail off with pleasure.

The trapper is a busy man when the weather is good. When I was with Uncle Stan at Big Gull one of us would go upriver and the other down, maybe ten miles between us. Each of us would take a week to travel up one side, cross over, and go down the other bank checking our snares and traps. Thursday or Friday evening, if all went well, would find us back at our base camp, unshaven, hungry for a good meal, craving a good wash, each with a pile of animals to pelt. All of those animals, otter and lynx and fox, would have to be skinned with care so as not to damage the fur — a small cut could mean a big loss in price. The pelts would have to be tacked, skin side out, on special handmade, tapered boards to dry, with a long narrow wedge or spreader inserted up the middle to stretch them tight, but not too tight. Every few days the oil and grease would have to be scraped off and any loose tacks replaced. When dry, the pelts had to be rolled fur side out and combed. Meanwhile there was always wood to split, water to fetch, and meals to get, emergency mending and darning to do, and the dogs to look after. We never trapped on Sunday: we needed the rest anyway. Monday we would go our separate ways again.

You had to check your traps often, or the jays and foxes and crows would get there first and peck and spoil the fur, especially in mild weather, unless the animal was alive. If it was, we dispatched it with a blow on the head from a stick or the axe handle, or by stepping lightly on its chest until breathing stopped. A bullet would ruin the pelt, and we couldn't afford the cartridges anyway. Now and then a bullet would have helped, especially with lynx. The lynx is very quiet in a trap. It will sit motionless for hours, even days. One time Howard and I had one in a trap held by the one talon and nothing more. This was half a mile below Rolling Falls on the north side. By the depth of the hollow it had thawed in the snow I knew the cat had been there a fortnight. We had left the gun on the slide back at the river so there was nothing to do but try to club him. The minute I raised the stick the lynx made a sideways lurch and was gone like a ghost through the trees: a big loss for the trapper, freedom for the cat. Billy John lost his favourite dog one time when a lynx got loose like this and clawed half the dog's face off so that he had to make away with her then and there.

Oh, we had our ups and downs. Sometimes a snowshoe frame would break or the filling get torn. You could mend the frame with wire or rivets, and we always carried a roll of pre-cut hide for filling. Above all, we had to watch the weather. One week it could be snow that would bury our snares a foot deep, the next it might rain and leave them high and dry over bare ground. More than once I've been caught in a blizzard or a fog miles from camp at night and had to depend on the dogs to find my way back.

One thing you could always count on in was the hospitality of other trappers. In an emergency you could use anybody's camp and anybody could use yours. That was the unwritten rule. Another thing was honesty. You could leave your stuff anywhere and have no fears of theft. Those two things saved a good many lives. For someone half-dead from exposure to reach shelter just in time, and there to find not only a stove but firewood and splits already clove, a box of dry matches in a bottle on the shelf, along with tea and sugar and flour, was like finding manna in the wilderness.

One time Elam Gillingham and I went across from Big Gull to Little Gull in March month to take up our lynx traps for the winter. For shelter we counted on a felt or tar paper wigwam along the way. Well, when we got there it was just after dark and the wigwam was just the poles with three feet of snow on the floor. We had to make in a fire for light, and put up a bough lean-to with stuff we cut handy. We used to have several lean-tos or whiffets like that every ten miles or so, mostly boughs but sometimes birch rind.

There was one time during the War when I was glad to have a wigwam to crawl into. I was trapping alone at Fourth Pond. It was late in November month, but the weather was holding mild and I was taking advantage of it, making my rounds by canoe with my five horsepower Evinrude Elto to save time. At the first sign of cold weather I planned to head home. Having caught only two lynx, I wanted to do a little better.

Overnight a cold snap struck. The next day I had some minor engine trouble. Before I got it fixed, collected my traps, took down my tent and stowed my gear in the boat, there was ice making around shore and across the wide cove at the lower end. Steaming through this was easy and once I hit the faster tide it was all open water down through Fourth Pond Chute and past Joe Batt's Brook until I reached the upper end of Third Pond. As I rounded Cleaves Island I saw what I feared — ice from shore to shore.

Thinking it couldn't be very thick, I took a chance and steamed full speed into it. At first it was all right, but then I began to lose headway. This scared me because if I got stuck too far out I might not be able to get back to shore and have to stay there until the ice got thick enough to walk on. By jumping up and down in the bow of the canoe with the motor running full throttle I managed to gain a few more boatlengths, but that was all. I was stuck like a fly in molasses. After all my thumping and crashing around, the sudden silence was strange. I could almost hear the ice taking hold of the sides of the boat. There was no time to lose if I was to get back to open water. Turning the boat around was out of the question: I could not reach bottom with my pole. All I could do was swivel the motor completely around and break the ice with my pole as I backtracked stern-first, trying to steer at the same time and not fall overboard. This took me a solid hour. While I was at this a *Liberator* bomber passed over, came back, and circled several times very low, as if the pilot was trying to decide whether I was in trouble. It was nice to have the company, but I had no time to wave.

When I finally broke free, my clothes were wet with sweat. The evening breeze out of the northwest cut like a knife, but at least I could get back to dry land. The only thing to do was to beach the canoe and try to lug my gear home, leaving what I couldn't carry.

While poling ashore I noticed that the ice there was strong enough to walk on. I thought to myself: why not carry everything down the pond toward Third Pond Bar, a load at a time, canoe and all, and then go on from there? Certainly it would be better than giving up like this. There was always a chance that First and Second Ponds would still be open down the middle, being less than half a mile wide and having a stronger current. Third Pond was almost a mile wide, and that made a difference.

My idea was to use the tent as a toboggan over the slippery ice, then take the canoe as the final load. In minutes I had unloaded the boat, unrolled the tent to its full length on the ice, and piled on my stove, duffle bag, lantern, blankets and what grub I had left. Grabbing the tent ropes, I laid them over my shoulder and set off at a trot down around shore toward the black line of open water. Already long blue shadows were creeping far out across the ice as the sun slipped behind the tall spruce and birch on the western shore.

The water was farther away than I thought. And I had to allow some for the freezing that would go on while I brought the other loads. By the time I turned back with my makeshift toboggan for the second load the stars were out. Figuring that in the dark the first load might be hard to find, I lit the lantern for a beacon and set it on top of the pile. On my next trip I brought the engine, five gallons of gas, my rackets and axe. I carried the packsack on my back, but left the traps because they were too heavy.

On the way back up for the canoe a tiredness came over me. And then I remembered that I hadn't eaten a bite since breakfast: no wonder my stomach was growling and my legs aching. I made in a fire beside the canoe, boiled the kettle, and had some bread and tea and jam from the grub box. It was now a bitter cold starry night with hardly a breath of wind. Very nice to gaze upon, that blue dome full of stars, but the ice would be making faster than ever, and no time to tarry; must get that boat back in the water and head for home.

But I couldn't budge her. A Gander Bay boat has several hundredweight of plank and ribs and keel and nails in her, and even when

I held her on an even keel my boots kept flying out from under me. After all my work I was still no farther ahead. I was ready to quit. My hand fell on the brin bag of traps and snares. I had been wishing for a pair of creepers like the old people strapped on their boots to get over the icy roads to the store or to church: wouldn't a pair of traps work just as well? Among my collection were some Number Four *Victor* otter traps with teeth. Kneeling on the ice I set two of them, tied the jaws open with wire, and fastened one to each boot, jaws to the ice. I took a few awkward steps, dragging the chains behind.

They gave me an excellent grip. I couldn't slip if I tried. By two in the morning I had the canoe into the open water above Third Pond Bar, and everything back aboard. Three miles farther on I reached the upper end of Second Pond. To my amazement it was frozen too. And since this pond joins on to First in a narrows, and I could picture the ice reaching clear to Booming Point, seven miles away. I lit a fire and had another lunch. Hauling the boat ashore, I turned her over and tied her on and stowed what I didn't need underneath, and walked to a wigwam I knew and crawled into my sleeping bag and slept like a dead man. When I woke the sun was high. I walked the remaining thirteen or fourteen miles home and was there in time for supper. The two lynx pelts fetched $60 apiece.

But that was nothing to the trouble my cousin Stanley and I had getting home for Christmas in 1933. We had gone up to our camp at the mouth of Little Gull in mid-October, planning to be home for the festivities either by boat or on foot if the River was frozen. As it happened, the River caught over around the end of November so we hauled up our canoe and kept on trapping until December 17 or 18, which would give us ample time to walk home. It was on a Monday we planned to start out, but Friday evening the weather turned mild with rain. All Friday night and Saturday it poured out of the heavens.

And of course the River began to rise and the ice began to creak and groan with the weight of the water above and the pressure of the water underneath. The noise was fearful, I can tell you. But it wasn't the noise that worried us. Our camp was on low ground in a stand of old fir trees at the junction of Little Gull and the Northwest, and we knew that if Little Gull broke out before the main branch, we would be flooded out, perhaps even buried under ice. Around ten o'clock that night we heard the roar of the ice breaking at Little Gull Falls two miles away. Expecting the worst, we hauled our boat up close to the camp and stowed all our gear aboard. The Northwest continued to rumble, louder now, but not as loud as Little Gull. It was just like being out in a big thunderstorm with no lightning.

At the last going off we could make out the pans of ice lurching and tipping and coming down Little Gull toward us — and then the main river broke. First the middle, then the sides, until everywhere we looked there was ice moving. Pans of ice eight or ten inches thick and longer than our canoe rafted up over the bank and into the trees by the camp. Several trees went down, torn out by the roots, others splintered above ground. The resulting barricade of wood and ice protected the camp. We watched until things quieted down, then turned in.

The next morning the River was free of ice except around shore, and the air was still mild. At Stag Brook we had some traps and snares we wanted to check one more time. This meant poling the eight miles upstream and paddling back — a full day's work — and the water ice-cold and freezing on the pole. After dinnertime the wind shifted into the north and turned very cold. From Stag Brook we hurried back to camp for the night.

Next morning we left for home. It was a beautiful cloudless day but cold enough to skin you. And by noon, when we stopped for a quick mugup near the mouth of Miguel's Brook, the ice had started to form. In little coves and backwaters, between islands and across steadies, thin sheets spread and joined and broke and joined again, making it harder and harder to paddle or pole. By nightfall we had reached Ron Francis' camp near Rolling Falls — only fourteen miles in eight hours. Ron was trapping the area and we hoped to find him home, but from signs in the snow we saw where he had tied on his rackets and left, forgetting his pipe on the chopping block. It was filled with tea.

At daylight the following morning we found the river running full of greenish slob ice under a wintry sky. Once out into it, we found poling or paddling almost impossible — all we could do was drift with the tide. In slack water we hardly moved; we were like ants in a porridge pot. Finally, just below Rolling Falls, which we portaged around, we found the River had burst through. So we got clear of the slob ice. But now we had to contend with the slabs that stuck out on either side in the narrow channels. Once, drifting along with our packs on our backs in case we had to jump, we went underneath an overhanging ledge so low that it broke the two thole pins on one side of the canoe. We just lay flat in the bottom and hoped for the best.

Two miles below Big Gull she was frozen solid again. We hauled up the canoe then, secured it for the winter and started to walk the sixty-eight miles to Gander Bay. First we walked to Gull Rocks camp. It was on the south side, and to reach it we had to cross twenty feet of water six feet deep. This was too wide to jump so we cut two longers to walk on and two poles for balance and got across. Most nights we reached a trapper's camp, usually a wigwam. If anyone was home they were glad of the company; if they weren't they didn't mind. And so we arrived home on Christmas Eve.

I trapped pretty steady until 1944. And from the late thirties on I was buying raw fur on the side. One good thing about the War was that it drove fur prices up. Queen Elizabeth's coronation in 1953 helped too. When King George VI died, the Hudson's Bay Company sent out letters asking fur buyers to collect as many large weasel pelts as possible for the ermine coronation robe. I sent in about two hundred of the very best — good guard hairs and good underfur, nice uniform colour, no signs of chafing, no tears or holes of any kind, no urine stains. I've often wondered whether any of my furs made it into Westminster Abbey.

Esau Gillingham: "White Eskimo"

While on the subject of trapping I must relate what I know of Esau Gillingham, the notorious "White Eskimo" of Gander Bay. I oftentimes saw him when I was a boy, for he trapped for a while with my Uncle Jim Shea. And only weeks before he died I chatted with him on the shores of Gander Lake.

Like his namesake in the Bible, Esau was a rough and hairy man of the outdoors. Thickset and of average height with bushy eyebrows and a big black beard, he put me in mind of a pirate. Give him a peg leg, a hook, and a parrot on his shoulder and he would have passed for Long John Silver, or so he seemed to me when I was young. And perhaps my youthful fancies weren't far off the mark. Whether Esau deserved it or not, a taint of violence, a whiff of lawlessness dogged his travels to the end. And he was superstitious: he claimed to have heard the spirits dance on his cabin roof.

Though Esau Gillingham lived a long time on the Labrador, he was no more Eskimo than I am. As a matter of fact, he was born a love child of an unmarried Gillingham girl in Gander Bay. This would be in the early 1870s. In that place and time he grew up to be an excellent woodsman and trapper. Although unschooled, he knew the three Rs, and at one time or another bought and sold fur, ran a fox farm, and managed the Queens Hotel in St. John's. After Prohibition in 1917 he and others in Glenwood made and sold moonshine, and in one drunken racket he is supposed to have shot a man. Sometime in the twenties Esau moved his wife and family to New York, where he worked as a motorman on the Long Island subway. But he soon got fed up with city life and came back to Newfoundland.

With a former trapping buddy from Conception Bay he then went to the Labrador; apparently his wife and children stayed behind, and they say she later left him. At Okak Bay north of Nain they built a cabin on some river — probably the North — and started in trapping. They did well, but in the spring of the year, coming down the river with their winter's catch, the canoe was upset and his partner drowned. Esau came out alone with the fur. Suspecting he had shot his partner, the Rangers investigated. When they recovered the body it was so decomposed that no bullet wound could be seen. Esau's story was that his partner had insisted on running the rapids, but that he himself had thought it too risky and walked along shore, only to see him capsize. Nothing more came of this, but the suspicion remained.

He must have been a hard ticket, for he kept running afoul of the law. In March 1938 an Eskimo trapper came to Esau's cabin at Okak Bay and got drunk on moonshine. The next morning some of his friends came looking for the trapper and found him near the cabin, dead in the snow. The Eskimos took their dead companion to Cartwright for an autopsy which revealed he had been struck in the back of the head with a blunt object, perhaps a bottle.

When the Rangers came to arrest him. Esau claimed he had put the Eskimo out for being drunk and disorderly, after which he must have perished in the snow. And he wasn't satisfied to go with them until he could go over his trapline and take up his traps for the season. So the Rangers went away and came back later. Hearing noises in the camp, the officers found Esau's two cabin-mates pushing containers of moonshine out through a back window. The jury in St. John's found him guilty of making moonshine and causing the natives to get drunk. Sentenced to six months in Twillingate jail, he pestered the jailer for a meeting with Magistrate B.J. Abbott. He told Magistrate Abbott that unless they let him catch the last boat before navigation closed they would have to put up with him all winter at taxpayer's expense because he had no money and no other place to go once his sentence was up. This was in June. As summer drew on Esau cursed and swore, sulked and ranted, and even tried to bribe them with promises of his best silver fox pelts for their wives. At last, by permission of the governor, he was given a reprieve. His sentence was shortened and he went back to Okak on the last trip of the SS *Kyle* that fall.

Much as he liked the Labrador, he was not well-liked by the people there. One man who fished out of Nain told me that the local Eskimo called him a name that meant "Bad Man." They said that he took an Eskimo woman to live with him, and Esau himself told me he had a seventeen-year-old daughter in Labrador.

During the last war his son Dominic was stationed with the Air Force at Gander, and after the war, in 1949 I think it was, Esau left the Labrador for good and came to live in Glenwood. This was only ten miles across Gander Lake from his old trapping grounds on the Southwest. It must have brought back memories. It was certainly a far cry from Okak Bay, with its 4,000-foot mountains to the north and south, the Torngat Mountains looming in the west, and no trees at all once he left the lowlands. Compared to that the Southwest was the sort of country where a man might come to retire or die: relatively good canoeing water, easy walking summer or winter, plenty of wood, and the highest hill, Mount Peyton to the west, a leisurely hour's climb.

One day in July I was guiding a party of three salmon fishermen from St. John's. It was such a nice day we steamed across Gander Lake to the mouth of the Southwest to cook our dinner on the sandy beach there. While I was tending the fire under our pot of salt beef and cabbage and potatoes, two of the party took a long walk down along shore, while the third had a drink and dozed off in the warm sun some distance from the fire. He laid the whiskey bottle by a rock.

Then I looked and saw this cedar canoe with one man aboard coming down the Southwest, and from the big beard I knew it must be Esau Gillingham. Paddling straight toward us, the man beached his boat next to mine. As he stepped out I saw two rifles, one a .22 semi-automatic, in the bow. In July there was no open season on anything but crows and ravens. Dodging over to where I sat tending the pot, he eyed me from under the rim of a battered grey felt hat.

"Hello, Esau," I said, rising. It had been twenty years since he had laid eyes on me, and for a long moment he studied my face. I saw that the hard years in Labrador had taken their toll. Although the beard was still as black as ever, his cheeks were gaunt and his eyes were red-rimmed and tired. "You don't know me now, Esau, do you?" I said.

" 'Tis'nt Saunders, is it? Nephew of Poor Stan Gillingham that drowned?" I nodded. He came forward then and pumped my hand. Looking around, he spotted the bottle of whiskey, still three-quarters full. He grinned.

"Like a drink, Esau?" I said.

"And that I would, you," said he. I handed him the bottle and he tipped it up. I was only being courteous, but seeing the bottle would soon be empty I reached out and took it from him, explaining that it was not mine and that I would likely be blamed for drinking it. He didn't seem to mind.

"That was some good," he said, smacking his lips. To take his mind off it I asked him if he could recall the time that he and my Uncle Jim

Shea were up on the Southwest hunting and Jim shot himself in the shoulder while putting his shotgun in the boat.

"Oh, aye, very well," he answered, gazing up the river. "Jim and me made up a song about that, you know. Would 'e like to hear 'un?"

"Sure," I said.

'First I'll need another nip," he said, cute as a fox. By now my fisherman was snoring, so I let him have one more gulp while I held his wrist. Then, in a deep bass voice he rambled through several verses to the tune of "The Star of Logy Bay." I can only remember these two:

I called to my companion,
Come quick, I'm shot, said I;
In less than many moments
He was standing up close by.

"Cheer up, don't get downhearted,"
The hero fondly cried;
"It's only in your shoulder, Jim,
It did not strike your side."

After the song he said, "Brett, yesterday evening I seen a big animal cross the river, like a horse. Is that what they calls a moose?"

"Yes," I said. By this time moose were fairly common, whereas when Esau left they were still rare. For a minute or two he stroked his beard thoughtfully.

"Are they any good to eat?" he said.

"Yes, the smaller ones are very good."

"Then I'll have the next one I sees!" he said with a hearty laugh.

I asked him then what he was doing on the Lake alone. Perhaps he had a premonition because he looked at me closely and said in a low voice, "Brett me son, I've come back for a last look at me old haunts, and then I hope the crows will pick me bones."

A few weeks later his canoe was found drifting on the Lake and a search was begun. They found his body on the sandy beach near Jack's Feeder at the mouth of the Southwest, lying partly in the water. His pants were down, and nearby was a fire ready to light, with his cook pot hung over it on a stick. It seems that he was getting ready to cook his supper when he felt the need to relieve himself and that while taking down his pants he suffered a fatal heart attack or a stroke. He had been dead for some time. Meanwhile, there had been heavy rain which raised the Lake several inches and floated his canoe away.

I wasn't with the search party, but I talked to the ones that found him. Two things have stuck in my mind ever since: in the pot was a fresh moose heart, and the crows had picked out both his eyes.

Rabbits by the Thousand

Many's the time I've wondered what would we have done in Newfoundland without the rabbits. Introducing the snowshoe hare from the Maritimes in the mid-1800s was certainly one of the few good things a politician ever did for Newfoundland. The credit goes to the Hon. Stephen Rendell, who had them brought in and who arranged for the different magistrates around the coast to release them in the woods. I suppose in our district, which was then called the Northern District, the magistrate would have been John Peyton, Jr. of Twillingate. Anyway, in no time these rabbits found each other and started to breed like rabbits will, and people started to catch and shoot them here and there. By the 1870s they were plentiful. Now, in a place like Gander Bay we could always get caribou, but for people on the coasts and islands who had no fresh meat in the wintertime but a scattered turr or bullbird, they were a godsend.

You didn't even need a gun. Anybody with a grain of sense could catch them with a shoelace. What they used around Gander Bay was salmon twine or sail twine. Sail twine was soft, so when they made a loop it would hang down limp. To cure this the old fellows would soap it so the cold would stiffen it up. Reuben Peckford, Allan's father, was the last I saw doing that, when I was around fifteen, in on the Southern Neck. The other problem with twine was that the rabbit might bite it off and get away if he didn't die quickly. The way the oldtimers got around this was to rig up a hoister. First they would bend down a nice springy birch or the like where they planned to tail the slip. Then they would make a little wooden toggle, tie one end of a string to that, and the other to a small tree, and hook the toggle in a notch cut in the bent sapling. With the snare fastened to this sapling, the slightest tug and up would fly the rabbit in the air. Not only did it die almost instantly, but the foxes and

160

weasels couldn't get at it. Another kind of hoister was made by tying the snare to the small end of a pole laid across a forked stick in such a way that the big end was up in the air and the other end held down by a toggle as before.

When I started rabbit-catching in earnest around 1923, canning was the big thing. Father had a licensed cannery, putting up salmon in the summer and rabbits in winter. He sold both in St. John's in one-pound tins. I remember the label on the rabbit tins:

NEWFOUNDLAND RABBIT
WITH PORK & ONIONS
F. SAUNDERS, GANDER BAY

Myself and some other young fellows often worked in the cannery, so we knew the routine of cleaning the carcases and of packing, boiling and sealing the cans.

In the fall of 1923, being nineteen and having nothing better to do, me and my cousin Stanley Gillingham decided to catch and can rabbits all winter. Instead of bringing them to the cannery, our idea was to take the cannery to the rabbits. We knew from older trappers there were all kinds of them around Fourth Pond that year, so in October we loaded a canoe with a month's grub and other supplies and left and poled the twenty-odd miles to the upper end of Fourth Pond. There we built a log camp to live in and another for our factory. A canning factory consisted of a cabin equipped with a five-foot special tin stove, a big boiler with a wire rack to hold the cans, a hand-operated crimping machine, and soldering gear. The latter items had to be brought in later. Around three walls we stacked boxes of empty tins — over thirty cases of forty-eight apiece — while the fourth wall we piled to the rafters with dry wood to feed the stove, with more under the eaves outside. By the time we were ready it was mid-November, with snow in the air.

It was plain from the well-worn rabbit leads or runways and the fresh mounds of buttons that the whole area around the camp was overrun with them. Using Number Two picture cord we started in catching them. Our idea was to make a stockpile which we could start canning when we returned after freezeup. For every dozen slips we would have eight or ten rabbits the next morning. We had no competition for miles. By Christmas, when we went home to wait for freezeup, we had cleaned and scaffolded three hundred.

Stockpiling them like that was a mistake. In January when we came back by dogteam with the canning gear we discovered that our rabbits were frost-dried and worthless except for dog food. But with the dogs to haul for us we went farther afield and soon made up for it. Between us we tended up to 150 snares on a five-mile trail. We worked hard, Stan and I, slogging along on snowshoes every day that was fit, returning to camp with the dogsled piled high, resetting our snares after every blizzard or thaw and cooking and canning until after midnight most nights. Our average catch was just over a hundred a week. The empty cases gradually filled.

And that winter we ate a lot of rabbit. In canning you only use the legs and back, so the rest we would make into soup, and sometimes we fried a batch of livers with pork and onions. To relieve this diet we had potatoes, turnips and carrots along with salt beef, and we had flapjacks, bread and blueberry or partridgeberry jam and tea. Roast caplin now and then was a treat. But rabbit in one form or another was on the menu most days. One day it was more than on the menu.

In rabbit-catching it sometimes happens that you snare an otherwise healthy one alive by the leg. One day we brought this one back to camp for a pet. It sat very still on the floor in its makeshift cage of boxes so we took it out to see what it would do. In the corner stood a big pot of leftover split pea soup. All of a sudden the rabbit jumped and landed on the pot lid, which flipped and dumped him head first in the soup. Well sir, you talk about go. There was pea soup flying in all directions as the poor creature scampered all over our bunks trying to find a way out. Stan and I were laughing so hard we couldn't do a thing. Finally we opened the door and let him go. The soup tasted as good as ever; better, for the bit of excitement.

Excitement was what we needed. We had no radio, and very few visitors, just a scattered trapper passing through. Above all we missed girls. Sometime in January we decided we needed some mail, someone to write to and get letters from. The *Family Herald & Weekly Star*, although a farm magazine, was very popular in Newfoundland then, and we happened to have a copy. One of its regular features was the Maple Leaf Pen Pal Club. So both of us wrote to several girls and sent our letters out by Billy John. We had a box camera with us and just for devilment took a bunch of snaps of each other, posing with the dogs and the rifle and the like of that. Most of the letters went to girls in Newfoundland, but I sent some to Toronto too. Sure enough, the next time Billy came by he had a handful of letters for us. We felt like youngsters at Christmas. After all, we were only lads. One of Stanley's letters was from a girl in Bloomfield, Bonavista Bay. She sent her picture — wasn't half bad looking either — and asked him to visit. Stanley never bargained on getting serious. Later he passed on her name to Hubert Gillingham, and even gave him a recommendation. Hubert took the train from Glenwood that spring and spent two days in Bloomfield with her. But the romance didn't blossom. "Too religious," was all Hubert would say about it when he got back. Among my correspondents that winter was a nurse at the Children's Hospital in Toronto. She was the one I met by chance a year later at the Ossington Rink.

That winter we caught and canned 1,100 rabbits, not counting the 300 we fed to the dogs. When the season closed on March 15 we made trip after trip up to Bridges Angle with the sled groaning under the weight of cases of tinned rabbits, each box weighing fifty pounds. At Bridges Angle, about five miles below Glenwood, we transferred them to the canoe because the River was open from there up. Then we made as many trips again to Glenwood, portaging around Big Chute each time. The water was so cold our poles would ice up and we'd have to switch them from end to end. And when the ice got so slick it was impossible to get a grip — and this was barehanded now; you can't pole with mitts on — we would go ashore and make in a fire to melt it off and thaw our hands. I sold our winter's catch for $12.50 a case to a merchant there. After paying my cousin the agreed amount of $35 a month and taking out the cost of tins, solder and so on, I cleared just under $200. That was a nice few dollars in those days — and we had had a good time too.

The time I got in trouble with the law was around 1939, when my brother Harold and I went up the Northwest to can rabbits. We went up the last week in November, with my three dogs Spot and Sprig and Jack pulling a dogsled loaded with as many cases of empty tins as they could — twenty-two altogether — along with Pop's canning gear and the big tin stove, and grub for the winter. Now Harvey John Thompson had a camp twenty miles above Glenwood at Upper Narrows that he would let me use, so that's where we went. It was a seventy-mile trip. When we got there we built a piece on the camp for our factory, laid in dry wood, set up the gear and settled down to work.

Rabbits weren't plentiful, Harold was never as keen on the trapper's life as me, and two weeks before Christmas he changed his mind. By now the River was well frozen, so he left and walked home to be with his wife Kathleen and their young family for Christmas. He and Kathleen were only married a few years before. Had we been handier I might have gone with him for Christmas, but it was too far and I had to tend the snares. So there I was in the heart of Newfoundland Island with no trapping partner, only my three dogs and a *Majestic* radio to keep me company. A short piece downriver there was a camp belonging to Billy John and his father Peter, and Billy came there regularly, so I arranged that on his monthly rounds from Glenwood he would be my mailman.

However, there was little time to be lonesome. By 7:30 most mornings, unless it was stormy, I was on the trail picking up the night's catch and resetting the snares. Most days the dogs and I would haul twenty to thirty rabbits back to camp. From dinnertime on I would skin and clean them, separate the legs and back meat and pack it into cans with salt and pork, then seal them in the canning machine. Meanwhile, I would put water on to boil. In the two hours and a half while the full tins were boiling I would eat my dinner and have a rest and a smoke. Then I would lift all the cans out with the rack, and, while they were still hot, exhaust the gas by pricking each one with a nail in a stick and quickly sealing the hole with solder, using a soldering iron kept hot in the coals of the stove. Any cans that were bad would bulge in a few days and these I would discard. The rest I would label and repack in the boxes. Any spare time went into keeping the woodpile up. Birch and black spruce was plentiful, but it still had to be junked with a bucksaw, split, and dried by the stove.

The radio was great company. With an aerial of foxsnare wire strung from the camp to a tree and insulated at each end by winding it around a small pickle jar, I was able to pick up St. John's most of the time. At night or before a storm I could get Boston and New York, and sometimes even Wheeling, West Virginia for some good western music.

"At this time we present the *Gerald S. Doyle News Bulletin*, bringing you the news from all over Newfoundland." This was the programme nobody missed if they could help it. It was broadcast after supper on VONF in St. John's, and the special thing about it was that anyone with access to a telegraph office could have a message put over the air. Doyle sent a notice to ours and every other post office in Newfoundland inviting anybody to send VONF a collect telegram with news or messages. So you got not only the regional news, but a glimpse of how other people were living. This was a wonderful idea Mr. Doyle had, even if it was started partly to advertise the patent medicines he sold. It helped break down the terrible isolation that had always plagued people living in our small outports or working away from home. As long as they had a wireless set in working order they could stay in touch. If one of my sons took sick in the morning I could know about it soon afterward.

The trick was to keep the radio working, and above all not to run down the batteries. This was hard when you were alone because there were other good programmes, like Joey Smallwood's "Barrelman," and popular music by groups like the McNulty Family from Ireland. In those days radio batteries were big and heavy to lug, especially in the woods. Mine consisted of two dry cells each about the size of a small rum bottle

164

and one wet cell much like a regular car battery except it was done up in shiny cardboard with black, white and red vertical stripes. These were wired together on a shelf beside the radio. Well, I spared along my batteries all right, but that didn't prevent a tube from blowing. One night in January it lit up like a Christmas tree and that was that — the radio was gone for that winter. Except for seeing Billy John once a month, I was completely isolated. Or so I thought.

Around the time Harold left, another trapper, Elam Gillingham, dropped by on his way home for Christmas. Elam was only sixteen or so, and when he saw my cozy setup he thought to spend the winter with me. I certainly could have used the help. However, Christmas was too much for him; he wanted to get home. Before he left I gave him a meal of fresh venison for his family, charging him not to let the Ranger catch him with it because it was closed season. As a precaution I cut the meat in small pieces and told him that if he saw someone coming towards him far away on the ice, to wait until he could see their headgear, and if it was the tall fur hat of a Ranger to throw the meat to the dogs. The evidence would disappear before they reached him, guaranteed. We figured a trapper had a right to fresh venison when he needed it. Anyway, Elam left for home and I thought no more about it.

Then, one night in March I was awakened by a loud crash. At first I didn't know what to think. Then I heard a man's tread and dogs panting. Jumping out of my bunk, I grabbed my rifle and swung the door open, ready for anything. There, smiling sheepishly, stood my brother Harold. "What in the name of God are you doing here?" I said. I was pretty vexed, and I told him it was a wonder he wasn't shot, crashing into the door like that. He said his dogs grew so excited when they got handy the camp that he couldn't hold them, and the sled ran right into the door.

"But why did you come? To go rabbit-catching with me again?"

"No," he said. "I had some business to do in Glenwood so I thought I'd better come up and warn you that you're in danger of being arrested any day for having venison without a permit." When I asked how they knew, he told me Jack Munroe and the Ranger had caught young Elam with the meat and made him tell where he got it; not only that, Elam had been convicted and put in jail for thirty days. So Harold had slipped away with his two dogs to tell me, taking care to pass through Glenwood after dark so nobody would see him, staying at Billy John's camp at the mouth of the Northwest the first night. While crossing Careless Cove on Gander Lake he went through the ice with one foot, he said, but the sled saved him. When he reached the mouth of the Northwest he found it had broken out a short while before, and the lower part was nothing but blocks and pans of ice piled every which way, with deep holes and black water between. But somehow he hung onto the sled and the dogs got him across. And on the second night he reached my camp.

I felt really bad about Elam, but there was nothing I could do now except look out for myself. I didn't intend to leave, nor to lose my winter's work. I knew it was no good to hide the venison in the woods: their dogs would sniff it out in no time. We decided the best thing was to build a log roof over my outdoor toilet and stow the meat up there under a covering of boughs. The toilet was just a pit with a log to sit on; it was in the woods behind the camp. So early the next morning that's what we did. We were pretty sure no dog would sniff around a toilet, or notice the smell of meat there if it did. As soon as this was done Harold took off downriver, hoping the wind would cover his track and that he wouldn't meet the Ranger.

Just before dark a couple of nights later my dogs ran out to the river bank and started barking furiously; I went out to have a look. Sure enough, two men were coming up the River, one of them with a big fur hat on. That would be the Ranger, escorted by Jack Munroe of Glenwood. They had dogs but were moving slow. This gave me time to carry out a plan I had. Winnie had sent in some pork chops by Harold for a treat, and I quickly put them on for supper. Soon my dogs barked again and I heard voices outside. Opening the door I saw Jack Munroe and the Ranger climbing up the bank, each trying to hold back their dogs, who were excited now by meeting mine and at the prospect of rest and food. I hailed the two and invited them in.

"Mind if we unharness the dogs and let them run a bit before I feed them?" said Jack.

"Not at all," I said. "Mine are untied all the time."

"Well," he said, coming to the point, "we heard you had venison and thought we'd check it out while the dogs are hungry."

"Go ahead," I said. "I'll finish cooking supper."

The dogs, glad to be out of harness, raced around but found nothing. I concentrated on the pork chops. After urging the dogs on some more, they gave up, fed them some dried caplin and came in and sat down. The Ranger was thickset with black hair and a beefy face and he looked beat out. Jack's keen blue eyes roved around my camp.

"That's some good smell," said the Ranger with a grin.

"Yes," I said, "and it tastes even better." Handing each a tin plate, I dished up potatoes and onions and chops, and took the hot pan outside on the pretext of feeding the fat to the dogs. Instead I dumped it over their snowshoes — an old trappers' dodge designed to encourage the dogs to eat the fillings. When I went back in Jack and the officer were gaffling into their supper. For a time we ate in silence. Then the Ranger turned to Munroe and said, "Jack, is this caribou meat?"

"No, 'tis not," said Jack, "this is pork." He chewed thoughtfully. A few minutes later he went out and brought their snowshoes in and stood them by the door.

They stayed with me that night. The next morning they went out and had another snoop around. The worst part was when we were standing outside the camp and the jays started coming down on the roof of the toilet and pecking at the fresh snow on top of the boughs. But the two of them never noticed this. I suppose that, having used the toilet themselves that morning, they didn't think of looking there. Just the same, it did me no good.

"Mr. Saunders," said the Ranger, "even though we can't seem to find it, we're certain you have fresh caribou around here because we have the word of a witness. I'm afraid I'll have to serve you with this summons." I took it from him and read it. The place they had on it was "Northwest River." Figuring I had nothing to lose, I said he must have the wrong man.

"Why?" he asked.

"Because Northwest River is on the Labrador, and I've never been there in my life. This is the Gander River, Northwest Branch. You should know better than that, Jack," I said. While the warden was explaining this — the Ranger was from elsewhere and didn't know the difference — I asked why the Ranger didn't serve a summons on his friend too.

"For what reason?" said the officer.

"For illegal possession of Crown property," I said, pointing to the faded coat-of-arms on Jack's canvas duffle bag. Like many Newfoundlanders before and since, he was using an old mail bag, which was strictly against the law.

"Where'd you get it, Jack?" asked the Ranger, his face turning an even deeper red. Jack mumbled something about a friend giving it to him fifteen years before. The officer got mad then and told me to quit fooling around or it would go worse with me when he got me in court. He ordered me to appear before Magistrate Bradley in Grand Falls on March 16. "Report to me in Glenwood the day before," he growled over his shoulder as they got under way. They left without even thanking me for bed and board. And I was going to lose a whole three days' work, if not more.

On March 15 I arrived in Glenwood to learn that Harold had waited there for me. The weather had turned mild, which made me anxious about getting back should the River break out. Leaving my dogs at Jim John's, I reported to the Ranger's shack. He told me that the westbound express would arrive around four o'clock the next morning and said if I didn't see him on the station platform to come and rouse him as he sometimes overslept. When the train pulled in it was thick of fog and not another soul around but me and the station master. When she pulled out I was aboard — and satisfied that the Ranger was not.

At ten o'clock that morning I walked into the courthouse in Grand Falls as the summons stated. Magistrate Gordon Bradley, a long-faced, balding man in his fifties, read the charge, asked if I was Brett Saunders, and eyed me over his glasses for a long minute.

"Possession of caribou meat out of season," he said, half to himself. "And where's the Ranger?"

"I guess he overslept, sir. He wasn't on the train, though I reported to him yesterday."

"I see." He folded and unfolded the summons. "I don't suppose you feel like waiting for him to come on tomorrow's train?"

"No, sir. I'm a trapper with seventy rabbit slips to tend on the Northwest Gander and spring breakup is not far away."

"No," he said gravely. "No reason at all why you should. But we do have a witness...." Then, frowning at the summons, he cleared his throat: "You are hereby fined $20." I didn't have $20 on me. He consented to let me mail it to him after I got home. Catching the next train to Glenwood, I returned to Upper Narrows while Harold went on home.

A fortnight later I had all the cases full. The sun was warming up now and pretty soon the River would burst out and it would be muskrat trapping time again. Leaving everything at camp, I went home, riding on the sled where I could and jogging the rest of the way. In April I returned by canoe and brought everything out. The twenty-two cases of tinned rabbit I sold to an agent in St. John's and, after expenses — including a new tube for the radio, and my fine — I ended up with almost exactly $200. And, thanks to my brother's 140-mile jaunt and that sleepy Ranger, I managed to stay out of the clink.

The River Was Our Road

Lots of people have heard of the Gander Bay boat, but not many know how it came to be. It's a special canoe developed by two or three generations of Gander Bay boatbuilders to suit the special conditions on the Gander River. Although these canoes can be seen today on the rivers of southern Labrador and a few other places, they haven't really caught on elsewhere. It's their name that has spread, carried to all parts of North America and even overseas by the stories of the hundreds, and maybe thousands, of sportsmen who have travelled in them on fishing and hunting expeditions that they have remembered fondly for the rest of their lives. For one of our fishermen, an American from Washington, D.C., that wasn't enough; he bought one and had it shipped home at great expense for cruising up and down the Potomac.

Now, when I was a youngster there was no such a thing. The real Gander Bay boat reached its present form in my time. Before that, if a man wanted to tend his salmon net he got in his punt and rowed out, just the same as if he was going across Main Tickle in Change Islands. Or if he wanted to go up the River he took his double-ender and poled the rapids and rowed the ponds and steadies. Before that the oldtimers used punts — but they were almost useless on the River. A double-ender was just a homemade copy of a cedar canoe. The Micmacs in Glenwood had cedar canoes, a scattered one; I suppose they got them in Nova Scotia or in Old Town, Maine. In those days outboard motors were unheard of, so every canoe was pointed at both ends for easier paddling. Being made of half-inch fir planking, with juniper ribs and keel, your double-ender was also too heavy to paddle well, so it was fitted with thole-pins fore and aft for rowing, just like a punt. They were sixteen or seventeen feet long, mostly. Some had a hole in the for'ard tawt (thwart) for a mast, and if there was a nice breeze the men would rig a blanket on the pole to help them along in the ponds.

Gander Bay was never a very good port for ships. At Clarke's Head there was less than five fathoms of water in the channel. Even the smallish coastal boats, the *Clyde* and later the *Glencoe*, had to anchor down off Sandy Cove to unload. So when the Newfoundland railroad went across the island around 1890 and linked us to St. John's and Port aux Basques, the River became our road. And for a long spell the double-ender was the workhorse of the Gander. We still depended on ships for heavy freight, but anything else, and passengers as well, we brought by canoe

To pole and row to Glenwood in one of those double-enders meant two or three days of back-breaking labour, staying in camps overnight. Coming back down wasn't so bad: it took about a day, depending on the load. One fall in the twenties the Horwood Lumber Company hired some Gander Bay men to bring down their full winter's provisions for forty men and half a dozen horses — a boxcar load of hay and oats, and another carload of flour, pork, beans, molasses, cheese, and the rest, along with a quantity of grindstones, axes, crosscuts and camp gear. A few years ago my son Calvin and his second oldest boy Jeff were picking up firewood at Bridges Angle and they found, half buried in the sand, three twisted pieces of rusty steel — two bandsaw blades and a rotary saw — lost overboard long ago and crumpled by the ice.

It was outboard motors that did away with the double-enders. Around 1926 or 1927 my father came back from his annual buying trip in St. John's with an ad from John Barron & Sons which told about this engine you could clamp on the outside of a small boat and steer with two ropes and a rudder. This was the *Evinrude Elto* — a 4.4 horsepower. It came with three dry-cell batteries in a box, and started with a knob on the flywheel that you spun around. My younger brother Harold, always quick to see possibilities, lost no time in urging Pop to buy one. So in the spring of 1927 they purchased one of the first outboards on our coast, if not in Newfoundland. I first saw it on returning from New York that summer, and knew I had to have one too. As it turned out, Winnie and I went to Boston that fall and on to Buffalo, and I didn't get mine until years later.

The Elto was a sensation around the Bay. Not that it was speedy — the engine weighed a good thirty or forty pounds, and at first had to be clamped to the gunwale near the stern — it was just the idea that a man could sit there doing nothing and travel faster than the ablest rower. Older gentlemen like Uncle Jack Gillingham, who had rowed back and forth to his salmon nets in Sandy Cove all his life, wondered out loud what the younger generation was coming to. But the young men were eager to take it for a spin, and even a few women tested it "for the sake of the cool breeze." Gander Bay would never be as quiet again.

That's how it began. The next thing was to make a proper stern to fasten the Elto's broad clamp to. Harold's father-in-law, boatbuilder Willy John Torraville of Victoria Cove, was called into service. Now whether he sawed the stern off a double-ender and rebuilt it or went to work and designed a new boat, I don't know; all I know is the square stern didn't pan out too well. It worked fine in the stillwater, but as soon as the boat got in the tide, a five- or six-knot tide, she would pull a wave along behind and couldn't get up any speed. Boatbuilders like Willy John and Nat Gillingham puzzled over this, sucking their pipes on long winter evenings around the stove. Their solution was to go back to the canoe shape under water, but keep the square stern above. That way they got rid of the drag but still had a place to clamp the motor on. This evolution didn't happen overnight, but gradually. When I came home from Huntsville in 1930 it was just beginning. In those years there were few models of outboard motor boats in existence anywhere, and even fewer in Newfoundland. As it was, the 4.4 Elto was so much faster than poling and paddling that nobody minded very much. Calvin recalls when he was eight or ten being given one of the first experimental canoes for his own because, with a motor on it, it was considered too short and too cranky for the River.

Word of the new, speedier way to get to Glenwood got around. Pretty soon Harold was not only bringing freight for the store but he was getting a few passengers. Once the River broke out in March or April there would be fellows going up to Millertown or Badger to work on the drive, driving the pulpwood down the Exploits to the Grand Falls mills. At the same time there would be other men coming out of the lumberwoods after working since Christmas. And there was always a teacher or nurse or a politician coming or going.

For a few years the 4.4 Elto was all we had. We shared it as best we could, as part of the family business, and came to rely on it for bringing out freight from Glenwood in the spring before the coastal boat could get around. In 1938 my father made up his mind to go into the lumber business again. He saw a good market, the logged-over areas were growing timber again, and it would give his boys steady work winter and summer. Harold and I went to Gambo in the green skiff — a voyage of nearly 150 miles — and brought back an engine Pop had located in a sawmill there, a big half-diesel. It was bad enough for us to go in an open boat with no compass, but every so often the engine would quit and we'd have to stop and clear the gas line. The trip home took us more than thirty hours.

171

So the new mill was built just west of the wharf, and the four of us took the horse and went logging. We logged in back of Clarke's Pond where Pop had cut pitprops during World War I — in around Joe's Steady, Floating Tart Steady, Dad's Brook, and those places — and we hauled it out onto the ice at Clarke's Pond and drove it out Clarke's Brook in the spring. Summertime we helped Harold in the mill. I mostly sawed and tallied. We shipped our lumber by schooner to Mark Gosse and Sons of Bay Roberts, and to Saunders & Howell of Carbonear. Some was sold in Fogo and Change Islands. In 1939 our youngest brother Don, now eighteen, enlisted in the Forestry Corps and went overseas. For a time Aubrey was sick with TB, which left him unfit for heavy work. Harold and I carried on like this for two or three years until one day in 1943 a board flew off the saw and struck me in the throat, driving splinters deep. I left the lumber business in Harold's capable hands and never went back.

That was when I made up my mind to get an outboard of my own. Not being able to afford one, I asked Pop to lend me the money. He thought he would if it could be used instead of the 4.4 — which had suffered from two or three dunkings and didn't work like it used to — for collecting salmon for the cannery and the like of that. But I wanted it for guiding as well. I pointed out that Ralph Francis now had one, and also Fred Hurley and Hedley Gillingham; that if I didn't soon get one we would lose out. In the end Gerald S. Doyle lent me his 3.3 horsepower, the one he used for getting ashore from his yacht. He used to always spend a day salmon fishing whenever he came to the Bay, and as I often guided him he did this for me. But it didn't solve the problem.

Vexed at Pop, I went to see Joe Peckford, then Horwood's manager of Gander Stores, and asked him to loan me the price of a new Elto. I believe it was $120. He not only agreed, but gave me the contract to bring out all of Horwood's freight that came through Glenwood. Since they were still actively logging in Gander Bay, this was a nice bit of work for me. It was too bad I had to go to my father's arch business rival, but I couldn't see any other way to be my own boss. In time he forgave me. I bought a five horsepower Elto with a flat, wraparound gas tank, a pull cord instead of a starting knob, and a steering handle instead of tiller ropes. With the money earned freighting I was soon able to repay my debt.

As time went on the Gander Bay boat grew longer. The reason was that the makers of outboard motors started turning out bigger ones. Soon Johnson outboards began to show up on the River. At first they were all five horsepower models, but soon the 7.5 came along, and then the ten horsepower. While these more powerful engines were not all that much heavier, their extra thrust pulled a boat down by the stern and lifted the bow away up out of the water. In a stiff wind this was dangerous. The low stern also raised the risk of breaking the propellor or skig on a submerged rock. Putting ballast in the bow solved the problem for an empty boat, but it was a waste of gasoline. In the end the boatbuilders solved the problem in a very straight-forward manner: they just lengthened the canoe. Not only did this provide the correct balance, it made the boat ride higher and gave us more cargo space. From then on it was just a matter of refining the shape to get the best combination of speed and capacity. The cuddy got a bit longer, the counter or transom became smaller to match the newer screw-on clamps, and the thole pins, withes and oars disappeared for good. A ten-foot pole for getting up the rattles, a spoon paddle for coming down, and that was it. The motor did the rest. By the early 1960s the evolution to twenty-four-foot and twenty-five-foot canoes and twenty - to twenty-five -horsepower motors was complete. Oh, different boat builders would come up with different variations — a sleeker bow line, a rounder bottom, and so on. Each builder had a style all his own, but as none of them used scale models or calipers, it was mostly hit or miss. One time I had a canoe that was faster than any of my previous ones and nobody could figure exactly why. Even so, you could look at almost any Gander Bay boat and tell who built it. In the 1940s they charged about $100. That was for two or three weeks' work plus materials.

The canoes seldom exceeded twenty-four or twenty-five feet because a motor over twenty horsepower is too heavy when the River is low in July and August. Twenty-four feet gives the riverman six feet of an advantage over the ordinary cedar freighter canoe, yet he can still slip between rocks and over shallows since his boat is less than four feet in the beam and draws only eight or ten inches loaded. Such a boat is quite stable in rough water too. A man in the water can climb right in over the gunwale without capsizing the boat. In fact, on civil days it's no trouble to go to Change Islands or Fogo in a Gander Bay boat. I've done it more than once. The sight of my canoe at the Labrador Export Company wharf with Winnie and our son Gary aboard created quite a stir in 1943. But the weather has to be perfect. (We ended up going home by the SS *Glencoe* in rough seas. Another small hazard of that trip was that while crossing Hamilton Sound under clear skies we saw the periscope of a submarine for several minutes.)

But it was on the River that this improved boat was at its best. It transported some strange cargoes. One time Harold brought out fifty feet of boom chain and a Holstein cow and her calf. He charged 1½ cents a pound for the load. In the early 1950s, after we got into the tourist camp business, I brought out a half-ton lighting plant from Glenwood to Third Pond and unloaded it myself with a tripod and block-and-tackle. Another time I recall bringing out 830 pounds of ⅝ inch boom chain for Harold, along with six fifty-pound bags of nails, and five rolls of roofing felt for the cabin, all in one load. We had to pass the chain down through the railroad trestle. In fact, every scrap of lumber, glass, et cetera for the fishing camp that we built in 1948, right down to the bed springs and kitchen cutlery, had to be brought that way.

I remember once being in a sort of contest with a small motor boat, taking hay in to one of the lumber camps in the fall. The skiff could beat me on the ponds because she could carry a lot more, but I made it up on the rattles where they had to get overboard and haul her along. As a rule, 1,500 pounds is about the maximum a modern Gander Bay boat can safely carry. One time my brother Don brought out a record load from Glenwood to our tourist camp on Cleaves Island. It totalled 2,100 pounds on the waybill. But his canoe was like a log in the water, and if the River hadn't been top high and Big Chute almost smooth, he could never have done it.

But the strangest cargo, if not the heaviest, we ever brought out was a *Hurricane* fighter plane that crashed in February 1943 on a bog just below Jonathan's Brook in Third Pond. This was being used as an advanced trainer that was flown solo by pilots who had graduated from the dual-cockpit *Harvard Trainer* and were getting ready to fly the faster and more heavily armed *Spitfire* overseas. The impact of the crash wrecked the engine, but the fuselage and wings were useable so the RCAF wired for somebody to bring them out to the Bay where they could ship them to Lewisporte via the SS *Glencoe* and thence by rail to Gander. Already the river ice was too thin for horse and sleigh, but I figured it could be done by boat. The distance was just under fifteen miles.

I wired the RCAF in Gander that I would bring her out for $300. They sent out a Sergeant King to supervise the operation and to sign the contract. Although a nice enough fellow, he just didn't believe I could do it by canoe, and said so. I said, "Give me the contract and I'll deliver your plane, guaranteed." I wouldn't let on how I planned to do it, see, until the contract was signed. My plan was to bring it out in three trips on two canoes lashed together catamaran-style. And that's what I did. I hired Harold and another man and we brought out the two wings, the easiest load, first. The canoes were held steady by two poles across the gunwales fore and aft, and a tarpaulin kept the waves from swamping us on the rattles.

With the wings safely unloaded, the sergeant told me he strongly advised against bringing the cockpit and fuselage the same way. "Look here, ol' man," I said, "it's me that has the contract and me that's paying the wages and the gas, so let me get on with it." He declared it would be impossible and announced he would wire his CO for permission to destroy the plane. "Well," I said, "if you people don't want it, let me have it to put in the meadow for the youngsters to play in." For he was making me crooked with all of his foolishness.

"Dammit," he sputtered, "if you can bring it out for the kids you can bring it out for us!" After that he left me alone. There wasn't room for him in the boats anyway. The fuselage was more ungainly than the wings, but we could manage to see along either side of it because the tail section had been removed as not worth saving. We got that to the wharf okay too. Inspecting it, Sergeant King noticed a triangular rip in the fabric where the red, white, and blue bullseye of the RAF was painted on. "Didn't notice this before," he muttered, taking out a pen. We assured him that it was there before. With the pen he marked the ends of each tear so he could tell if further damage was done during the trip to Gander.

To tell the truth, I was worried about the cockpit section myself. Not only was it five feet high and too wide for us to see around as we steered our motors, but it was heavy from all the steel they put in it to armour it against bullets. The way we solved that was for me to sit in the cockpit and give hand signals to Harold and the other fellow. We had a few scary moments coming down Second Rattle — especially the right-angle turn — and expected more than once to end up sideways on a boulder. But we made it safe and sound. The sergeant was some relieved. Watching from the deck of the *Glencoe* a week later as her derrick swung the last piece aboard, he even smiled down at us.

With all the glamour of the outboard motor it is easy to forget the importance of the art of poling. All rivermen learn it at an early age and perfect it by practice. Describing the motion of a skilled poler is hard, but to pole well is harder still. In fast water he needs good balance and quick reflexes, for he is standing in the stern, which is less than two feet wide, and at the end of the push stroke he's even leaning out over the water. With a whip of the wrist and forearms, he then shoots the wet pole up through his hands until the tip clears the water. Reaching it forward with one hand and planting it firmly down on solid bottom before the boat loses headway, he grips the pole with both hands near the top and drives the canoe ahead. If it's windy he has to compensate for that. Jim John was the best man I ever saw to pole.

It's no trouble to make a good pole, but it should be done in May or June when the sap is running and the rind can be peeled with ease, leaving a very smooth surface. A little work with a spokeshave to remove the small knots, a few minutes with a sharp axe to put a point on the butt, a couple of weeks drying to cure the wood, and the pole is ready. To find a suitable tree we would go to a thick spruce stand — what the oldtimers called red spruce but the young experts call a form of black spruce — where the trees are tall and tant from reaching for the light.

There's a story told about Skipper Billy Blake who worked in Phillips' mill, how he and his son Noah were poling up the River when Noah broke his pole. This didn't go over too well with the old man, and when they got the boat under control he sent his clumsy son ashore to cut another. Just as Noah was going in the woods with the axe he turned and sung out: "Father, what kind of a tree will I cut?" Skipper Billy bawled back, "Damn you, cut a var or a whatnot, I don't care!" A fresh-cut fir would have been very uncomfortable indeed with all that sticky myrrh, and it liable to break besides. But a spruce is perfect.

In fact, except for nails and oakum, everything Skipper Billy's generation needed for navigating the River by canoe could be found growing along its banks. By adding the outboard motor and six or seven feet to its length, my generation changed that — but the Gander Bay boat is still very much a local product, designed to fit our unique River, and nothing else can really take its place.

A Trip to Twillingate

In the thirties and forties Notre Dame Bay Memorial Hospital out on Twillingate Island was our nearest place to see a doctor. At fifty miles it wasn't exactly handy, but St. Anthony was 130 miles away by water and St. John's twice that far by land. In summer we used to go to Twillingate by motor boat, taking one day to go and one to come back. Wintertime it meant an overland journey by horse and sleigh across Dog Bay Neck, Chapel Island and New World Island — a hard, hard trek for a sick person.

During those years the *Matilda* was gone and we had another small passenger boat, and got a bit of business carrying people back and forth between Gander Bay, Carmanville, Fogo, and Change Islands. And I made a good many trips to Twillingate with sick people, especially in the fall. The patients would stay overnight at the hospital or with relatives. I would eat and sleep on the boat, which had a cabin with a drop-down table, benches, and a stove on which to cook. Back aft there was a small closed-in wheelhouse. She was thirty-two feet long, not so pretty as the *Matilda* but a bit faster, with a four-cylinder Lycoming engine. We never gave her a name, she was just "the passenger boat."

I liked those trips. I always did like the salt water, never got seasick, and it was a way to pick up a few dollars when I wasn't guiding sports or trapping. Most trips were just routine, and because we picked our day we were seldom caught by dirty weather. Very few of my Twillingate passengers were what you would call emergency cases: in the early years those stayed home and prayed, and later — once the hospital was built after 1940 — they might get a mercy flight to Gander, .

But one trip I will never forget. It was in October of 1943 or '44. I left the wharf at 9:30 a.m. with three women, Dot Squires and two others, and when we got to Victoria Cove I picked up Sam King. We had the green canoe in tow with the five horsepower Johnson outboard on the back. My son Calvin was with us too. The wind was light from the southwest with a hint of rain, but it was a mild day and they all sat around on deck laughing and chatting. Fifteen miles from home, while crossing Dog Bay, we sighted this schooner beating up to Horwood. With the spyglass I made out that she was the *Miriam May* out of Carmanville, and I knew she was skippered by Theo Blackwood. I figured she was going for a load of lumber. By now there was some fog. She was on a tack that took her away from us and into the mists, and then it came on to rain so we took cover and thought no more about her.

The next thing we knew there was a splintering crash, the boat shuddered and I was knocked off my seat in the wheelhouse, which tumbled down on top of me. The steering wheel was torn from its moorings with me hanging onto it. For what seemed like a long while I lay there holding it in both hands with the engine pounding away, trying to think what had happened. I stopped the engine and crawled from the wreckage.

"Anybody hurt? Anybody hurt there?" a voice sang out from a distance. I looked and there was the *Miriam May* hove to, and Captain Blackwood standing by the rail, hands cupped to his mouth. Now I knew what had happened: the schooner had come back on her starboard tack, and though he had seen us soon enough, he figured we had seen him and would alter course any minute. It so happened that anyone sitting in our wheelhouse, unless they leaned well back, had poor visibility to the sides. So it was partly my fault. At the very last moment the captain had tried to avoid a collision, but it was too late. One of the passengers saw her looming and so did Calvin. Her jib boom passed right over us, but the bobstay cable underneath knocked down our stovepipe, sheared through the wheelhouse and ripped off a section of our after railing. And the schooner's bow, passing between us and the canoe, put such a strain on the tow rope that the top of the stem head popped out and left her drifting. It was a good thing for us the schooner was empty and high in the water or she'd have raked our deck as well. And if she'd struck amidships, all hands of us might have perished. As it happened not a soul was hurt. But the women were crying and all of us were badly shook up.

With a sculling oar we worked our way over to the schooner, got a line aboard, and put the wheelhouse to rights with some boards that hadn't floated away. Captain Blackwood couldn't do enough for us. But one of the women, recovering her wits, cursed the poor man up and down for several minutes until the others got her quieted down. After an hour things were more or less in order. We made our way to Twillingate without further mishap, and in time for everyone to see the doctor that day.

The surgeon in charge at the hospital was Dr. John Olds of Windsor, Connecticut, who came to Twillingate in 1929 as a twenty-three-year-old medical student from Johns Hopkins University in Maryland and upon graduation returned to stay. To the thousands of people he served from Cape St. John to Cape Freels, this lanky man with the piercing eyes and gruff manner became a hero. He was one of us. They say that when he arrived in 1932 with his young wife Betty to become superintendent, she looked in dismay at Twillingate's treeless, rocky hills and said, "Oh well, Johnny, if we don't like it we can always go back home." To which he replied, "This *is* home" — and that was that. We thought the world of Dr. Olds, and people flocked to his hospital in numbers that he and his staff, no matter how dedicated, could hardly be expected to handle.

The next morning my passengers were back from the hospital and ready to go home. One of the women had been fitted with a plaster cast to her back and hips. This cast, along with some other things, would give me some bad moments before the trip was over.

When we left Twillingate Harbour the wind was breezing up from the northeast, which meant that once we left Burnt Island Tickle and cleared French Point we were butting a headwind. The boat started to pitch up and down a bit and one of the women got seasick, but otherwise we were doing all right. Then, about halfway to Baccalieu Island — less than half an hour out and the engine still running normal — we lost headway and began to drift toward the land. Giving Sam the wheel, I jumped in the canoe to check the propellor. Sure enough, when the motor boat's stern rose on the next swell I could see where one of its three blades was bent, bent right over so the tip was resting on one of the others. The propellor was just churning water.

We were just past Baccalieu Island. I looked ashore. At the rate we were drifting it wouldn't be long until we'd be on the rocks. I shut off the engine and Sam hove the eighty-pound anchor overboard, both of us hoping it would strike bottom before my eight fathoms of rope ran out, and that it would hold. We stood and watched the rope uncoil and go hissing down out of sight in the black water. Around six fathoms it went slack. After some dragging a fluke dug in and held, bringing our bow into the wind. Everyone heaved a sign of relief; the rocks were less than a quarter-mile away, close enough for us to see the yellow kelp swinging as the waves broke over them in creamy white froth. To the southwest we could just make out the houses of Cobbs Arm.

With my passengers safe for the moment, I put my outboard motor on the canoe and set out for Cobbs Arm where I knew there was a limestone quarry and a chance of help. It was pouring rain now. The manager of the quarry was a fine fellow who, despite the rain, got his boat going and brought me back and towed ours into harbour. His wife saw that the women were made comfortable. As soon as the showers let up, Sam and I went to work piling rocks on the bow to raise the stern out of the water, the only way I could get at the propellor. After an hour we had it out of the water. Working from the canoe I broke off the damaged blade. Without a spare, and nothing in Cobbs Arm that would fit, we would have to cripple home on the remaining blades. I kept the broken tip just in case. We dumped the rocks, got the women aboard and resumed our journey. We had about twenty-five miles to go.

In spite of some vibration and loss of speed, the propellor seemed to work well enough, even with the sea getting rougher. An hour or so later, however, I noticed the bilge water rising. We must have sprung a leak, I thought, but where? Had the vibration loosened the waterproof stuffing around the shaft? If so, it could be bad. The rain was pouring down again. Without telling the women in the cabin I alerted Sam and set him to pumping. It wasn't enough. Disconnecting the water intake hose that cooled the engine, I plugged the intake hole and put the hose end in the bilge so the engine would suck that instead and pump it overboard. Still the water kept gaining on us.

Then in the distance I saw another motor boat. I think it was the *Constance* from Joe Batt's Arm. Imagine my relief when I realized it was heading in our general direction. The only trouble was, he was barely moving. Either he had engine trouble or she had one of those four-stroke Guarantee or Coaker engines. To make better time he was using a small leg-o'-mutton sail. But I still had some headway, and after a long, worrisome spell we finally came abreast. He took us in tow and brought us into Boyd's Cove, a larger settlement ten or twelve miles to the south where we had a better chance to beach her. One of the women, the one who tongue-lashed Captain Blackwood, was giving me black looks as I led them ashore for the second time, this time to a friend's house. Boyd's Cove was a nice piece out of our way.

Again we ballasted down the bow with rocks — that's one good thing about Newfoundland; you're never short of rocks — until the propellor rose clear. It was no trouble to spot the problem this time: one of the two screws holding the stuffing box to the stern had broken with the vibration. We'd have to have a new propellor. While one of my helpers went to ask around the community, I took off the bad propellor, removed the other screw, reversed the box so the good material faced out, then replaced the missing screw and tightened them both up good. In the meantime, a propellor was found that looked like ours. I put it on. We dumped the ballast.

To my surprise, now the boat would only go astern. She would go ahead with the engine in reverse, but this was no good. Thinking I had put the propellor on backwards, I cursed myself for being so stunned and went through the whole business with the rocks a third time, reversing the propellor and trying the engine one more time. Still the boat wouldn't go ahead. We stayed there two or three days, trying different propellors. But they all had the wrong pitch.

Baffled and disgusted, I wired my brother-in-law Roy Reccord in Victoria Cove to come and tow us home. While waiting for Roy I got out the original blade and looked at it. By drilling three holes along the broken edge and in the matching stub, I was able to bolt them together with two steel plates. By now we must have moved five ton of rocks; but it was a fine morning so we gave it one more try, and it worked. We all went aboard, and, watching the bilge like a hawk, I started for Clarke's Head. Two miles out we met Roy. A quizzical look crossed his mild face. I explained that the stuffing box could give out any minute. We put a line aboard him just in case and came along home with no more problems, arriving in time for supper.

As I let my long-suffering passengers off along the way, there was a lot of laughing about our adventures and some goodnatured ribbing about the boat. When it came time to take leave of the woman with the plaster cast, she threw her arms around my neck and kissed me. Caught me by surprise, she did. Yet considering what happened on the way, I suppose it was only natural. Remember how, after we left Twillingate, the boat started pitching and rolling? Well, this got steadily worse as the wind picked up and by and by, between Cobbs Arm and Boyd's Cove, she came back to the wheelhouse to ask could I do something because the cast was chafing. At first I hesitated. All I had was a hunting knife; there wasn't even a file on board. Already the plaster was hard as a rock, and the boat rolling like a cradle. What if the blade slipped? What if the boat started to sink again? I asked her where the cast chafed. Blushing, she indicated her groin. Why, I said to myself, did I ever get into this passenger business anyway?

And while all this was running through my mind she began to whimper with the pain. The others all knew something was wrong by now, so I called Sam to take the wheel, led her forward to the cabin, and explained to the two what I had to do. They looked away as she raised her dress and pulled up her bulky bloomers on one side. To me she whispered: "I don't care what you see so long as you stop the pain!" With that we braced ourselves against the motion of the boat and I began chipping and scraping at the edge of the cast where it was sawing into her groin. The flesh was so raw she had started to bleed. It was a good thing she was a thin woman or I might have cut her. Someone at the hospital must have been pretty rushed, I thought, to have made such a poor fit. After a long time I succeeded in removing about a quarter of an inch from the bottom edge of the cast. The woman had tears in her eyes, but she said it felt much better. That's why she kissed me.

Maybe I should have been a doctor. I certainly did a better job on her cast than I did on that propellor. For when I went down on the wharf the next morning to have a look at the boat where she was moored off on the collar, there was nothing showing above water but the wheelhouse.

Man Overboard!

It's a queer thing, I know, when you've been all your life around boats and water, but I never could swim a stroke. No matter how many times I tried, I would sink like a rock. Once I even had my brothers heave me overboard in the middle of the Bay to see if that would work. They had to haul me out; I was going down for the third time. A doctor I was guiding one time told me it was all in my mind, that the human body will float whether we think it will or no, and that mine was no different than anybody else's. That didn't help either. Although this inability never bothered me, there were times when even knowing how to dog-paddle would have saved me a lot of worry. And considering that two of my uncles — Jim Shea of Glenwood and Stanley Gillingham of Gander Bay — were among the four men known to have drowned on the River in our time, I might have made more effort to learn. Not that the Gander is all that dangerous or wild as rivers go — you just have to know what you're doing and stay alert. The other two who drowned were Billy John and Orlendo Gillingham, both of whom seem to have fallen overboard in the daytime during a heart attack or something. The times I nearly drowned were at night and there was nothing wrong with me.

But first let me tell about Harold's experience. In the spring of the year, as soon as the ponds went out, we were always going back and forth between the Bay and Glenwood with freight and passengers, especially after Father and Harold bought the Elto in 1927, making it possible to do the round trip inside of a day. One spring around 1928 or 1929 — I think I was in the States at the time — Harold and his buddy Ron Francis were coming out with a load of freight. They were making good time because the River was top high. On board they had the usual cargo: a box or two of apples, a dozen or so pairs of thigh rubbers, a few sacks of potatoes, some tinned goods, a keg of nails — the like of that. The eighteen-foot canoe was heavily loaded, but the high water was smooth with hardly a rock showing. To make better time they were taking short cuts over boulders and low islands and sandbars that they would have run aground on in the summertime. It was around duckish or twilight, but already they were below First Pond and, knowing the April evening light would linger, they hoped to be home by dark. Harold was back aft steering with the tiller ropes while Ron watched up forward. Suddenly, up ahead they saw this old birch sticking out of the water where it was growing on one of the submerged guidy islands. Ron yelled a warning, but when Harold yanked the steering rope to pass to one side, it broke. Before Ron could grab a paddle the bow of the canoe ran up the trunk of the tree and fell to one side, leaving the canoe broadside to the current and filling rapidly. Both of them jumped for the tree. The canoe, caught amidships by the full force of the current, and sluggish with the weight of water and freight, was jammed so tight they could not dislodge her. The freight was soon washed away; the boat stayed fast.

Well, the two of them spent the whole night in that birch. Harold said the tree was shaking all night with the vibrations from the tide. And dark, you know; they couldn't see the water and kept wondering if the tree would tip over by the roots. Just hanging on they were, and the water freezing cold and waiting for them. To rest their arms they used to take turns standing on the gunwale. And the worst part of it was, at daybreak they could see that the nearest island was a couple of feet under water. The only high ground where they might light in a fire was a larger island farther away. And another thing was that, with the River so high, anyone using a pole boat would keep in the proper channel where the current was less. So they knew nobody would come past there because they were the only ones with a motor.

The only thing was jump in the water and swim to this larger island, and when it got light enough to see better, that's what they did. Ron was a good swimmer, but Harold wasn't. So Ron swam across first with a rope. The current was so swift he was carried downstream, but he managed to reach the island and to help Harold across with the rope. They made in a fire — every riverman carried dry matches in a pill bottle — and dried their clothes.

Now at the end of this island there's another run, a back angle which in high water conditions is about thirty yards wide and ten or eleven feet deep. They didn't attempt to swim that, but they knew that whoever went by would be poling along there. Sure enough, about dinnertime Levi

Gillingham and Maurice Thistle — that's Howard Thistle's father, who always made moonshine — came along carrying someone to Glenwood. They took Harold and Ron and landed them ashore on the mainland down at First Rattle and went on their way.

The two now left to walk home. After being awake all night they were tired and sleepy; when they got in the woods a mile or so — it was a nice sunny day — they laid down and went to sleep. And when they woke up it was dark again. In the meantime some of the freight floated down to the Bay. The box of apples drove ashore at Wings Point, and since it had Father's name stencilled on, the word went around that Harold and Ron might be drowned. But of course they arrived soon after and everything was all right. Later they salvaged the canoe — it took several men to get it out of the grip of the current — and recovered the Elto, which was all right once they got it home and cleaned out the sand and water. Fresh water doesn't hurt a motor the way salt water does.

There was another time — in April month it was, the same as before, but in the thirties — when Harold and his father-in-law William Torraville and myself were coming downriver with three caribou in the same boat. Again the canoe was loaded to the gunwales and again it was pitch dark. We were travelling after dark because we were carrying meat out of season. And to make sure we arrived home after dark we had stopped to boil the kettle at Casey's Angle, just out of sight of the first houses. We were just getting under way again. I was up in the head with a pole. Soon I could hear a rock gurgling, getting closer. But I couldn't see it. I gave the boat a shove the way I thought she should go — and put her right up on that rock! It was the big smooth boulder just below Casey's Angle.

Well, I knew there was about ten feet of water in that spot. Harold could manage to swim, but I couldn't and neither could Willy John. When the canoe capsized, Willy John grabbed the paddle and I hung onto the pole. The boat came up below the rock and out of reach. We had a white mailbag — a lot of people used them for duffle bags in those days though 'twas against the law — and when I came up I threw my arm around it. I was six feet from the boat then. The thought struck me, "Well, this bag is going to get soaked and sink, and then it won't float me." Somehow I thrashed my way to the canoe and climbed up on her bottom. Harold did the same. But Willy John couldn't reach her. In the dark I could hear him come up and blow and puff to get his breath. And I was hollering to him, "Keep goin', keep goin'! There's a sandbar inside where it's shallower." I couldn't tell if he heard me or no, but he made that sandbar and waded ashore from there. My brother and I were on the bottom of the boat. Having lost all the meat and our packs, we didn't mean to lose

185

the canoe as well, so we tried to pole her ashore. We couldn't do it. The same engine, the 4.4 horsepower Elto, was still on her and every time we'd take our weight off the pole the boat would sink down aft, the engine would strike bottom, you know, bump, bump, and drag as the tide took us downstream. After a spell of this Harold said, "I'm gonna try and swim ashore." He took off his sheepskin coat then and threw it away, he took off his long rubbers and threw them away, and jumped overboard and went on, because he could at least swim. But before he jumped Harold said, "You better come with me." I said, "No, Harold, you know I can't swim." And that was the God's truth, I couldn't swim to save my life.

So Harold went, and there was I alone on the boat in the dark, drifting. I tried then to right the canoe. I'd put one foot against the keel and get the pole down, and push and push and try, but I couldn't break the air suction along her gunwale. And once, when I was doing that, my foot slipped and I fell backwards in the water. I never saw the boat after. I went down. My feet touched bottom. Cap came off. Lungs bursting. But I had the presence of mind to hold on to that pole. I put it down behind me until I found solid bottom, and the current would lift me. I used to climb the pole then, hand over hand. And when I'd come up, I'd breathe. And then I'd put the pole down again, I'd sink down, but I'd get to work the pole just the same as if I was in the boat. That's how I finally got ashore. But it took me all of half an hour.

Well, I reached the bank and I couldn't get up. I was beat right out — couldn't get up over the bank. I held on to the alders and threw the pole up on top. After a while I got strength enough to crawl up. The first step I made, I fell headlong because my thigh rubbers were full of water. I was beat out anyway and I just fell down. As I emptied my rubbers I heard Harold and Willy John singing out. They seemed to be in the woods farther up the shore. With my boots lighter I started to walk towards them. It was pitch black; you couldn't see a thing. There were trees and you had to put your hand before your face to favour your eyes. Finally I got up where they were.

Willy John was just about gone. "Leave me here, b'ys," he kept saying, "I'm all right." But he wasn't. He was full of water and his face and hands were cold as ice. Now two hundred yards upriver from where we upset we had a fire a few hours before. By this time it was about ten o'clock in the night. I said to Harold, "Don't leave him, b'y, because he'll die there. Make him walk and I'll go up to where we had the fire and see if there's any coals, any sparks left."

I got up there, and soon had a good fire going. By and by they came. Willy John was so glad of the fire he just stood over it steaming, his mitts

186

hanging down and the water running out of them; he looked just about dead. We bent him over then and got the water out of him, and after that I took hold of him and raced him around the little clearing as well as I could, for he kept stumbling and his legs wouldn't work. Finally I got a bit of life in him. Then we got the clothes off him. A big fire was blazing now. With some poles and forked sticks we rigged a drying rack. We took off every stitch of our clothes and wrung them all out and dried them by the fire, turning and turning them so the flankers wouldn't burn holes. And by the time this was done Willy John was himself again.

We stayed there until we heard the first robin bawl in the morning, then we left for home. We had to walk through the woods and stay on the main shore. Going down to Gander Bay we had the Gut Brook to cross, wading to our waist. So we followed the shore down. This was just at dawn, about five o'clock in the morning. We wanted to get home before anybody was stirring, before the people got up, because of the illegal caribou, you see. Along the way I picked up our paddle and pots and a pair of snowshoes — but not a sign of the boat. We reached the house without seeing a soul, made in a fire, and boiled the kettle.

After a mugup we got ourselves another canoe and left again. Our plan was for Harold and his father-in-law to search the south side of the Bay by boat while I would walk the north side. We were determined to pick up our meat before anybody else happened along. They dropped me off and I hurried along, finding a kettle here, a mitt there. On the south side they never picked up a thing. Just below where we overturned we found the venison. But all we could hook up off the bottom was five quarters and a liver. The rest still had the hide left on and must have floated away. As for the boat, her painter had fetched up on a sunken log not far downstream and she was moored there bottom up. The motor was nowhere to be seen. Although fastened with screw-clamps onto the stern, all that banging on the rocks and boulders had knocked it off. Just after we got the boat put to rights, and while we were still hooking around with the pole, Jim Snow and another fellow from the Bay came along. Naturally they wanted to know what we were looking for and whether they could help. "We shot a seal up there," I said, "and it sank here somewhere." That satisfied them and away they went. After a while longer we gave up, couldn't find any more.

In the meantime there was another boat had started up from the Bay. Now I had lost a clothesbag with some clothes in it and a fox skin, and those two fellows picked that up. And knowing it was my bag, they went back and carried it into the shop where Father was. "Skipper Frank," they said, "we know this is Brett's clothesbag and we think they must have upset. But we never seen their boat." Now this might have driven Father wild — his two oldest sons maybe drowned and Willy John too — but he knew something they didn't. He knew we had been home that morning when he came in from the shop for his breakfast for he saw the three teacups on the kitchen table where we'd had our mugup, and some wet clothes drying over the stove.

That was quite a night, quite a night. We later found the Elto. Another valuable item we lost that time that we never expected to recover was the spyglass that the British hunter Dr. Seccombe Hett gave to Billy John on their 1919 caribou hunting trip, and which Harold later bought off Billy for $10. Harold went back next August when the River was low, and after a good while managed to hook it off the bottom with a wire on a pole. The brass tubes had gone slop or loose from the soaking, and the leather case was all hardened, but otherwise it was still all right. Harold still has it.

There was one other night when Howard Thistle had a like to drown. It was the night he got drunk and fell overboard at Bridges Angle in March month, the winter we were up there rabbit-catching in the early forties. Rabbits were plentiful and fetching a good price in Glenwood, and as we had nothing else to do, so we set ourselves up in the same spot where my cousin Stanley Gillingham and I had worked some twenty years before, even staying in the same camp. The beauty of it was that from Bridges Angle up, the River stayed open all the way to Glenwood, which meant we could take our rabbits by boat and sell them while they were still fresh. Roland Richards used to buy them at eighty cents a pair — cash on the barrel head, all we could supply — and sell them to the train crews. We went up in the fall and worked at it, hard at it, through the winter, taking Rol a boatload every week or so.

Now Howard was a hard man for the bottle. He got that way while he was overseas in the First World War. Perhaps the fact that he was badly wounded in the neck had something to do with it; perhaps it was because his father Maurice always made moonshine. Anyway, I made a rule against drinking in the boat. And even though he was ten years older than me, drink was rarely a problem. Still, I always tried to make sure there was no liquor around. I liked a drink now and then myself, but Howard, once he had a drink, couldn't rest until he saw the bottom of the bottle or the case. And it would bring out a mean streak in him, making him as contrary as the devil and wanting to row and fight and stir up trouble.

Howard and I had trapped together in harmony for years. He was a fine woodsman and a boon companion. I remember one time we were trapping at Big Gull. It was in November and although we had the canoe, this day we were on foot. And for some reason we forgot and crossed over upstream so that when we came back down our boat was on the wrong shore. The water was only about three feet deep in midstream, but ice-cold.

"That's nothin', I'll wade over and get her," says he.

"No you won't," says I. He was prone to chest problems and I didn't want him catching penumonia. "I'll go."

"No, no, I'll get her," says Howard.

"And that's what you won't," says I, half vexed.

He looked at me then in that way he had, with his head back and that mischievous twinkle in his blue eyes, and he said, "Hell, we'll both wade over!" I'll never forget that.

Well, there was no liquor store in Glenwood, so I wasn't too worried. But on one of our trips Howard got a thirst for something stronger than tea and ordered two bottles of rum from St. John's. The next trip, while I was unloading the rabbits, he went to the station and picked up his grog. Knowing I would disapprove, he soon found some friends to help him drink the first one, and by the time he returned they had killed it and he was half on. He was all for opening the second one, but I wasn't fussy about going down Big Chute after dark with him drinking, so I coaxed him aboard and we left just before sunset. He wouldn't give me the bottle though.

We had no motor and were rowing and paddling. Howard sat up forward, facing me, rowing while I steered with the spoon paddle in the stern. Every so often I would notice him stop and turn around and reach in the cuddy. I knew then that he had the other bottle open. This worried me because by now the sun was gone down and the stars were out — a tricky proposition for steering even at the best of times. By and by a full moon rose to starboard and I could see the rocks a little better. We got past Big and Little Chute, the two worst places, without a mishap — only a couple of miles to go. Then he took another swig and said to me: "Brett, I'll steer now."

"Why?" I said.

"To make sure we finds the camp," he said. I could tell by his voice he was fairly well loaded. "We're in the wrong channel and I'm gonna straighten us out before 'tis too late."

I knew full well we were in the right channel, that it was just the rum talking. I said nothing and just steered while he let his oars trail in the water.

"Lard Jesus Christ," he yelled, "gimme that paddle. You don't know how to run a boat, you never did. You're no damn good anyway." He was rising to his feet, the bottle in one hand. There was nothing I could do but quickly trade places, only I sat facing ahead, the better to see where we were going in case he headed for a rock. The stern was narrow and, as the boat turned and rocked in the waves, it was all he could do to keep his balance, even sitting. And about a quarter mile from camp he fell overboard in about twelve feet of water. Rowing backwards I quickly stopped the canoe, and when he came up, sputtering and blowing, I managed to grab his collar. It was quite a struggle to get him over the gunwale in the dark without capsizing, and if the bitter cold water hadn't sobered him up some it would have been harder. By the time we reached the landing his clothes were frozen stiff.

All day the ice had been making around shore in the coves. At the camp it was already out several feet from the shore. The minute the bow touched the edge Howard stepped out and broke through and fell down. This made me so crooked I had a mind to leave him there to perish. But I pulled him out again and wrestled him up the trail and into the camp. With a good fire blazing I peeled off his ice-caked clothes, rolled him into his bunk, and hung everything up to dry. Before I finished he was asleep. The last thing I did was go down to the boat and take the bottle from under the cuddy and hide it under my bunk. In the night I heard him fumbling for the door latch in the dark and muttering to himself "Need a piss, where's the goddamn door, need a piss."

Early the next morning, while Howard was still snoring, I took the boat and went downstream and found the paddle he'd lost. When I got back he was sitting on his bunk holding his head in both hands. "Brett," he said as I came in, "is there any rum left? I need a drink real bad this morning."

"No, b'y," I said, "you lost the bottle when you fell overboard."

"Fell overboard?" he said, rubbing his eyes hard. "Wondered why all my clothes were hung up like that." We had a cup of tea and I told him the story, ending with the fact that he'd lost his cap. "Oh, to hell with the cap," he snorted, "it's the rum I'm sorry to lose!"

With that I pulled the bottle and poured us both a good snort. "You sleveen!" he said, happily downing his. "I knew you were lying." What he didn't know was that the night before I had poured half the rum in the River.

That winter we caught and sold 1,600 rabbits, or about five thousand pounds of meat. Rol paid us $640, which we split between us. That worked out to a daily wage of just over $5 apiece. And not long after, it was Howard's turn to save my life — but that's another story.

Shot!

Three times in my lifetime I've been shot, once very seriously. But I was never in the war, and no man ever shot at me. Each time it was my own fault, and each time I was old enough to know better.

The first accident happened in my late twenties, not long after we came back from Huntsville, and it was with a shotgun. At that time I was helping Father around the shop, carrying freight and so forth. In the fall of the year he used to buy berries from pickers around the Bay, pack them in twenty-gallon kegs, and sell them to W.A. Munn Limited in St. John's. These were blueberries and partridgeberries mostly, and if people couldn't bring the berries to us, we would go and collect them.

This day Father asked me to take the canoe and go down to Victoria Cove and bring back three barrels of partridgeberries from Mrs. Lemuel Oake, and some more from Liza Jane Harbin in Rodger's Cove, the last house down. It was a nice calm October day and I took along my twelve-gauge in hopes I would see a seal or some ducks. Sure enough, off Wings Point a seal was sunning itself on a rock. As I steamed by he dived, but I slipped a BB shell in the shotgun and swung the boat in his direction, hoping to get a shot when he breached. But the seal was too cute for me. So I went on, leaving the shell in the gun in case I saw another one. I lodged the gun on the after tawt, muzzle forward, within easy reach.

After coming from Mrs. Harbin's, I landed near the Oake's house in Victoria Cove, rolled out the barrels, and got some help to hoist them aboard and stow them. They weighed two hundred pounds apiece and had to be laid side by side at right angles to the keel, between the forward and after tawts. That didn't leave much room, and to reach the motor after shoving off from the wharf I had to walk on these barrels. While doing this I chanced to kick the muzzle of the loaded shotgun. This drove the hammer against the tawt, and the gun went off. Suddenly my left foot felt like it had been smashed with a red-hot maul.

Some men rushed to pull the canoe back in and help me. I felt all right, but I had to get to a house and get my boot and socks off. I hobbled back to Mrs. Oake's. She had heard the shot and met me at the door. Explaining what had happened, I asked her for some Jeyes Fluid disinfectant, water and a pair of sharp scissors. After we worked the long rubber boot off I snipped and peeled off two layers of bloody wool sock, and placed my foot in the enamel basin full of warm water to inspect the damage.

The BB charge had entered the sole of my foot at pointblank range, angling upward into the ball of my foot. At the sight of the ragged hole Mrs. Oake felt queasy and went away to scorch some cloth for bandages. There were shotholes in the thick skin there, and more in the loose skin between my toes; at the far end of each hole were one or more pellets. They all had to come out — and the sooner the better, while the flesh was still numb from shock. I sharpened several matchsticks with my pocket knife, dipped them in the Jeye's Fluid, and went to work. After half an hour there were over a dozen black shot in the red water of the washbasin and the life was starting to come back to my foot. Altogether I hooked out sixteen. Between my big toe and the next there was one I couldn't reach, so I left it; it's still there today. (The thought came to me that it would make a good mark if ever I was drowned.) After bandaging my foot Mrs. Oake put the sixteen shots into a matchbox for a keepsake. Fortunately most of the charge lodged in the thick sole of my long rubber or else glanced off. Two went in my right foot as well — one in the big toe and one in the instep.

When all was nicely bandaged I sent Mrs. Oake's daughter-in-law to the Post Office with a message asking Pop to send the motor boat for me. But after we got the boot back on over the bandage it didn't feel too bad, so I hobbled back out to the canoe and left for home. Halfway to Clarke's Head the motor boat met me and towed my canoe and cargo home, for which I was thankful because I was in some pain.

The next day, while I was resting on the couch, there came a rap to our door and Skipper Johnny Squires was standing there with a grin on his face.

"Hear you shot your foot yesterday," he began.

"Yes, that's so, Skipper John." I stuck out my bandaged foot. But the details of my accident didn't seem to interest him.

"I was wonderin'," he said, grinning more than ever, "if ye'll be needin' your right long rubber now that the left is ruined?"

"No," I said, "I s'pose I won't." And although my foot was paining like the devil, I had to laugh. "Mr. Squires," I said, "that was a lucky shot for you, and you're welcome to the other boot if it'll fit."

"Oh," he replied in high spirits, "that jes' suits me fine, 'cause I got a hole in me right one." And off he went with my long rubber under his arm, full of the pleasure only a tightwad can know. I never bothered to tell him it was leaky too.

My worst mishap with guns happened in the late forties on the Northwest Gander. Howard Thistle and I had a moose licence and we went up to Big Gull looking to get our meat for the winter. He went in one direction on the south side of the river; I took the boat and went out on a large island, one of three that moose frequented. When I was walking up around the shore there, I saw a moose come out of the woods on this other island about 150 yards away. The gun I had was my brother Harold's, a Remington .44-40 full magazine pump action rifle.

Well, anyway, I shot this moose. It fell down, and I was going over to paunch it and clean it up. There was some clear black ice in a little cove that I was walking around, and underneath this, as I went along the shore, I saw a muskrat swimming out from shore. I watched him for a while and then reached out with the rifle butt, to turn the muskrat back. Now the safety on this gun was underneath, just behind the trigger guard, and you had to push it one way for On and the other for Off — I never could remember which was which. And the muskrat was nearly out of reach, but if I could turn him I was going to break the ice and pick him out. As I reached with the gun I overbalanced, and had to let the backstock go down on the ice, and when it hit the rifle went off.

The bullet went through my mitt, creased the side of my hand, went right through the centre part of my thigh and came out behind. I made two or three quick steps — thought maybe my leg was broken, I didn't know — but I could walk all right. So I left to walk across the island, back to where the canoe was. On reaching the other side I felt giddy, sort of weak, like I was going to black out. I lay down. Then I took to shivering — shivering and shaking pretty hard. After that was over I hauled off my rubber, poured out a pint or so of blood, and got my pants down to look at the hole in my thigh where the bullet went in. The hole was big enough to put my little finger in. A bit of pink muscle was throbbing in and out.

So I hollered out to Howard, and finally he came out of the woods just across the River. But I had the boat and it was about two hundred yards away, down on the other end of the island. To reach me he had to wade across in that ice-cold water to his waist. This was about four o'clock in the evening. It was too dark to start for home that day. All he could do was get me back to camp and try to make me comfortable. We had no pain killers with us, not even rum. As luck would have it, I didn't lose much blood.

At daybreak the next morning we left for home, a distance of seventy miles with outboard motor, pole, and paddle. I had sense enough to keep the leg elevated. On the second day around dark we reached Clarke's Head. Father wired Roy Reccord, my sister Marion's husband, in Victoria Cove to meet us with his motor boat and from there we started right away for Twillingate Hospital.

It was a stormy evening with wind and rain from the north and a chop that got worse as we cleared Dog Bay Point. By and by we got in the lun of Dog Bay Islands, sixteen miles from home, and anchored for the night in a sheltered cove. In pain from the rolling and pitching of the boat, I couldn't sleep. At four the next morning we reached Twillingate. Roy naturally wanted to call Dr. Olds and a taxi to take me to the hospital right away, but I said we would wait until eight o'clock when they opened. Dr. Olds met us at the door.

"And what happened to you, Brett?" he said gruffly. I had guided with John Olds' hunting parties since 1938 and we knew each other pretty well.

"I was up moose huntin'," I said, "and shot myself."

"Are the moose that scarce?" he said, winking at Howard. After washing the wound he pulled a piece of my underwear out of the hole, snipped away some proud flesh, and bandaged my leg. "Well," he said, straightening up and turning serious, "you're a very lucky man. An inch either way and you'd have hit either the femoral artery or the femur. A severed femoral artery and you would have bled to death; shattered femur and you might never have walked normally again. As it is, a bit of clean-up, a few stitches and some rest and you'll be as good as new."

It so happened that my wife Winnie was in there at the same time. When Dr. Olds had me squared away I asked about her. He went to her ward and said in his brusque manner, "Like to see your husband?"

"Certainly I would, Doctor," she replied, "but he's up on the Northwest with Howard Thistle hunting."

"And that he isn't, my dear," he said. "Brett is here in the hospital — I was just talking to him."

"Oh, Doctor, he's not shot again is he?" she said, much to his amusement.

The third time I shot myself was on another moose hunting trip a

194

few years later, with the same Remington .44-40 rifle. Harold had a logging camp on the south side of the Bay in a good area for moose, and since it was December and the snowshoeing was good, I was hunting late in the day before heading back to camp. There was plenty of sign — tracks and browse marks and droppings — so I left a bullet in the chamber just in case. By now I thought I knew the gun much better. The safety was on, and this time I had even checked it by hitting the rifle two or three times on a blowdown tree to see if it would go off. It didn't, so I put it on my right shoulder and dodged on. We trappers always carried our guns with the muzzle forward, not like the military people with the muzzle behind. And as I was walking through a thick bunch of woods, the backstock caught on a tree. My little finger must have been fair over the muzzle, because when the gun went off I felt it tear away.

It was just about dark. I still had a mile to go to camp. Making a snowball, I pushed my finger in it to stop the bleeding and then went on, cursing myself for being so stunned. Back in camp I washed off the caked blood and saw that only the tip of the finger and part of the nail was gone: this time it was nothing serious, didn't even need a bandage.

When I got home the next day I told Harold, but never let on to Winnie — I was too ashamed. But a few days later as she was getting ready to do some mending, she picked up the mitt with the bullet hole and asked what happened to it. "Cut it with the axe, setting a rabbit slip," I said. A week or so later Harold came in. The three of us were having a cup of tea.

"How's that finger of yours coming along, Brett?" he said.

"Oh, very good now," I said, trying to catch his eye.

"I'm not going to loan you that gun anymore," he said. So the cat was out of the bag. After that Harold tried to set the gun off while the safety was on, but he couldn't, so he kept her. In some ways this third accident was my worst, because it was the hardest to live down. Perhaps that's why I never had another one. But when Calvin reached fourteen and wanted to go by himself with a gun I worried perhaps more than most fathers. And this made me do something rash. I had this lovely ten-gauge shotgun — that's a bigger bore than a twelve-gauge, with a longer reach — and I had charged him never to take it unless he asked me first. But one evening after school he wanted to go hunting ducks so badly that he took this gun and went up to the Gut in the boat without permission. When dark came and he wasn't back I was worried and waited for him on the wharf. After a while he came. Without a word I took the gun, went up to the forge, put the barrel in the vise, and twisted it in a figure eight.

One other time he went to tend his rabbit snares after school and took the Winchester single-shot .22 without permission. Coming back he was afraid of what I would say or do so he hid it in the sawdust road near Harold's barn. When Harold took the big horse out the next day it trod on the exact spot and split the forearm. Calvin felt so badly he had to tell me. I didn't have the heart to punish him. We fixed the cracks with screws and putty and he used the .22 for many years after that.

Norseman and Fox Moth

Although there was an airstrip at Norris Arm as early as 1934, flying mercy missions and winter mail with *Fox Moths*, an airplane was a rare sight over Gander Bay until World War II. Previously the loudest noises we heard in Clarke's Head were the sawmill in the summer and the muskets on New Year's Eve. Hitler changed all that. Since we were only forty-odd miles from the seaplane base at Botwood to the west it wasn't unusual to see a big, lumbering *Catalina Flying Boat* come skimming up the Bay on some practice mission. And with Gander Airport only twenty-five miles away to the southeast, the sight and sound of yellow *Harvard Trainers* became commonplace. Sometimes two or three would roar past at nearly rooftop level, rattling the windowpanes and shivering the cups and saucers, sending the horses and sheep racing off the roads and into the woods. It was enough to split your eardrums.

Now in Gander Bay the quietest time of all was a Sunday morning early. And that seemed to be their favourite time. I remember one Sunday they made me so vexed that I picked up a rock and fired it at one as it skimmed over our house. I thought I heard it strike, too. Afterwards someone told me the fighter might have crashed if that rock had hit its propellor. Sometimes we could see the faces of the pilot and his instructor in the double cockpit; they were just young fellows getting ready to fight the Luftwaffe in the skies over Europe and having a bit of fun first. So I never did that again.

Gander was the centre for all wartime air traffic in the western North Atlantic. After the United States came into the war in 1941 a steady stream of bombers and pilots passed through there. With all that traffic there was bound to be accidents. In 1942 or 1943 a *Lancaster* went down in a snowstorm a few miles in from the south shore of Gander Lake, killing all hands. Later, on a hunting trip, I saw the wreckage. For several hundred yards, lower and lower as she came in, the big plane had sheared off the tops of the trees. We fellows thought it all right to pick up odds and ends that we could use — aluminium tubing, life-jackets, K-rations and the like of that. One time I found a fat billfold full of money. But it was only sample bills from countries all over the world, to help a pilot know the currencies. There was no name in it.

Except for the *Hurricane* that crashed near Third Pond, there was never a major crash near Gander Bay. But we did have two minor accidents involving bush planes in this same period — one a *Norseman* and the other a *Fox Moth*. I was away trapping on the Northwest with Howard Thistle when the *Fox Moth* incident took place, but I was very much involved with the *Norseman* because I got the contract to salvage it.

The trouble with the *Norseman* happened this way. Early in January of 1945 Susie Gillingham took very sick. They sent a telegram to Gander for a plane to come and take her to hospital right away. I think it was appendicitis. Now Susie lived on the north side, the Clarke's Head side, but the pilot landed on the ice near George's Point on the south side. Group Captain David Anderson had never been to the Bay before, and since his map had *Gander Bay* marked on the south side — where the old post office used to be — he assumed that was the right place. Somebody at George's Point having explained the mistake, he turned the plane and started to taxi across. The Bay at this point is almost a mile wide. Because of the River current the channel is always the last to freeze. It had caught over in December and the ice, being covered with a couple of inches of snow, looked strong enough. George Harris of Harris Point, always the first to test the new ice each winter, had already walked across to Point Head with axe in hand, leaving little spruce tops to mark the safest route. Others had crossed on foot as well. And, as Group Captain Anderson sped along, sending up clouds of snow, he spotted a man walking towards him. I believe it was Reg Bath. Still unsure of where Susie Gillingham lived, he turned toward the man and cut the throttle, intending to ask the way. And when he did the ice collapsed under the *Norseman*'s sudden weight and her nose went down.

Well, it was a scramble I can tell you, with the hot engine bubbling and throwing up clouds of steam, for the pilot and his engineer Angus Steele to haul themselves up through the escape hatch, run across the wing and jump to safety. For all they knew the wings would break through as well and the whole plane would sink — she weighed about four tons. But the wings held her up. She came to rest with her engine and skis out of sight and the waterline just at the cockpit. There was fifteen feet of water underneath. So there she was, and Susie no closer to hospital than ever. Another wire was sent. Before dark another plane took her away and she was saved. And this other plane, a *Fox Moth* piloted by Joe Gilmore, Chief Engineer for the Royal Air Force's Ferry Command in Gander, was the same plane that was to crack up in Gander Bay only a few weeks later.

After sizing up the *Norseman* situation, Joe came in the shop to look for somebody to take a contract to get the plane out. I told him I would do it for $1000. Now the *Norseman* had four strong hoisting rings on its roof, and I knew that if we could rig a block and tackle from a strong framework and put enough men to it we could lift the plane out. Joe said he would send out a double-sheave chain block which only required one or two men because it had a ratchet to keep the load from slipping back. So that would make it easier. The other thing was, would the ice hold once we lifted the plane up and set the skis down on it? We would just have to hope for frosty nights and in the meantime get ready.

I hired Roland Gillingham to help me. We cut two thirty-foot poles for uprights. Chopping holes in the ice on either side of the fuselage, we set them firmly in the bottom mud. Across the top we laid a twenty-foot spruce stringer and notched and bolted it into place. This gave us fifteen feet clearance above the ice, enough for the skis to swing free so we could shove planks underneath when the time came. The last thing to do when everything was ready was to take up the strain of her weight on the chain block and chop her out of the new ice that had formed around the fuselage. Slowly, chopping very carefully with our axes for fear of gashing her fuselage or wings, we went all around the hole until she was clear and there was room for the skis to come up through. A crowd was watching as we hoisted her out; I made them stand back in case the ice collapsed. It proved easier than we thought. But what a sad sight, a fine plane like that with water streaming out of her engine and ice candles hanging from her struts! In a few minutes we had the planks in place. The ice held. She was safe and sound.

Joe was delighted. He was busy flying back and forth now in the *Fox Moth*, bringing supplies for the next phase of the operation, which was to dry out the engine before the water damaged it. I told him the Bay water thereabouts was nearly fresh — that in fact it was the River current which had made the ice thin. But he was worried about rust just the same. When the ice was strong enough we gathered a crowd of men and hauled the *Norseman* in close to shore at Thistle's Mill, just above where the causeway comes ashore on the north side today. That way, if a thaw came she wouldn't sink, and there was less wind. Rigging up a tarpaulin shelter over the front half of the plane, with two gasoline heaters and a blower to drive out the moisture, he left a mechanic to work on it. Our job was to guard the plane day and night and keep the heaters going. Rol and me lived in canvas tent right there on the ice. The mechanic stayed at Mother's. In all it took him a fortnight.

Finally the big day came. Group Captain Anderson arrived in a little green and gold two-man *Piper Cub*, looked the *Norseman* over, and climbed into the cockpit. Meanwhile, we had marked out a runway with spruce tops and pointed her in that direction. He pressed the starting button. Nothing happened. The battery was dead. And I knew why. Several times, after the mechanic and Joe had fixed her up, they started the engine. And when they weren't around I had started it myself, showing different people how. One time I did it and the tarp got tangled up in the propellor and rolled up in a big ball. I also shot off the Berry Pistol one night — taking care to aim the flare low so they couldn't see it in Gander. Anyway, Group Captain Anderson was none too pleased that he had to go back to Gander without the *Norseman*. They flew out a generator, then, and a couple of days later she flew away and the excitement was over. I got my $1000 and paid Roland and was well satisfied with my two weeks' work.

After this was over Howard Thistle and I went up on the Northwest trapping. It was while we were away that Joe Gilmore had the mishap with the *Fox Moth*. Joe was not a certified pilot, but he had taught himself to fly bush planes and liked nothing better than taking a short trip away from the pressures at Ferry Command. During the *Norseman* episode he had become a friend of the family and would sometimes drop in for a visit. One day he parked the little biplane just off the wharf and stayed for dinner. After buying a jug of molasses at the shop, he walked out to the plane. As usual, a crowd had gathered to watch the takeoff. Even Uncle Dick Gillingham, though feeling "wonderful bad" all winter, managed to hobble out to see it. Pop was there too, and a bunch of children on their way back to school.

Now the VO-ADE *Fox Moth* had no starter: you had to hand-crank the propellor. And because all the struts and cables between the upper and lower wings made it hard to reach into the cockpit, there was a rig that let the pilot set the throttle from the outside. To prime the engine he would crank the prop over three times with the ignition switched off. He would then switch on the ignition and give it one more half-turn to start her. But this time he no sooner touched the propellor than the engine caught. 'Twas a wonder he didn't lose an arm. She not only caught, but was going at full throttle in a second, and moving ahead the next second. Father later told me Joe ran and jumped onto the lower wing to try to climb into the cockpit and hit the switch, but she was already moving too fast. He fell to the ice, got up, ran again, but the *Moth* was picking up speed. Just like a plane taking off, she was. She went on like this for a hundred yards or so, going downwind toward the centre of the Bay, when a strong side gust struck her. With that she swung around like a windjack facing into the wind, made a wide turn, and headed right back toward the crowd.

When Father, who had followed after Joe for a piece and was standing watching, realized she was coming right for him with her engine roaring and her skis fairly bouncing off the ice, he knew it was too late to run. Besides, he was too fat. So he dropped flat on his face. The bottom wing grazed his shoulder. Meanwhile, people turned and ran every which way from this little plane gone berserk. Now there was a rock-filled pier near the wharf, one of the piers we used to tie our log boom to. Very solid, it stood fair in the *Fox Moth*'s path. The impact stopped the plane in its tracks, curling the tips of the metal propellor, breaking one wing, and ripping the canvas off the fuselage. But nobody was hurt.

So that was two plane crashes in one winter. The youngsters were tickled. They dogged Joe's footsteps as he and his mechanics — this time Sam Blandford and Harry Young — set to work with wood and canvas and glue to rebuild the *Fox Moth*. I believe Angus Steele helped too. They took off the wings and carried them up into the sawmill, leaving the rest of her covered against the weather. Shaping new pieces of wood to replace the broken framework of the wings, they stretched and tacked canvas duck over it. To tighten the canvas they brushed on strong-smelling dope. A new propellor was brought out and installed. All of this took two or three weeks. A final coat of light grey paint and she was ready. Calvin recalls that on the day Joe flew her out, he arrived in a *Harvard Trainer* that landed on the ice with wheels and taxied in close to the wharf. Again the youngsters were watching. When the *Harvard*'s pilot stepped down from the cockpit in his helmet and goggles and leather jacket, with his "May West" life preserver on and a .45 automatic pistol in a holster at his side, their eyes were as big as saucers. First VO-ADE and then the yellow fighter roared into the sky, leaving the crowd with snow stinging their eyes, the smell of exhaust in their nostrils — and exciting memories to talk about for years to come.

That winter Howard and I did well with the fur. And for a couple of years I had also been buying quite a bit around the Bay. The spring before, I even went to Horwood by canoe to buy muskrat pelts, getting stormbound so that I had to come back on the *Glencoe*, canoe and all. Joe Gilmore, during his trips back and forth, said he might be able to sell some pelts for me to the bomber pilots and crews going through Gander. This worked out quite well. Then it came about that the *Norseman* would have to go to the Noorduyn plant in Montreal for a new engine. He would be flying it there by way of Stephenville and Prince Edward Island. He offered to sell about a dozen of my best lynx and fox skins, about $1200 worth. I brought them to Gander in a mailbag. Joe happened to be away repairing another downed plane on the Southwest Gander. Not wishing to leave my furs with just anybody, I got clearance from the commanding officer to leave them with Joe's wife. But my bag of furs never did make it to Montreal. Joe Gilmore did indeed fly the *Norseman*, along with a Squadron Leader Radcliffe who was on furlough and went along for the ride. For the over-water flight from Harmon Air Force Base to Prince Edward Island they were accompanied by a *Catalina Flying Boat*, but it wasn't over water that they needed help. On May first, twelve miles out of Charlottetown Airport, the *Norseman* burst into flames and crashed in a farmer's field. The impact was so great that the engine buried itself several feet in the earth. Both men died instantly. Joe's body was flown back to Gander for burial. The funeral was a large one, for Joe was known far and wide for his skill and dependability, and everybody was stunned that such a misfortune should have happened to him of all people, and felt sorry for his wife and family. I later heard that Joey Smallwood, then running his pig farm at Gander, had expected to go to Montreal with Joe, but was grounded by the CO; he raised a large sum of money for Gilmore's family. As for my furs, perhaps they made a fine present for the farmer's wife, or perhaps they burned in the crash.

Pike Pole, Chrome Iron, and Cod

Three more things I did to make a dollar were log driving, prospecting and inspecting fish. I did none of them for long, but each occupation was interesting in itself, especially the river drive.

"Going on the drive," as we called it, was something most young men in the Bay did at one time or another. After the spring breakup it was the only way of moving logs to the mill. Most of the larger brooks around Gander Bay have had logs driven down them, especially Joe Batt's, Miller's, Bellman's, and Barry's. Even Clarke's Brook, though less than two miles long, had a scattered drive. I remember during the First World War Father drove pitprops down to tidewater on Clarke's Brook in the spring, and after we started the new mill in 1938 we drove wood from Clarke's Pond for several years. We even had log chutes to get by the roughest places.

A lot of the men who went on the drive didn't pride themselves on it, but only took the winter's cut down and then worked in the mill the rest of the summer. Others, like my Uncle Stanley Gillingham, made a name for themselves. Depending on the year, a full driving season could last from early April, with snow squalls and ice still lingering along the shore, right into the end of May, when the nippers and blackflies would make life hellish but at least the water was not so cold. After Phillips' sawmill closed down, these professional drivers found work on the big Exploits River drives, bringing pulpwood down from Millertown on the main river and also off the tributary streams like Noel Paul, Tom Joe, Mary Ann, Badger, and Sandy. Other years they would drive sawlogs off Barry's or Dog Bay waters for the Horwood Lumber Company. It was while on one of those drives, in May of 1912, that Uncle Stan was nearly caught in the big forest fire that almost burned the village of Horwood out. He was only nineteen or twenty then.

A young fellow like that, in the prime of life and catty on his feet, made one class of driver, the class that had the job of rounding up the rear or picking up the stray sticks and moving the logs along through slow water or steadies with their pick poles. Sometimes they would send one or two logs out to bump the others in midstream and hurry them along. A second class of driver was the fastwaterman, the older driver with years of experience under his belt who knew just where to expect trouble and how to untangle a jam when it occurred. And a fourth group were the wing men, fellows who went ahead of the drive to set up "wings" or guide logs where they figured the logs would run aground or get snagged in bushes or whatever. The first run of logs would "grease the river" for the rest.

In the spring of 1943 I worked as a wingman on the Bellman's Brook drive for Horwood Lumber Company. We drove sawlogs down Bellman's Brook — that is, about ten miles from Bellman's Pond to Gander River and from there another eight miles down to the Bay. At George's Point the logs were boomed for towing by the company's tug, the *Beatty*, to Horwood fifteen miles away.

We lived in felt or tarpaper wigwams set up at strategic points along the brook. Each morning we walked about two miles upstream to the head of the drive, where we left it the night before, and each evening we would walk two miles down below the last of it to the next lower camp. Walking up was on company time and walking down was on our own time. It was a twelve-hour day, with breakfast at about 5:30 a.m. and supper at 6:00 p.m., a lunch at 10:00 in the morning and another at 3:00 p.m. and at bedtime. We had ravenous appetites. Bread and tea and molasses buns was the staple for lunches, baked beans and pancakes was the main breakfast meal, and salt beef and vegetables or fish and brewis was the main fare for supper. By suppertime all of us were soaking wet — some to our waist, some to our neck. We never changed during the day. There was less chance of a man catching cold or pneumonia if he let his clothes dry on him. Beef, Iron & Wine Tonic and Buckley's Mixture were our only medicines, with liniment for aches and pains. At night we hung our wet socks and other garments around the stove and tried to dry our underwear. That was one thing about working on the drive: we never needed a bath. Our clothes consisted of what we always wore: long woolen or cotton underwear, one or two pairs of double-knit wool socks, cotton shirt, homespun wool sweater, and some kind of coat and cap. Sometimes it was cold enough for mitts, but mitts were clumsy for handling tools.

On their feet professional drivers wore leather boots with sharp caulks or "sparbles" that wouldn't slip on the wet logs and slubby rocks, but we just wore rubber boots. The two main tools were a peeled ten-foot spruce pole with an iron point, which we called a "pick pole," and a stout, short-handled version of this with a curved, swinging iron hook for rolling logs, called a peavey. Some mornings the handles of both were soon coated with ice. We would leave them on the banks wherever we finished the evening before. Some logs would keep moving during the night, but most would not. It was the job of the river boss to gauge how far we would go each day. This varied with water depth, rainfall, current, and the wind. On the basis of these he would have to figure the location of camps, amount of food needed, and so on.

Once during the drive we were visited by Mr. George Horwood from company headquarters in St. John's. Harold brought him up from the Bay and landed him at the mouth of Bellman's. He came walking in the trail by the brook wearing a three-piece suit, mopping his brow with a big hankerchief and swiping at the files with his hat. I was sitting on the bank with a bunch of the fellows when he came in sight of us, just sitting there watching the logs go by. Seeing a quantity of logs along the shore, he cleared his throat and said, "Come on now, boys. Let's not lie around wasting money; get those logs out of here." I told him we had placed them there so the logs wouldn't hang up.

"It's what we call a wing, Mr. Horwood," I said. "And when you see all your drivers sitting down and the logs sluicing through it means you're making money." He seemed to like that idea a lot because off he went then, up the brook to inspect the rest of the drive, whistling to himself.

Bellman's Brook is a nice brook for driving because it has a good bit of water behind it and several feeder streams along the way. There's Bellman's itself, Southern Pond, Rocky Pond, and Little Rocky Pond emptying in along the way. If it was a dry spring Horwood's would open the splash dam below Bellman's First Pond, and then the splash dam just down from Rocky Pond, to flush the logs along. The spring I worked on the drive we had no trouble with water.

"Picking up the rear," which I mentioned earlier, was the last job on a drive. It meant going back after the main drive had gone through and picking up stray logs, including boom logs and wing logs. Any place there was a steady or cove, or where they wanted to hold the logs for a while, there would be boom logs strung end to end to guide the rest along so they wouldn't hang up the rocks and alders and marsh grass. Being longer than average, they would float a man. Riding them was much easier than walking along shore through the trees and bushes and brambles, but staying on top of one as it turned and twisted its way downstream through rough water and calm took great skill and concentration. And if, as often happened, the log struck a rock, the only safe place to be when it struck was up in the air — and come down a second later. Just a little jump at the exact right time. Otherwise the sudden jolt could throw a man headlong. For if a driver fell in among the moving logs he had a good chance of being crushed. I don't recall anybody getting hurt on the Bellman's drive that year, but now and then somebody did.

With some brooks you have ponds to cross. In the ponds the current is weak, and if there is any wind against you the logs won't move where you want. We didn't have that problem on Bellman's either, but when we got down to the River we did, because Bellman's empties out into First Pond which is almost a half mile wide. From there to Booming Point, where the tide takes in again, it's about two miles.

The solution was a headworks — a homemade winch mounted on a raft with an anchor to pull itself along. The winch or windlass consisted of a horizontal wooden drum about four feet long and two feet in diameter that held about three or four hundred feet of strong manila rope, and a crank or handle at either end. The raft was built of logs from the drive spiked or pegged together — hardwood pegs were better since the logs could later be sawed without damaging the saw — and big enough to carry a thousand to twelve hundred pounds. Two men operated each crank. The procedure was simple. Once all the logs were down and waiting in the boom, it was made fast to the rear of the raft and the anchor was rowed forward in a dory or punt as far as it would go and heaved out. The four men would commence to winch the rope onto the drum, while a fifth made sure it would wind evenly back and forth by placing guide pegs in a bar in front of the drum. After five or ten minutes of this the boom would start to move — first the anchor rope would tighten, then the boom rope would tighten, and then the real scoting would begin as the boys on the cranks bent their backs to it.

It was dog's work. The windlass would creak, the men would grunt, the sweat would roll. If the boom was too big or a wind came against them, sometimes the strain would drag the raft under water and the men would be up to their knees for a while. Every three hundred feet or so they would get a short spell while the anchor was towed forward, but that was it until the logs were in the tide again. If there was a breeze all day but it dropped at sunset, then night work was ordered. The trip down First Pond took around a day. We took turns on the windlass. The only good thing about it was you got clear of the flies for a while.

Once the strays from all the feeder streams were safe in the boom the main river drive could start, and so down to the salt water. I never worked at it long enough to become a real driver, but I had the greatest respect for the stamina and skill of men like my Uncle Stanley who were true professionals. Yet, despite their skill, none got much more than a couple of dollars a day. My wage was a dollar a day. Small as it was, it helped me earn enough to pay off Joe Peckford what I owed on my first outboard motor, the five horsepower Evinrude Elto.

Before we got down to Gander Bay the cook quit. For a few days I got stuck with his job. I didn't mind being dry for a change, but I did mind lugging the camp gear and grub to a new location every couple of days. The goodnatured complaints at mealtimes reminded me of another fellow who, when he got in the same predicament, vowed that the next person to complain would automatically become the new cook. That night before turning in he baked several pies, and in one of them he put some horse manure. The next day at suppertime somebody burst out: "This pie tastes like horse shit!" Then, just as the cook was about to nab him, he added, "But it's good!"

My prospecting wasn't for gold, it was for chrome iron. In the early 1940s I worked two summers with a government geologist, surveying east of Gander Bay and up along the River. And in the winter of 1951-52 I helped cut lines for a mineral survey crew camped at First Pond, where an airplane survey had shown high tungsten and asbestos readings along Weir's Brook.

The chrome iron surveys were directed by Claude K. Howse, then chief geologist for the Newfoundland Department of Mines, and he sent out a Mr. John Horwood as party chief. Horwood came to Clarke's Head and hired myself and Leslie Gillingham to collect samples and to look after the camp and grub. Leslie was a small man, but tough and wiry and a good woodsman; he always wore a felt hat and smoked a stubby pipe.

We started in June month at Alder Harbour near Carmanville. We travelled on foot and slept under canvas, lugging all our grub and gear on our backs, as well as the samples we collected each day. Some days we made five miles; other days we never broke camp. Horwood was an easy-going, studious man. Many's the night he still would be poring over his maps when the rest of us were turned in. It was mostly serpentine rock he was looking for, a waxy, greenish, and smooth rock often associated with iron. He would go on ahead while we struck camp in the mornings, and if he found something we could always tell by the clink, clink, clink of his rock hammer somewhere up ahead. He had a wealth of prospecting experience and his sharp eye never missed much. If it was a good find he would load us down with samples to lug to camp for closer study. Before the summer was over Leslie and I were as strong as horses. And we got pretty good on naming rock samples.

All summer we worked our way south and west. It was some of the same country I'd traversed in my teens for the Reid Newfoundland Company. We passed Island Pond at the head of Ragged Harbour River. We came to Barry's Brook waters and detoured a few miles to Gander Bay to replenish our grub and tobacco. For a few weeks we took samples along the serpentine band between Weir's Pond and First Pond. Here and there along the whole route we struck good veins, but nothing in abundance, nothing exciting. It began to look as if Gander Bay's future in chrome iron was shaky. In late July we struck the River at Second Pond. From then on we travelled by canoe, camping along the shore a few days at a time until our work inland was done. We came to Glenwood and stocked up again, then kept on going up along the west shore of Gander Lake and on up the Northwest. By the end of August we had tramped and canoed seventy-five miles. There had been little rain for weeks and now the River was almost dry in places. Our goal was Red Cliff, fifteen miles above Big Gull River, but when we finally reached Big Gull we knew we'd have to turn back or else wait for rain.

Sixteen days we waited. Our grub was running low. Still no rain, not even a sprinkle to cool the air. I knew that if we waited too long our chances of getting back downstream in boat would be poor, for we had a fair load of heavy samples to ship to St. John's from Glenwood. While we were there two Micmacs from Conne River and a white man by the name of Sawyer from Herring Neck came out of the woods, heading north. They had a mugup with us and said they were walking from Bay d'Espoir to Glenwood, a 130-mile trip, to find work. For food they carried a large chunk of venison, around ten pounds I'd guess, which they used to boil on the outside, the first inch or so, so it wouldn't spoil. This they carried wrapped up in thin birch rind to keep the flies off. When they left I wished I was with them; at least they were going somewhere.

Finally, more for something to do than anything else, I started picking out a channel through the deeper places, prising rocks out with my pole and digging through sandbars with a frying pan. Then we gave up waiting and left for Glenwood. It took us five days to get back to Gander Lake, a distance of only twenty-six miles; normally the trip would have taken less than half a day. From there we went ten miles along the south shore of the lake to the mouth of the Southwest. Here the water was even lower. After the first mile upriver we had to leave our canoe and continue on foot. As a precaution, I hid our gas can and chained the Elto to a birch tree on the riverbank. The three of us then walked five miles to Little

Dead Wolf Brook where we spent a couple of nights sleeping under a birch rind tilt and checking outcrops. Again, nothing of value. We felt discouraged. We were even more discouraged when we got back to the boat and found that a bear had chewed four holes in the tank of the Elto, causing all the gasoline to drain out. Besides that, he had thrown down my toolbox and gnawed on a tube of gear grease. To make the tank tight again I whittled small pine plugs. There was barely enough gas in the can to get us back to Glenwood. We finished up the summer prospecting around the north side of the lake. Our most valuable find was ten gallons of partridgeberries that Leslie and I picked on Sundays.

Red Cliff had to wait until the next spring, when Claude Howse wired to ask if I'd take him up there. I replied yes, but that we'd have to go right away because of the low water later on. At Glenwood we hired Harry John, Jim John's son, to help. Eight miles below Red Cliff, at Rolling Falls, we had to portage. After a few trips with gear we were ready to rope the canoe up. Normally this is no trouble if you watch your footing on the rocks and slack off the gunwale rope when you see her start to tip. To save work I had left some of our gear and instruments in the boat. I never expected Dr. Howse to ask if he could haul her up. I was against the idea and told him so, but he insisted. No sooner had he started than the canoe began to wallow by the head and he, being too slow to give her rope, had all he could do to keep from being dragged into the boiling tide himself. In a twinkling the canoe went bottom up. We lost a lot of stuff which we later picked up, but some valuable instruments we never found.

In 1945 our older son Calvin was seventeen and wanted to take a commercial course. We moved to St. John's at Eastertime, rented a place on Bennett Avenue, and enrolled both sons in St. Michael's School. Next fall Calvin started Grade 11 Commercial in Prince of Wales College. After some searching, I got a job with the Newfoundland Fisheries Board as an inspector. At that time salt herring was being packed all around Newfoundland for the United Nations Relief and Rehabilitation Association, otherwise known as UNRRA. One port alone — Curling, on the west coast — shipped 50,000 barrels, each weighing two quintals or 225 pounds. Every shipment had to be inspected to make sure the barrels were full and that the herring was good. That was my job. Of course we didn't examine every single barrel; we just sampled here and there and estimated from that.

My starting salary was $125 a month — not bad for Gander Bay standards, but barely enough to pay the rent and feed my family. Still, it was the best I could find. That winter I was assigned to Placentia Bay, with headquarters at Harbour Buffett. We inspected shipments of dried cod, salt herring, and lobster in season. We made our rounds on the MV *Cinderella*, stopping at settlements along the east and west shores of that huge bay, and on Woody, Long, and Merasheen Islands. Fish was also brought from Fortune Bay ports by schooner to Harbour Buffett for inspection. The winter of 1946-47 I was stationed at Curling. To save some money on rent I shifted the family to Gilbert Street, a short street of wooden row houses running from Casey Street to Springdale Street a few blocks above Brazil Square. Everyone burned coal there, the houses were grimy, and we had to share the bathroom with the family in the next house. But it was within our means. The third winter I made the rounds of Notre Dame Bay. Calvin was now graduated and working with Bowaters in Lewisporte, so we moved there to live in the rambling old house where Senator Fred Rowe grew up. It had hop vines trailing along the verandah and a shed out back for hens and goats. That fall we bought a gray and white nanny goat that had been bred, and before long there was fresh milk and two frisky kids. Meanwhile, I travelled to wherever fish was being packed for UNRRA, as far north as Fleur de Lys near White Bay, to the central loading depot at Bridgeport on the western end of New World Island, and many other places.

I didn't mind the work or the isolation from home life. It was what most men had to do in those times, and we accepted it as such. It was no worse than being away for weeks at a time in the woods. Besides, I always liked the salt water and beating around in motor boats and schooners. Having a small schooner, like my father before me, is a dream I've always had. But on this job I did get to meet all kinds of people and see most parts of the Island, places I'd never been. And then there was the fun of trying to outwit the merchants and fish packers.

I well remember one barrel we opened. It was from a firm in Fortune Bay. On the outside it was stamped with the usual "225 lbs.," but on the inside we found only 167 pounds of herring. The rest was just pickle. We turned around then and opened eight more barrels. All of them fell short. The lowest had 160 pounds of herring; the highest only 180. So we ordered the whole shipment opened and repacked to 225 pounds a barrel. I can guarantee you there was some muttering and grumbling around those premises for the next few days.

Most of this kind of double-dealing was the work of the business firms, not the individual fishermen. And because a fussy inspector could mean long delays and loss in revenue, a good many companies took pains to sweeten him up. When a new man was sent to a place he was taken on a tour of the premises. They showed him the herring factory, the saltfish packing sheds, the wharves, whatever they had. Just about every time this tour would end at the engine house where the diesel generators were, and before you left there your guide might casually remark, "Oh, and any time you wants a drink, this is where we keep the bottle; help yourself." They knew it was breaking the law to offer an inspector a drink outright, but planting the temptation was just as good. One inspector I knew spent a whole week at a fish plant and never saw a fish packed. Yet his stencil and initials went on every cask just the same. And he was known as one of the Board's best men.

Each summer on my two weeks vacation from inspecting fish I would guide for a Mrs. Murphy who ran a tourist hotel at Glenwood. In the fishing party I guided in July of 1947 was Ben Wright of New York City, a former editor of *Field & Stream* magazine. Ben and his wife Dolly enjoyed excellent salmon and trout fishing that trip. Before they boarded the train in Glenwood for the airport he said, "Brett, why don't you build your own fishing camp and go into the catering business yourself? You know the River, you like people, and I fancy you have a head for business. If you decide to try it, let me know and I'll help you. I'll print a thousand folders and get the word around New York State for you." Well, that made me think. All winter, beating around the islands of Notre Dame Bay, I pondered on it.

In the spring of 1948 I resigned from the Board and moved my family back to Clarke's Head. Paying rent on a small salary, we'd never have anything. In Gander Bay we owned our own house and I felt sure we could make a go of the tourist business. I wrote to Ben Wright and told him my plans. He wrote right back with suggestions for the folder and other ideas. On the whole, the next nineteen years were to be the happiest of our lives.

PART IV

Better Times

Blue Charm and Silver Doctor

The first thing was money. Our savings were small. Lumber was no problem because we had a sawmill in the family, now being run by Harold. But roofing, paint, windows, wallboard, stove, refrigerator, cots, mattresses — all the like of that would take hard cash. My youngest brother Don was a good guide and good with people, and he agreed to go partners with me. With the money we had between us, we figured about $300 more would do it. We decided that in order to make a decent living we would need a cabin big enough to sleep ten guests. And to take advantage of the 1948 fishing season we had to build it as soon as possible.

A loan was the only way. Before resigning from the Fisheries Board I made up my mind to try two of the St. John's firms my father had dealt with for forty years. With all the business he had given them, I couldn't see how they could refuse. First I went to Steers Limited: they turned me down. Then I went to Gerald S. Doyle Limited. Mr. Doyle, then about sixty, ushered me into his office and asked about my parents. A tall, soft-spoken man with broad shoulders, he was known all over Newfoundland as the man who started the "Gerald S. Doyle News," and for his travels all around the coast in his yacht the *Miss Newfoundland* promoting his patent medicines, cod liver oil, and other products. "What can I do for you, Brett?" he said. I told him our plans, and ended by saying I needed a loan of $300. "Glad to help," he said, adding, "are you sure $300 is enough? You can have a thousand if you like." I told him just the $300 would do, and that was that.

The second thing was permission to build. We already had the land picked out, but the government had the say in who built cabins on the rivers, including the Gander. So far they had allowed only three lodges on the lower Gander, namely the government guest cabin on Joe Batt's Brook, built in 1938; F.M. O'Leary's camp at the outlet of First Pond, which me and Tom Gillingham and another fellow built in 1944; and the Anglo-Newfoundland Company lodge at Burnt Rattle, dating from about the same time. All three were strictly guest lodges for non-paying clientele. The first commercial fishing camps were those of Robin Reid who, before the war, had operated a main lodge — "Gleneagles," located just above Glenwood — and four small cabins on the lower Gander. So we would be the only commercial outfit on the River. Still, I worried that Don and myself, without political connections, might not stand a chance if someone opposed us.

At that time the government man in charge of land grants and leases was Ted Russell, later to become well-known for his radio stories and his writings about life in the outports. That same spring, in April, I went to St. John's to see him. Somehow even in his office clothes he struck me as one of us. He had more the look of a fishermen, and that gave me hope. I told him what we planned to do. He thought for a minute or two, then stood up and said, "Just a minute," and went off down the hall. I supposed he wanted to check on something and would be right back. After waiting for half an hour I asked his secretary if she thought he would, and she replied "I don't know." So I left his office and came home to Gander Bay, and in May we started to build.

The spot we picked was on an island halfway between Gander Bay and Glenwood, the island where Old Man Cleaves had a drivers' camp in Phillips' time, and known as Cleaves Island ever since. We picked it because it was central for bringing supplies up from the Bay or fishermen down from Glenwood, and also because it was midway between all the best pools, from the Sunshine Pool just below First Pond to Salmon Brook Pool a few miles below Glenwood. It also had two excellent pools within a few minutes' steam — Joe Batt's just over a mile upstream and Third Pond Bar three miles down. If other fishing lodges came to be built and the pools got crowded, this would be an important advantage. Then it would be first-come, first-served. As it turned out, the only other lodges of any size to be built were that of the Allied Aviation Service of Newfoundland Limited at Third Pond Bar in 1951 — a guest lodge for staff and clients; and my son Calvin's "Minnehaha Lodge," a commercial venture started near Booming Point on First Pond in 1952.

Cleaves Island had two other advantages: it was high enough to escape the annual flooding, and there was a fairly good beach for unloading supplies and tying up six, eight, ten canoes. And it was a very pretty place, a level grassy ground in a grove of tall birch and aspen, some of them over ten inches in diameter. Many's the time I had admired the spot when passing by, and now and then I used to spend the night there. It was the first place Jim John and I camped the time we went up the Northwest in 1919. The old people said that the reason it was so level was because Old Cleaves had once grown potatoes there.

The first big job was to bring in the building supplies. Everything, every roll of felt and stick of lumber, had to come by canoe. Thank God for the outboard motor or we'd be at it yet. Even so, we could only carry four hundred feet of lumber to a trip. The lodge was going to be thirty by twenty-six feet, one story high, with an L-shaped kitchen joined on the back. We figured on maybe twenty trips, and that's about what it took, counting the bags of nails, the hardware, and so on. We hired Melvin Francis and Roy Hodder as carpenters at three dollars a day. Don and I worked hard too, and on August 1, 1948 we were ready for business. This was much too late in the season to get started, but still and all we managed to get a few fishermen. We took in $244 — our rate was $12 a day with everything included — and after deducting $128 for expenses, we had $116 to share as profit.

That first year we did all the cooking ourselves, making the beds, peeling potatoes, as well as guiding. For the next year, when we hoped to have a full quota of ten fishermen at least part of the time, we would need a guides' cabin, outdoor toilet, ice-house, and perhaps a lighting plant. There was lots to think about and plenty to do, but it was a happy summer for me because I was finally getting on my feet, doing what I liked. I hammered my thumb more than once helping the carpenters, but I learned a lot too. One of the interesting things that happened was that while digging holes for the foundation post we came across a leather driver's boot, complete with metal sparbles or cleats, and slits to let the water run out. It reminded me of how cold my feet used to get on the Bellman's Brook drive. Before freeze-up Don and I laid in a supply of firewood, framed up the toilet and guides' cabin, and even managed to guide a couple of moose-hunting parties, using the camp as a base. That gave us a few hundred dollars more.

Meanwhile, Ben Wright had been at work. Enquiries began to come in from the States. A thick brown envelope arrived containing over nine hundred glossy folders featuring "Saunders' Camps — Excellent Salmon Fishing," with good black and white photos of fish we had caught the summer before at Mrs. Murphy's. With these I was able to advertise through the winter months, and by March we had several fishing parties confirmed and others interested. As soon as the ice went out Don and I were at it day and night, carrying more lumber, stocking gasoline for the guides' motors and our own, laying in grub and supplies for the cook, and so on. We barely got the toilet finished before the first party arrived; the guides' cabin had to wait for another year and we had to set up canvas tents for them.

That summer of 1949 we had a full camp for most of the season, starting in early July and ending in late August, and the fishing was excellent. According to our camp register, among the first to come was Ben Wright, who brought his friend Ebb Warren, outdoor editor for *True* magazine. Another guest was Dr. H. Ford Anderson of Washington, D.C. who came every year thereafter until we closed in 1965. Such faithful guests spread the word and soon we had a regular clintele who came for a week each July and booked space a year ahead so they wouldn't be disappointed. Among these were Dr. Lewis Flinn of Wilmington, Delaware; Dr. Austin P. Ellingwood of Manchester, New Hampshire; Dr. Frank Hand of Chevy Chase, Maryland; Drs. Richard TeLinde, Charles Wainwright and B.H. Rutledge, all of Baltimore, Maryland; and Dr. Benjamin Rones and his wife Evelyn of Washington, D.C. There were also regular guests from Nova Scotia and other parts of the mainland, and a scattered fishermen from France, Belgium, and England. Every year a few came from St. John's too — mostly businessmen or lawyers like the Ayres, Geoffrey Carnell, G. Rex Renouf, Henry Collingwood, and sometimes a doctor, among them Dr. G.M. Brownrigg.

Most of them reserved a week in July, the peak month of the salmon run on the Gander. In the early years we had no indoor plumbing or electricity, but very few complained. We had no telephone either — they especially liked that. What they came for was the fishing; that and a lot of joking and yarning, a little drinking, and the good clean air and the quiet. We provided them each with a guide — in the seventeen years we were open there were dozens, but some worked for us year after year, and a fisherman would be disappointed if he couldn't have such and such a one. Since we normally catered to three dozen or more anglers during each six-week season, each guide would get to know several fishermen pretty well. Among our regular guides, besides my brother Don, were Leslie Gillingham, Dominic Francis, Mose Downer, Heber Peckford, Victor Coates, Lester Vivian, Peter Downer, Victor Bauld, Lee Bath, and Leonard Francis. And whenever I could spare the time, I guided as well.

The Gander isn't noted for big salmon like the Humber. Most of our fish are what you would call grilse — under six pounds. For example, our camp register for 1960, an average year, shows that of the 294 salmon taken between July 3 and August 17, only eight were over six pounds. Of these, the largest weighed thirteen pounds, twelve ounces. Nobody complained about the grilse because as any salmon fisherman will tell you, it's your smaller fish that put up the best fight. A big fish is much more likely to go to bottom and wedge himself in among the boulders until the guide prods him loose with a pole. The largest salmon ever taken on the Gander by flyrod weighed forty-two pounds. This was the famous fish hooked at Joe Batt's Upper Pool at seven one evening and landed at the Lower Pool eleven o'clock that night. Jim John was the guide — but it isn't true, as one writer stated, that Jim tied the fish on for the night and landed it the next morning at Petries Rock.

The summer of 1949 I received a letter from Mr. Roland Goodyear, a Gander businessman, advising me that he owned the land on which our lodge was built and furthermore that he had a lease on the whole island. He went on to state that either I would have to sell the lodge to him or move it. This letter gave me some sleepless nights until I figured out that the land he was referring to was on Third Pond Island, not Cleaves Island. Third Pond Island is at the lower end of Third Pond, over three miles downstream. But his challenge did prompt me to straighten out my own title. This time I had no trouble. We secured a twenty-year lease to that part of the island.

Every year we made improvements. The cook needed a refrigerator, so we ordered a Servel, a model that ran off kerosene. After a while kerosene lamps got to be a nuisance as well as a fire hazard, so we installed an electric lighting plant. Like everything else, this quarter-ton monster had to come by canoe. To hoist it out of the boat I rigged a tripod with block and tackle and swung it ashore myself. As expenses went up we raised our daily rate to $17.50, still with board and lodging, guide and boat supplied. For seventeen years we continued under the name of Saunders Camps — which we painted in large white letters on our black roof as a marker for pilots who occasionally landed parties on nearby Third Pond. Most of our guests Don or I met at Gander International Airport and brought down from Glenwood in boat.

In 1952 Calvin built a lodge on First Pond. This became his main source of income. Between us and the non-commercial camps, all available fishing space was now taken up. By the early 1960s our guides were complaining of overcrowding. To be sure of a place they sometimes had to leave camp before daylight. One rival guide got everybody's goat by painting his surname on a rock in one of the best pools, thereby hoping to reserve it for himself and his clients. What annoyed me was that half the fishermen on the lower Gander at any one time were non-paying guests of either the government or private firms. While this gave jobs to guides, it hurt the fishing for paying customers and made it harder for the bona fide caterer to keep his clients happy. When the Gander Bay road was put through in 1961, opening the First Pond area on the south side to any Ganderite who didn't mind walking a mile through the woods to fish, this situation got worse. Meanwhile, the fishing had gone downhill for other reasons — summers were too wet or too dry, poor runs of fish that some blamed on the Greenland salmon fishery, and increased poaching. For these and other reasons we reluctantly got out of the business in the fall of 1965, selling the cabin and lease in the winter of 1966 to the Buchans Mining Company Limited, a subsidiary of the American Smelting and Refining Company.

Nevertheless, they were good years and we had some good times. The part I enjoyed most was meeting people. In my opinion fishermen, in particular salmon fishermen, are a special breed. To be a successful salmon fisherman of the rod-and-reel kind you have to possess patience, humility, and good humour — or at least be willing to learn them. From 1949 on Don and I also catered to caribou- and moose-hunting parties under canvas on the Northwest Gander, and I can state from experience that among hunters you see those traits less often. Male hunters are inclined to be more aggressive, less impatient, more concerned with proving themselves.

We had anglers from as far away as Belgium — in particular a lawyer and his daughter who still came to Calvin's camp in the 1980s. They landed salmon with ten- and twelve-foot rods, real two-handed oldtimers compared to North American lightweight rods. One party of doctors from Baltimore, Maryland, fished at our camp for sixteen successive summers, always booking next year's space before they left. One of them, Dr. Richard TeLinde, later gynecologist to the wife of the Sultan of Morocco, was still writing to me in 1983 at eighty-nine years of age. Quite a few of our anglers were women who came with their retired husbands. And I recall one widow, a heavy drinker, who brought her daughter-in-law. Don was guiding the latter and one evening the two of them did not return for supper. It was after dark and the widow asked if I thought Don had seduced her. I told her not to worry, that they had probably hooked a salmon about dusk and would be in shortly. Much to the widow's relief, this is what happened.

Several times in the early years I guided Lee Wulff, the well-known salmon fisherman and flycaster. That he is an expert caster there is no doubt, for I've watched him time and time again place his fly exactly where he wanted it. In fact, he could cast without a rod — just the line in his hand — better than some people using a rod. But when the magazine reporters and newspapermen make him out to be an expert salmon fisherman, I for one have to disagree. His habit of wading through all the pools disturbed the fish and moved them out of his reach. Maybe that's how he came to be such a fine long-distance caster. One time I watched him at Jonathan's Pool in Third Pond, a pretty good place at certain times. I knew the salmon were there. As usual he had on a pair of chest waders and before long he was standing in four feet of water, casting and casting without a single rise. After a spell of this he looked at me and called out, "Brett, where's the best place to fish?"

"Right where you're standing, Lee!" I replied. "It's best to stand on the shore so the fish won't see you." He moved back to shore.

It was Lee Wulff who introduced dry fly salmon fishing to the Gander. Before, everyone used the wet or underwater fly. A dry fly floats; a wet fly sinks. Most dry flies are tied with the hair or feathers fluffed up and sometimes they're treated with water-repellent oil. Deer or caribou hair is a favourite because it floats naturally. Wulff took advantage of this and designed the "White Wulff," a caribou hair salmon dry fly that's still used.

But for some reason the dry fly never really caught on with our fishermen. They preferred the standard British wet fly tied on a Number Six to Number Eight hook with turned-up eye. Some fished the tiny Number Ten, but that was more for the challenge than anything else. The most popular patterns were "Dusty Miller," "Thunder & Lightning," "Black Dose," and "Blue Charm," all drab-looking lures. The most brightly coloured one they used was probably the "Silver Doctor," which sported "married" red, yellow and blue feathers in the wing and fancy silver body winding. Many a novice fishermen protested when his Gander Bay guide took a pocket knife and trimmed such handsome lures down to the essentials — a bit of silver winding on the body, perhaps a wisp of golden pheasant for the tail, some plain brown or speckled black hackle, and a wing stripped of all but the drab colours. But he stopped protesting when he saw the results. The reason dull colours work better may be that the Gander's pools are shallow. Even the deepest are seldom over six feet in summer. Since salmon rest near the bottom, it could be that whereas in deep water they can see bright colours more easily, in the well-lit shallow water the darker colours show up well enough. Whatever the reason, one of the most successful lures of all is the "Moosehair," a wet fly modelled on the "Black Dose," all black except for its brown wing, yellow tail, and silver winding. About the only time brightly-coloured flies were used was for trouting, usually in May or June month when the sea trout came in. For this such lures as the red and white "Parmachene Belle," the white and brown "Royal Coachman" with its peacock body windings, and the red and yellow "Mickey Finn" streamer are among the best. But the drab

"Black Gnat" is good too, especially later in the season.

I still have our camp register. Sometimes to while away the time I scan the names and dates and recall all the personalities that came and went, the numbers and size of fish they caught, and what they said and did. One person that stands out, as I mentioned before, was Dr. Richard TeLinde. Because I knew he had a knack for writing, in 1976 I asked him to recall some of those people and times for a book my younger son was planning. His reply forms the text of the chapter that follows.

An Old Angler Recalls the Gander

Dear Brett:

You asked me if I would like to write of my experiences fishing on the Gander. I am very glad to do so for I had many a happy vacation there.

Dr. John Olds, who was chief surgeon at the hospital in Twillingate, is an old friend of mine, having been a surgical interne at Johns Hopkins while I was on the residency staff. He had often asked me to come to Twillingate to see him and his wife, Betty, who as a Hopkins nurse used to scrub for me in the operating room. Johnny finally got me to make the trip by telling me that he had a friend, Brett Saunders, who had built a fishing camp on the Gander River, and that he could arrange for me to do some salmon fishing there. That did it.

I have a friend, Donald Sherwood, an industrialist in Baltimore, who has fished all over the world. When I asked him if he would like to go, he accepted immediately. We took off on an old British Overseas Airline plane. In those days this company made daily flights to England, stopping for refueling at Gander. It was a four-engine propellor plane. On the way one engine went dead. We arrived at the old Gander airport a little late and spent the night in the old army barrack. The next day there was a two-hour ride down the River with an outboard canoe. You were my guide, and we stopped at Third Pond Bar to make a few casts before going into camp. On the second cast I hooked and landed a salmon. After a few more casts I had another. I decided there was nothing to this sport, landing two out of two. Over the next twenty years of salmon fishing I found out that I was somewhat in error. Still, it sold me on the Gander. My friend Don Sherwood and I had a week of great fishing.

That first trip was more than twenty years ago. It was so successful that I resolved to return as long as I was physically and financially able to do so — and so I did. In addition to Mr. Sherwood, future trips included Dr. Charles Wainwright, an internist from Baltimore on the Johns Hopkins Hospital staff; Dr. Lewis Flinn, an internist from Wilmington, Delaware; Dr. Benjamin Rutledge, also a staff member of Hopkins; Dr. Thomas Harrold, a prominent surgeon from Macon, Georgia; and Dr. Benjamin Rones, a well-known opthalmologist from Washington. Dr. Rones came frequently with his wife who had also been a Hopkins nurse. More recently, Mr. Ellis Ellicott, an engineer, joined the group.

To really know a person one should go fishing with him. Dr. Wainwright apparently can't sleep after 4:00 a.m. Addicted to coffee, he often woke the camp knocking about in the kitchen, making himself some. After tolerating this for a few years we insisted that he make his coffee the night before and keep it in a thermos so he could drink it quietly in bed. Then there was Dr. Rutledge, who nearly always brought in the most fish. He was guided by your brother Don, an expert flycaster. We suspected that Don was doing most of the casting. Rutledge invariably denied this, but on several occasions we passed him on the River and noted that he was either dozing or reading a paperback while Don was casting. Wainwright and Sherwood were the most persistent fishermen. Wainwright was generally the first on the River in the morning and the last in at night. Sherwood held the record for tolerating cold rain while the rest of us were sitting around the stove. Dr. Rones kept his good humour when his wife brought in more salmon than he did — which was often. Dr. Harrold's great contribution was in the evening, when he regaled us with stories from the Deep South. Flinn and Anderson took their fishing leisurely; after all, they were on vacation and not in a fishing contest. Dr. Anderson carried a great big mug which he used for coffee, soup, dinner, everything; in between courses he would simply rinse it out. "Saves washing dishes," he explained — though you had a cookee or cook's helper for that. Rumour had it that he sometimes used it as a urinal when he was too tired or lazy to go outside; but this was just teasing, since you had overnight pails in each room for emergencies and bad weather. And I know for a fact his nighttime visits to a certain spot burned a bare place in the grass. Mr. Ellicott had a marvelous disposition which was never upset even though he didn't bring in a fish. Whiskey and rum usually brightened our wonderful evenings around the stove, but seldom to excess. We knew you wouldn't stand for it. Once or twice you had to caution us about letting the guides get too free with the sauce, but that was all.

You had some wonderful guides. They not only worked hard to find the fish for us, they were real gentlemen. Some of their names have slipped out of my memory but I do recall some. There was your brother Don. There was Dominic Francis of Indian stock, swarthy and strong with a fine Roman nose. There was Flinn's guide Lew Gillingham, and Dr. Wainwright's guide Leslie Gillingham, who also built canoes. Then there was the oldest one, Mose Downer. I'm sure the older ones have gone to the fisherman's heaven, but we remember them with great affection.

Getting to the Gander was often half the fun. I recall one time when four of us left New York bound for Gander, when once again engine trouble developed and one engine failed and we were forced to land in Boston. We spent the day there watching the Red Sox play ball. The next day we took off again. It was dark and foggy when we arrived over Gander. The plane swooped down over the airport, then climbed again. The pilot made another try. I could just make out a few twinkling lights. He took us up once more, then came back to talk to us. He said he was afraid to land and would take us to Sydney, Nova Scotia. I was greatly relieved.

We left our duffle in the Sydney airport and put up at the Belle Isle Hotel at about midnight in adjoining double rooms with a doorway between. We all had different sleeping habits. The next morning Wainwright rose about 4:30 and went out on the street in search of an all-night joint where he could find a cup of coffee. Sherwood got up around 7:00 and went down to the lobby looking for breakfast. I arose shortly afterward and joined him. Rutledge was still asleep. I asked the waitress if she would call the room and tell the one who answered the phone that a plane was leaving for Newfoundland in twenty minutes. This was pure fabrication. He answered the phone, and thinking we were still asleep, ran into the other room to give us the news. Now, since we had left our duffle in the airport, we had had to sleep in our underwear or in the nude. Rutledge chose the latter. There were two maids in the room making beds when he rushed in, naked as the day he was born. Rutledge then dressed and ran into the dining room to tell us to hurry up and get to the airport. We laughed and told him to sit down and eat his breakfast — and that afternoon we were all fishing on the Gander.

That week I landed eight salmon. The crowd that followed included a Mr. Middendorf who was half blind but a very good fisherman. He landed eighteen salmon. We had an earlier week when conditions were better and there should have been more fish. I wrote you afterward saying "I can only conclude that I'm a poor fisherman." You wrote back agreeing with me. You said I was all right for the first half hour, but then I began to watch the beauties of nature instead of keeping my eye on the fly. I'll forgive you for that, but I would rather watch the beauties of the Gander River now and then and get a few less salmon.

We met some wonderful guests in the old camp — but they weren't all great. I recall one named Kelly who ran his canoe over Wainwright's line when he had a salmon on. If Wainwright had been a little huskier there might have been a murder in the camp that night and we all would have sworn it was justifiable homicide. Then there was that surgeon from Muskegan, Michigan who landed seventy-seven salmon in two weeks. He was in a bad humour because he wanted to catch one hundred, and he never tipped his guide. From this I conclude that salmon fishing doesn't make a gentleman; but it did help most of us in that direction.

One of our best years was the year of the great flood. The River was nine feet above its usual level. The government had placed a net across the mouth to count the fish. The flood took the net out. The guides said the pools had all been erased and they had no idea where they would find the salmon. People say the salmon is one of the smartest of fish, but on that occasion they weren't very smart. After the net went out they still stayed on the lower side of where the net had been! So we fished there, and I have never seen so many fish in one area.

Well, Brett, it's about twenty-five years since our crowd first discovered the Gander River. We loved the old camp and the owner. I recall the day the bear got into the camp. I think we were the last group of the season and you said you would have to shoot the bear or he would wreck it. So, one Sunday evening when Bruin appeared you did just that. At about one hundred yards you hit the bear in the neck. It didn't struggle an instant — just dropped to the ground without moving a muscle. I examined the animal and found you had hit it in the exact centre of the front of the neck. The bullet must have severed the spinal cord just as it leaves the brain. That was the best shot I have ever seen; but in doing that you broke at least two laws. It was against the law to carry firearms on the River, and it was out of season. Still, if I ever have to face a firing squad I want you to do the shooting.

We didn't just enjoy the River, we enjoyed Newfoundland. Every journey was an adventure for us and our trip to Twillingate in 1949 was one of the best. After Sherwood and I returned to Gander we rented a small plane with pontoons and flew there to take the Olds up on their invitation to visit for the weekend. Sunday was Johnny's day off but there were two surgical emergencies. When the third one came in I suggested to Johnny that I do the operation since he had been working hard and I had just had a week's vacation. He agreed and I operated. While in the OR I heard some scuffling outside the room. I asked Johnny what it was. He told me that a certain prominent citizen who was a sporadic alcoholic was in the hospital. While there he had wandered around and entered the supply room off the operating room, where he found a bottle of wood alcohol and proceeded to drink it. The scuffling had been due to an attempt to get him back to his room.

Johnny and I, as soon as we were done, went to him and tried to pass a stomach tube to empty his stomach before too much harm was done. He was as strong as a Newfoundland moose and we were unable to accomplish it. We had to settle for a dose of Epsom salts and hope that the wood alcohol would pass rapidly and thus minimize the absorption. The amount he drank was, according to the books, enough to blind him. The next morning he was sober and Johnny asked me if I would talk to the man. I agreed, and our conversation went something like this:

"Mr. — , you're going to kill yourself if you keep on drinking the way you do."

"Oh, Doctor, don't try to scare me. I've drunk five times that much and I'm still in good health."

"I know, but there are different kinds of alcohol and the kind you drank yesterday could kill you or at least make you blind."

"There's nothing wrong with my eyesight; I can see as well this morning as ever I could."

I changed my tactics: "Mr. — , I understand you were in the gutter for several years because of your drinking. Then you stopped and became a very prosperous businessman, outfitting sealing ships. Now tell me, haven't you enjoyed life more since you made such a success of yourself during your years of sobriety?"

He said, "Doctor, to tell the truth, I had the best times when I was drunk!" After that Johnny suggested I let him handle the psychiatry and I agreed.

On Monday morning it was too foggy for the float plane to come and take us to Gander as arranged, so the Olds suggested that they could arrange for a boat to take us to Lewisporte. Lewisporte is the port of entry for the airplane fuel for Gander airport, and before that, at the turn of the century, it was the shipping point for lumber from Lewis Miller's mill at Millertown — hence both place names. The trip proved entertaining. Newfoundland had just voted to become a province of Canada, and the man who ran the passenger boat and his first mate were discussing the pros and cons of Confederation. The captain wound up the discussion with these words: "Well, they can't expect nothing from we."

At Lewisporte we took a taxi to Notre Dame Junction, a matter of about twelve miles, to take the train to Gander. The station master was on duty. I approached him and asked when the next train was scheduled to leave for Gander. He said, "There's a freight train coming through here at 3:30 p.m."

"That's fine," I said, "we'll ride in the caboose."

"I'm sorry," he said, "only doctors and ministers are allowed to ride in the caboose."

"Isn't that fortunate," I said. "I am Dr. TeLinde, and meet my friend the Rev. Mr. Sherwood." Don, the industrialist, stepped up and solemnly shook hands with him. So we rode to Gander in the caboose.

I will never forget that ride. The day was cold and rainy. The caboose was heated by a pot-bellied stove and we were quite comfortable; but we were hungry. We hadn't had a bite since 5:00 a.m. It seems that the railroad crews cook their own meals. A brakeman came in and put a big kettle of water on the stove and then threw in a large chunk of beef. From time to time he would come back and throw in some carrots, potatoes, and onions. I have never smelled such fragrance as was wafted up from that kettle. Finally the temptation became unbearable. When the brakeman came in again I asked, "When do you fellows eat?"

"Right after we leave Gander," said he. So we got off at Gander and satisfied our hunger at the airport restaurant.

Well, Brett, we have all gotten old. I have attained eleven more years than the three score and ten allotted by the Bible, Dr. Wainwright is about the same age and the others not far behind. Drs. Harrold and Rutledge have left us. You have sold the old camp and I understand the new owners have built bathrooms and installed a television. In the old days we didn't need television. We got our entertainment on the River. Can you imagine anyone wasting his time looking at TV when he could be on the River hooking a salmon? After building the bathrooms the fishing declined. I have always maintained that salmon don't like flush toilets, and I believe that this is the cause of the deterioration of the fishing. But now you tell me that the salmon have returned. Maybe I am wrong and I sincerely hope so. Maybe the netting off the coast of Greenland had something to do with reducing the salmon in the River. But what I really believe is that no one knows how salmon think. That even includes you, Brett. You once told me, "The lower the water, the better the fishing." Yet, the best year I ever had was the year of the flood.

Confucius said, "The time a man spends fishing is not counted against him." So perhaps we'll have a few more years. But the Gander River flows on forever.

Dr. Dick TeLinde
Baltimore, Maryland
U.S.A.

Moose Hunting

Some of the best hunting trips I ever had were with Dr. John Olds of Twillingate and a bunch of his friends. Although Dr. Olds got a nice caribou one trip, moose was what they were after. There was him and Dr. Reuben Waddell and Ern French and Ned Facey and Joe White, and several times Beaton J. Abbott came. The guides were Billy John, Mose Downer, Nat Gillingham, Harvey Francis, and myself. One time my brother Don came too. It was my friend Howard Thistle gave Dr. Olds the idea. Howard didn't exactly guide, but came along on several trips to help. As I recall, there were trips every year from 1938, when the moose season opened, until 1946 or 1947. During the war Dr. Olds seldom came because he was alone at the hospital. Seven years I guided for that party, and after that Don and I opened our own hunting camps. I think the only year I didn't go was in 1938, the year Howard Thistle lined up a caribou hunting trip for Dr. Olds and Dr. Rueben Waddell. Howard at that time was a long-term patient at Twillingate with stomach problems, but he persuaded Dr. Olds to let him go and got Billy John to be the guide. That was the time, as Dr. Olds told it, that "Billy walked the hell out of us up on the Harvest Fields." But they got two caribou for their trouble, de-boned the meat, and brought it out in stages to Billy John's camp and so down to Glenwood.

The rest of our trips, as I say, were for moose. Moose are not found up on the barrens but mostly in the woods and along the River and its tributaries. The season was generally November month, and usually we would meet the party at Glenwood off the eastbound train from Notre Dame Junction and either go downriver or up the Lake. Some years we returned empty-handed, but most times somebody got their animal. "Some of the best trips," Dr. Olds told me in 1979, "were when we didn't get

229

a damn thing." For him the trip was the highlight: a chance to get away for a week from the heavy pressures of a busy hospital serving twelve thousand people in scores of outport communities. A trophy head was nice, but nobody was after one. We made ourselves comfortable in canvas tents outfitted with tin stoves; everyone smoked a pipe; and there were always a few bottles of rum to ward off chills.

The first time I went, we left Gander Bay in the afternoon by canoe with a northeast wind and snow flurries at our backs. We moved upriver twelve miles and it was so dark we decided to make camp. We set up our two tents early and turned in. Next morning it was still miserable outside, but Dr. Olds wanted to go for a swim, and he did, leaving his footprints in the snow along the beach. This was at Second Pond. The water was shallow and it took him a while to find a good spot. That day we moved upriver another thirty miles and camped two miles above Glenwood at Kings Head Cove on the shores of Gander Lake. By now there were three inches of snow on the ground. Again we set up the tents, collected boughs for our beds, and cooked supper. The wind was blowing thirty-five miles an hour with slop snow falling. About 10:00 p.m., after several drinks, Dr. Olds suggested we all go for a swim. Dr. Waddell was in favour, but Ern French wouldn't hear of it, and neither would we guides. To tell the truth, we thought they were not quite right in the head. Finally the two doctors stripped off naked, and we led them to the lakeshore with a flashlight. Dark as the grave it was, and the big lops rolling in. When they dived in we thought sure we'd never see them again, or that they would catch pneumonia. But next morning they were number one.

That same trip Dr. Olds had a meal of lynx. We had gone a few days with no fresh meat, only beans for breakfast, when one of us came across this dead lynx caught in a snare. Knowing whose it was, I removed the cat, brought it back to camp and skinned it in order to give the owner the pelt when we got back. Dr. Olds was studying the carcass, smelling it and poking it, and then he said, "Let's have some of this for supper." Although the cold weather had kept it from spoiling, I knew it must be two or three weeks old. Of course none of us would eat lynx, especially one that old, so he went ahead and cooked some up for himself. After dining on it he claimed it was better than chicken by a long shot, and even better than moose.

Poor Ern French! He used to get buck fever. He was such a bad shot that we used to keep his ammunition from him until something turned up big enough and close enough for him to shoot. A big gruff fellow, he was one of the sons of the T.& J. French & Sons lumber family that had mills at Birchy Bay and Mann Point, Gander Bay. Ern himself had a general store at Summerford on New World Island.

I recall one trip: we were coming home and the others had their moose, and Ern, who was with Dr. Olds, had missed several and was in a cranky mood. Dr. Olds had struck a rock and cut a shear-pin on his motor and was fixing it when out came this bull moose, wading the shallows not twenty-five yards away from them, walking across the River. We stopped our boats and pointed for Ern to shoot. When we stopped, so did the moose — just stood there staring. You could have struck him with a rock. Ern was shaking so bad he couldn't hold the gun steady at all, and the moose standing so still and us egging him on made him worse; the poor man fired and missed. Slowly, the bull walked ashore and turned broadside to stare some more. Ern fired again, twice, and missed both times. Then the moose dodged up over the bank and disappeared.

As I said, this sort of thing would make Ern French crooked. One time at Gull River he was so mad he slung a bar of Palmolive soap at a jay and killed him stone dead. Another time — it was November 5, Guy Fawkes Night — Ern wanted to have a bonfire but none of us wanted to help him with the wood. So he took all our birch rind we'd saved for the morning and made a bonfire for himself. I think that was the time we hove him in the River. Being a merchant, Ern liked to keep up with the news. On one trip he brought along his radio. Dr. Olds was disgusted. The last thing he wanted to hear that week was news, he said, and after a few drinks he picked up Ern's two dry cell batteries and chucked them in the River. Ern sputtered for a while, but it didn't spoil the fun.

Joe White was a better shot but he was very nervous in the woods. On the salt water he was great, none better; but you take him out behind the camp and he was lost. Well, on one occasion we left him in a good spot by a beaver dam to watch for a moose while we hunted the brook farther down. And after a while we heard a shot. Thinking for sure Joe had got a moose at last, we rushed back up to congratulate him. But there was no need to. Unknown to him a beaver was chewing down a tree not far away, and when the tree struck the water the noise scared Joe so badly he pulled the trigger. As Dr. Olds put it, "That's the only moose Joe ever shot."

For a few years Beaton J. Abbott — later Magistrate Abbott at Grand Falls — was a regular in our party. As he was a teetotaller, Mr. Abbott was appointed liquor controller, with power to punish any who broke the rules. One of the rules said there would be no drinking in the boats. One evening, as we landed to set up camp, he discovered a bottle of beer missing. He reported this to the skipper of the party, Joe White. "I bet you that was Ern or Ned," he said. "I'll find out and we shall have court after supper." Magistrate Abbott had told him to look in Ern's boat for evidence. Joe found an empty bottle. After supper Mr. Abbott briefed Joe on what to say when he opened court. Ern was brought before him and charged. Joe gave the evidence and Ern pleaded guilty. Mr. Abbott then lectured Ern on breaking faith with the hunting party and committing such an offence, and sentenced him to six slaps on the naked back. Ned Facey was called to administer the slaps. Court was adjourned, Ern took off his shirt, and Ned gave him four wallops that sent him dancing around the tent. Ned reported the accused was in no condition to receive more punishment, and the magistrate let him go.

They were none of them used to walking like we were. This caused some comical sights, like the time Ern lost his balance jumping across a small brook and fell ass-over-kettle in the cold water. After that we always called it French's Brook. And there was the time Dr. Olds and Don and myself left the others and tramped several miles in over the bogs looking for caribou. Now there is nothing so wearisome on the legs as a Newfoundland bog, and Dr. Olds sat down on a rock for a spell.

"This rifle is getting too heavy to lug," he said.

"Come on," I said, "let's dodge over to the next bog before it gets too dark."

"And what're you gonna do with that damned bog when you get there?" he wanted to know.

"Hell, I don't want the damned bog," I said. "I just want to have another look for caribou." But it was this kind of searching by Billy John that got Dr. Olds his fine thirty-four-point stag on his first trip, a trophy that came third in the Boone & Crockett Club awards for that year and which he still had on display at his home in Twillingate in 1979.

They didn't know much about canoes either. Dr. Olds had his own outboard, and one time he was towing two canoes down the Lake, each with a good load. We sung out to Dr. Olds to watch out but he wouldn't listen. Suddenly a big lop swamped his boat and took the motor right off the counter. It was still running when it hit the water, but of course the hot spark plug cracked and that was that. Ern was up forward when the lop struck. The wave came over his knees and he was bawling and screeching, and if the other canoes hadn't come along he might have gone overboard face and eyes. Dr. Waddell took the motor to Brookfield, Bonavista Bay — where he later went to practice — and got it fixed, after which Dr. Olds gave it to Howard Thistle.

Those trips were some of the best times of my life. We had long, hard days on the River and in the country, but then in camp at night we had fun and jokes and tobacco and a bit of rum. We all got along with each other; even Ern, who could act so gruff, always had something comical to say. The last time I saw him was around 1977. He was sitting in a car outside my brother Harold's gas station in Gander Bay South. I walked over and said, "What are you doing around here, Ern?" He looked at me and he didn't know me: "None of your goddam business," he said.

I thought about that bunch a lot the fall of 1977 when I was seventh-three and got a moose licence and went up alone. I camped over there by Robinson's Brook, opposite the Gull Islands. And I went in to Robinson's Bog — just to see the bog again, not to see any game or anything like that, but to see the bog — and I couldn't help thinking about them all. I thought of one time we were in there hunting and I was coming out the trail with half a caribou on my back. Dr. Olds was right behind me and I started zig-zagging, couldn't keep in the path, and he said, sort of worried like, "What's wrong with you, Brett?" But I was all right; my load was over a hundred pounds and I had this headstrap that was cutting off the blood supply and making me giddy I suppose. After adjusting the strap he said: "Any man that would carry half a caribou is foolish anyway."

My moose hunting trips after those years were more in the line of business and not so much fun. My hunters, the most of them, were sportsmen from the United States — some very fine ones, but not the same as Dr. Olds' crowd. We had parties coming and going week in, week out. There was food and gas and other supplies to think about, guides to be hired and paid, and always the worry that no moose would be found.

Not that moose were scarce. In the late forties and through the fifties they were plentiful, still building up, I suppose, from the introduction in 1878 of a cow and a bull near Tibby's Point, Gander Bay. From being a novelty when I was a youngster — the first one ever shot on the River was a big bull killed by Pierce Francis in 1912 at Hatchet Point on the south shore of Third Pond, which he and Maurice Thistle claimed they did in self-defence — moose gradually spread and multiplied. So most of our parties went away happy. A lot of our hunting we did by canoe. There was no need to slog through swamps or tramp through the woods when you could paddle quietly up a brook late in the evening or early in the morning and sooner or later find one. If none were in sight, in mating season you had only to imitate a cow urinating by dribbling water into the brook from a kettle, or else thump your paddle on the gunwale, to toll any bull within hearing distance. Sometimes we called them as well. But we never bothered much with birchbark horns; we just cupped our hands and made the moaning sounds of a lovesick cow or the grunting challenge of a rival bull.

One of the biggest moose we ever got in that way was shot by a hunter named Metzer near Walt Harris' camp just above Forsey's Rattle. I had him in to Jonathan's Brook first, but no luck. It was a strange day; the sky was a yellowish shade and the sun looked bluish and about half its normal size. The date was September 1951. Some said it was caused by faraway forest fires; others claimed a huge volcano had erupted somewhere or other in the world. Anyway, around supper time I went down to the shore and did some calling, and right away I heard crashing and grunting in the woods on Betsy's Island. Early the next morning I went out and called again, and out came this fine bull, eyes blazing. Without a pause he came down the bank on the trot and splashed into the shallow water, heading right for us. By this time I'd alerted Metzer. He was for shooting him as he ran, but I wouldn't let him for we'd only have to paunch him out in the River and drag the carcass ashore over the sandbars. "Wait 'till he's almost ashore," I said, and he did. That moose had a big rack and weighed almost half a ton dressed.

Moose can be bad-tempered; so can caribou, but because of its size a moose is less afraid of humans. I've never been attacked by either, though a cow moose once drove me up a tree and kept me there for two or three hours because she thought I was bothering her calf. Both moose and caribou have sharp hooves and know how to use them. I've never been in a bad situation with a bull moose, though I have watched some grand battles.

One of the best was while I was guiding a party of two hunters from Fort Fairfield, Maine. Rommie Haines was a farmer and Gilbert Peterson operated a gas station. The other guide was Dominic Francis of Clarke's Head. We were camped on the Northwest at Greenwood Brook. Rising at daylight I went to the River to get a kettle of water, and across the river I saw two bull moose and a cow, and the cow was lying down. I went to the tent and woke up my two hunters and told them about the moose, and of the likelihood of a fight. Now both were home movie buffs and wanted pictures almost more than they wanted trophies. Dressing hurriedly, they put their cameras in order and we crossed the River to an island near the animals. By this time the sun had risen, washing the whole scene in golden light, and the two bulls were squared off, heads down, shaking their antlers and bellowing, and every now and then making a fake lunge. A few minutes later the younger bull charged. Their antlers clashed like rifle shots. Peterson ran out of film; I sent Dominic back to the tent to fetch another roll. The sun rose over the trees. With his camera reloaded Peterson decided to get as close as possible. We were standing on a sandbar in the centre of the River a hundred yards from our boat, with roughly two hundred yards of water between us and the three moose.

Peterson started wading toward the bulls, camera to his eye. The two enraged bulls seemed to pay him no heed. Peterson filmed away. Suddenly the larger bull broke off the fight and came running toward him. Peterson kept on filming and walking. "Get out of there!" we yelled, "he's comin' for you!" When Peterson took the camera from his eye and saw this freight train of a bull bearing down on him in a cloud of spray he turned and ran for his life. And when he did, the bull stopped and turned back. It seems he saw Peterson as a second rival and only wanted to scare him off. Well, that he did, all right. Both men filmed the rest of the battle. The bigger bull won; as for the cow, she didn't even bother to stand up during the whole episode. It was just as well, as both animals later fell to the hunters' bullets and she was left alone. Some years later I visited Haines and Peterson at Fort Fairfield and saw the footage from that morning. It was excellent and brought all the excitement back.

Another hunter who liked to make movies was Eugene Potter of Ossining, New York; and he got a good scare too. Potter came with George Lesser, a taxidermist from Johnstown, New York who had previously shot a forty-four-point caribou stag, a Boone & Crockett Club winner. Potter got his caribou early in the hunt too. Since he had plenty of caribou footage, I offered to take them to the lower Gander to film moose. They were delighted. So I took them down to our fishing lodge, and from there we poked around in the most likely places.

One evening, walking quietly along an old logging road overgrown with alders, we heard a moose grunting in the distance. "Want to film a lovesick bull moose, Mr. Potter?" I asked.

"Sure do," he replied. I wondered if he realized just how big a bull moose was up close.

The alders made it hard to see very far, so I chose a small clearing farther along the trail with a tall white birch in it, and stationed the two of them in some thick fir on the side opposite where the sound had come from. "Make sure you can see the base of that birch," I said, "because I'm going to climb it and call that bull right up to you." We were in a thick droke of old black spruce overgrown with green and brown moldow, and I figured the sound wouldn't travel very far if I called with just my hands. While they were getting well stowed away, I peeled a piece of birch rind about eighteen inches long, shaped it into a long cone, and pinned it together along the seam with little wooden pegs the way Billy John had taught me.

"All set?" I asked. They were, so up the tree I went. When I'd found a good perch and everything was quiet, I put the horn to my lips and gave the call of the female moose in heat. In no time we heard the answering call of a bull, not half a mile away. Within a few minutes we could hear him coming, crashing through the fir thickets, knocking his antlers against trees, splashing through swamps. At times he would stop, listening. Then I would call again and on he would come. Just before he burst into the clearing I stopped calling and whispered to Potter to start his camera going so it wouldn't spook the animal.

Out into the little clearing he came, a fine specimen of perhaps a thousand pounds with brown, shiny antlers (twenty points at least), his mouth open and bits of foam on his lips, eyes wild and his bell swinging back and forth across a massive chest. He halted less than thirty feet away. I could hear the camera whirring, but the bull seemed too excited to notice. Tossing his grand head this way and that and snorting, he was looking for a cow. He never even looked overhead, and he never spotted Potter and Lesser. When I figured they had seen enough, I said to the moose in a low voice: "Satisfied, ol' man?" At the sound of my voice so close he wheeled and, like lightning, was gone with hardly a rustle.

"Well," said Potter, stepping out from hiding, "I'm certainly satisfied, even if he isn't! But I'm damned glad he's gone, too. For a few minutes there my hands were shaking so bad I had to rest the camera against a tree!"

"I got the jitters too," said Lesser, breathing a sigh of relief. "Next to him, my big stag looked like a Newfoundland pony!" We went back to camp well satisfied. I never did see that footage, but at Christmastime Eugene Potter wrote and told me it turned out fine — "except for a few minor tremors near the end."

Caribou Hunting

When I was a youngster moose were a rare sight in Gander Bay, a novelty introduced from the mainland only thirty-odd years before. The caribou was different. Caribou were hunted from time immemorial by the native peoples, and the early settlers told how herds of them would swim the Bay in the fall on their way to their wintering grounds on the Southern Neck in back of Musgrave Harbour. Other herds would migrate south from around Gander Lake to the headwaters of the Gander, and the old people told how the Notre Dame Bay men would go up to the Lake with their muzzle loaders and take all they wanted. Sometimes, to save on powder and shot, they would fire into their legs to cripple them and then finish them off with axes and knives. After that they would raft them down the River like logs — a caribou floats high because of its hollow hair — and carry them home on schooners.

Later, in G.L. Phillips' time venison was a staple food in the lumber camps. They even had lookout trees near the tote roads so they could track their movements. One of those was on the ridge west of Jonathan's Big Pond, a tall white pine long since dead, and I recall it had eight or ten long railroad spikes driven in on each side to make a ladder up to the first branch. Arthur Hodder worked in the woods for Phillips as a young man. When I asked him about it in 1975 he said, "Yes you, I knows all about that. That was our caribou lookout." I climbed it once. You could see the valley of the River to the west and parts of Fourth Pond. In Phillips' time caribou still frequented the lower Gander through the summer months. Arthur and his fellow loggers, laying in their winter provisions early in the fall, would have had no trouble picking up all the venison they wanted.

237

But in my day caribou were seldom seen north of the Lake. The first I ever saw in the wild was when I went to the Northwest with Jim John in 1919. There was plenty up there then, and for years later. I can mind sitting on the bank at the mouth of Big Gull in the fall and watching hundreds upon hundreds cross the Northwest there, going into the water, swimming, and coming out and shaking themselves dry like dogs, a moving sea of brown and gray, their hooves making that dry clicking sound, and them looking neither right nor left because the first snow had fallen and they wanted to reach the high southern barrens before winter set in. It was mostly us Gander Bay men and a few Indians that were after them then. The lumber camps were all gone and we never took many. There was no Trans-Canada and no snowmobiles to torment them, so they prospered.

One of the early sport hunters was Dr. Seccombe Hett, an English surgeon who served as a major in the British and French Red Cross during the First World War and was later a noted ear, nose and throat surgeon in London. In August 1918 the British government rewarded him with a caribou hunting trip in Newfoundland. Along with him came his wife and daughter and a Newfoundland clergyman. My uncle Stanley Gillingham was one of the four guides they hired; the others were Billy John, Richard Gillingham and Elijah Francis. Uncle Stan often told me about that trip; it's a wonder he got home alive.

At that time the caribou season opened August 1. They went as far as Big Gull River and hunted from there. After two weeks they ran short of whiskey so Dr. Hett sent Uncle Stan back to Glenwood, a distance of thirty-eight miles, to order two more cases from St. John's. The River being very low that year, he had to wade and drag the canoe over the shallow sandbars. Ten miles down from Gull River on the north side he saw the smoke of a campfire. Knowing that Billy John's father Peter always hunted in that area and had a camp there, he left the canoe and started to wade ashore to have a mugup and a yarn with him. Then he saw Mr. John walking in the trees along the river bank with a rifle under his arm and looking in his direction. My uncle was wearing a pair of white hip waders and realized at once that Mr. John, over eighty and with failing eyesight, had taken him for a caribou.

Now this was just above the Plough Island. He decided to run back to the canoe and then move downstream far enough to put the island between himself and Mr. John. But as he ran a shot rang out and he was showered with rocks and sand from the bullet. To his dismay he now saw the hunter hurrying to get below the island for a better shot. Uncle Stan knew that he must run for his life. He easily outran the old Micmac,

238

and when Mr. John arrived at the lower end Uncle Stan surprised him by waving his arms and singing out. It took the Indian several minutes to get over the surprise of seeing his caribou turn into a man. Finally he grinned and said, "Me should have struck you in the back," meaning that he had aimed above the white rubbers just as he would have with the white shanks of a stag. After that Billy never let his father hunt alone any more.

In Glenwood my uncle ordered the whiskey, waited a few days for it to come, and then went back to Gull River. In the next week or so they got their quota of caribou and started home. Dr. Hett was something of a naturalist and it seems his daughter turned after him, for while they were at Big Gull she came back one day with a live weasel. This she caught below Miguel's Brook, and the place is called Weasel (we always said "Wizzel") Point to this day. Another day she brought a hornet's nest into camp and drove everybody out, but she never got stung herself. By the time she left she had the weasel eating out of her hand. She also tamed a gray jay. How she kept the weasel from eating the jay I don't know; she must have had them in cages. Coming around Careless Cove Point on Gander Lake, her canoe was swamped close to shore. In the confusion the poor jay nearly drowned. But Dr. Hett wrapped it in a towel, gave it three drops of whiskey, and by the time they reached Glenwood that night the bird was as good as new. At the train station the major offered his guides anything in his outfit; he was pleased with the racks they got. I don't know what the others chose, but Billy John picked a fine brass spyglass that the doctor used for spotting caribou. Before giving it to Billy, Dr. Hett had his name and the date inscribed on the barrel: "G. Seccombe Hett, August 14, 1918." That glass, made by W. Gregory & Company of London, England, is now in Harold's family.

My trip with Jim John, as I've said, was a turning point in my life. But it was my trips with Billy John that really sold me on the woods. What stands out in my mind is not just the hunting and trapping lore, but the Indian outlook. Billy had a camp at the head of the Lake, a mile above where the River empties out. From there what we called the Venison Path went eight miles through woods and bogs up to Mount Peyton. An excellent caribou country in the old days, they always called it the Harvest Fields.

I mind one time Billy and his son Lawrence walked in there looking for caribou to sell to the train crews at Glenwood. This was when you were allowed three caribou and selling venison was legal. We shot two does, but that night it came on to snow. It got so rough we had to backtrack to camp empty-handed. But before leaving we bled and paunched both animals and hung them up so we could find them when we got back.

When we finished that and were picking up our gear to go, Billy said, "Too bad we got no pot to cook a nice heart in with salt pork and onions." It was true; all we had was a fry pan. "Yes," he went on, "with salt pork and onions, a heart would be nice." And with that he rolled up the two hearts in a piece of birch rind, stuffed the bundle in his rucksack and away we went, heads down into the storm, with night coming on, bound for camp, with Billy in the lead.

When Lawrence and I got there Billy already had the fire roaring in the tin stove and was slicing the hearts into small chunks. "What's the good, without a pot?" I said. Laughing — he had the same merry way about him as Jim John did — he took something white out of his pack and held it up. It was an empty caribou stomach. "See my pot?" he said. After washing it out he put in a layer of salt pork and a layer of heart, one on top of the other, and now and then a bit of onion and salt, until the bag was full. After that he gathered the top on a three-inch nail and tied two parts of rabbit wire about six feet long to the nail. He hung the bag from a nail in one of the rafters so that it hung directly in front of the stove, and at the same time he twisted it until it would turn and keep turning, first one way and then the other. Opening the stove door, he let the heat and light pour out on this Indian-style pot he'd made in just a few minutes. I can see his ruddy smiling face in the firelight now. There was a bed of birch coals, very hot, but the pot spun so fast it never scorched one bit. And the wire was so long that it kept turning one way for several minutes before reversing. For about five hours Billy sat there smoking his pipe contentedly, his dark eyes fixed on the flickering fire. It was just like the time he cooked the caribou head. Every so often he would shove in a junk or two or wood. Outside we could hear the blizzard moaning around the eaves and the trees creaking. Wet snow plastered our one small window and sifted in under the door. The smell from the pot got better and better. Finally the meal was ready. I never tasted anything so good. We ate it all — including the pot. Then, while the storm raged, we turned in and slept like babies.

Six inches of snow fell that night, quite a bit for October. The three of us walked back to the kill site, crossing some deep drifts here and there along the barrens. Billy deboned two hind quarters, packed them neatly together, and tied the bundle up in his Indian string, which also formed two shoulder straps. Myself and Lawrence took the rest and so we toted them back to camp, resting our loads against a rock or tree along the way whenever we wanted a spell, but never taking them off our backs. The next day we paddled down to Glenwood and sold our meat and some rabbits to the train crew.

There was another time some years later that Billy and I were up at this same camp and this time we had some caribou out of season. He went down to Glenwood for something and when he came back that evening he told me he had a way for me to make a few dollars. In Glenwood, he said, he had run into the game supervisor, Ronald Tilley from Clarenville. Mr. Tilley was looking for a way to Gander Bay. "I told him you got a boat and motor and will take him out for $15," he said.

"That's fine, Billy," I said. "Only trouble is, he's a game warden and it's closed season and I'd like to take a quarter of caribou home to my family."

"Oh, that's OK," he replied, puffing on his pipe and grinning. "Put your meat in the boat, in under the cuddy, see; cover it up wit' your tarp and don't worry."

Billy knew his man. When Tilley stepped aboard my canoe I was nervous as a cat, especially when he put one knee on the venison to steady himself before he sat down. If he suspected anything he never let on. After all, he wanted to get to Gander Bay. Those were the good old days when everyone had to work hard for a living.

In 1949, when my brother Don and I had Saunders Camps launched and going good, we advertised moose and caribou hunting trips under canvas, one week to a trip. By now our reputation as guides was getting known, so we had no trouble finding business, especially trophy caribou hunters. Moose you could get almost anywhere, but Newfoundland had the only herds of woodland caribou that far south. Some of the finest animals roamed the watershed of the upper Gander, especially the Northwest. And that was our stamping ground. We knew the country like the palm of our hand.

After a couple of seasons we settled on two areas for our base camps — Webber's Pond about seven miles north of Rolling Falls on the high country between the Gander and Exploits watersheds (actually it empties into Great Rattling by way of Haynes Lake), and Berry Hill Pond on the headwaters of Little Gull River. This gave us plenty of good caribou country to hunt, but more important, it gave us two good float plane bases. We figured we'd never make much money so long as we had to bring hunters in by boat. The Northwest is shallow. Even the lower Gander is not very deep, but at least you've got the Lake to keep the water levels more or less steady. But the Northwest and Southwest branches have nothing much behind them, nothing, you might say, of any size to back them up but Big Gull Lake and Big Berry Hill Pond and a lot of bogs. So as soon as the weather warms up in May or June your water is gone, and it doesn't come back again until the fall. And with the season opening

241

September 1, it took the best part of a week just to go and come by boat, whereas by plane you could be there in an hour and hunting the same day. From pitching canvas tents we went to canvas tents on plank floors and then to permanent camps; that saved time as well.

Neither one of us had a pilot's licence, but we soon had two small airlines to draw on, namely Newfoundland Airways and Eastern Provincial Airlines, both new and both eager for work. Since their main activity was flying mail to the outports after navigation closed in November, they welcomed our business. Newfoundland Airways folded in 1951. In 1954 EPA moved its headquarters to Gander and appointed two veteran bush pilots, Marsh Jones and Bill Harris, to run it. Their fleet consisted of *Otters*, *Beavers* and *Cessnas*. One or two trips could take care of our largest parties, which at most would be two or three hunters and their guides. We rented the planes for so much an hour, more for the bigger *Otter*, less for the other two. The time they saved us in travel meant we could do twice as much business. We never had a mishap.

The worst thing that happened in all those years was one spring when we were building one of the camps and the plane couldn't get back for us because she was tied up with mercy flights and with bad weather. We went three days without grub that time. First of all, in weighing our stuff for the plane we left a bag of flour behind. This meant that we soon ran through our tinned goods, of which I had allotted too little. I shot a caribou but left the hind quarters on a hill where they would stay cool, and a bear took them. My brother Don set out for caribou but came upon a bad-tempered cow moose with two young calves — all fuzzy they were — and left them alone. Another moose got away while Don was trying to drive it toward me, because while crawling into position he met a deep ditch and the backtracking took too long. I got one muskrat — I was afraid to shoot for fear I'd miss — and we caught one rabbit. I tell you that plane was a welcome sight.

Until I retired in 1966, and occasionally afterwards, we used these two camps. Our base in Gander was Deadman's Pond, which EPA also used from 1953 on. For moose hunting we sometimes flew parties to the fishing lodge on the lower Gander, landing on Third Pond and using canoes from there.

During the fifteen years or so that Don and I ran the business we guided dozens of caribou hunters ourselves, and, counting the guides we hired, I suppose we catered to and outfitted over two hundred hunters from all parts of the world. Except for the firearms, sleeping bags, binoculars and personal gear, we supplied everything and did all the cooking and most of the lugging. In the beginning we charged $250 per trip; later we had to increase the fee. Most of our hunters went away content, and a lot of them took out fine trophies. Because we operated on a small scale, we usually had good success. From our base camps we could set a man and his guide up under canvas right in the middle of caribou country and away from other hunters. If it was a trophy head they were after — and most of them were — they could scout the country to their heart's content, taking their time until they found something good. For frosty nights and dirty weather I supplied a homemade portable tin stove with four lengths of pipe.

In 1951 our outfitting business received a boost when one of our hunters took a world-class woodland caribou. I had hired my cousin Orlendo (Lindo) Gillingham to guide George Lesser of Johnstown, New York during the latter part of September. On the twenty-second, returning to camp after hunting all day with no luck, they spotted a big stag crossing Robinson's Bog. The stag was running and far away, but Lesser wanted to try for a shot anyway. Lindo, knowing caribou habits and not sure how good a shot Lesser was, advised him to be ready when the animal stopped. The puzzled hunter kept the stag in his sights and, sure enough, it hove to and looked at them, presenting a good broadside target though at long range. And thanks to Lindo's knowledge, the caribou's curosity, and Lesser's good shooting, they got him.

This exceptional animal had forty-four antler points on a very symmetrical head, and earned a score of 405-⅘ points, enough to win Lesser first prize in the Boone & Crockett Club awards for woodland caribou that year. It was the best Newfoundland caribou trophy since 1910, and the second best ever taken anywhere. In addition it won the 1951 Sagamore Hill award set up by President Teddy Roosevelt for the best all-round animal. That same year one of Edgar Baird's hunters took second prize in the Boone & Crockett competition with a stag from the Walls Pond area, and my son Calvin guided E.B. Warner to a third prize trophy.

When George Lesser got back home and told his friend Ken Davis about his world-class trophy, Ken was eager to try his luck too, so in 1955 Lesser brought him. With them came Ken's wife Flo, their son Blair, and a friend by the name of Bill Forster. Don guided Flo, Eldred Snow took Blair, Leslie Gillingham guided Bill, and I had Ken. Lesser just went along to observe and take pictures.

I hired EPA to fly us in to Webber's Pond. Webber's (or Jack's Pond) is nice and deep for float planes and only eight miles north of the mouth of Big Gull. I told the pilot to come back for us in ten days.

From the outset I was given to understand that Ken really wanted a trophy. Now trophies like Lesser's don't come along every day, and can't be ordered up. And the worst of it is, any hunter with a trophy on his mind has to pass up some respectable specimens and take a chance on getting nothing at all. Just to make sure we understood one another, I explained this to Ken. He told me not to worry, and early the next morning we struck out across the nearby bogs. After tramping for an hour or so we rounded a droke of stunted black spruce and came suddenly upon two young stags. But their racks were small and basket-shaped so we passed them up. A short while later we topped a bedrock hill in the rolling tundra and spotted, upwind and within range, a fine stag slowly grazing on the white reindeer moss. Dropping behind a small bush, the only cover around, I examined him through the glasses. Ken raised his .300 Weatherby, studied him through the scope, and prepared to fire. The stag's spread was a good four feet and well proportioned; but I saw he had a major flaw.

"Don't shoot," I whispered, laying my hand on Ken's shoulder. The look on his face was one of utter disbelief. "Sorry, ol' man," I said, "but he's only got one brow shovel. That alone would disqualify him as a trophy." Ken lowered the rifle. "But don't worry," I said. "They're running good today. We'll find a better one." Meanwhile the stag, attracted by Ken's black-and-white-checked mackinaw, took several steps towards us. To console himself Ken got out his camera and took a few snaps. When we stood up the stag jerked to attention, eyed us for a few seconds, and then slowly turned and trotted off. After lunch we did see another good stag, but he was several hundred yards away and moving right along — and he too had only one shovel.

Well sir, for the next nine days Ken and I tramped the bogs and barrens several miles in all directions without laying eyes on another male. Ken became convinced that they had all left the country. And his legs were bothering him. In the muskeg a person sinks at every step, and unlike Lesser he was new to Newfoundland caribou hunting. The only thing that buoyed his spirits were the reports from the other members of the party. His wife Flo, though she had never gotten close enough for a shot, was seeing lots of game. Bill got a nice animal on the fifth day. Blair had come close to getting a trophy. But Ken never did get a shot. George felt as badly about it as I, because it was he who had persuaded Ken to come. As Ken wrote to me years later, there was only one thing that sweetened the trip for him: his son's success on the last day. And when I told him we planned to do a book, he had Blair recount that experience in a letter. Here it is in his own words:

> As our trip neared its end we found the tempo of our hunting increasing. We hunted harder, covered more territory, and ranged farther and farther from camp. Finally we were down to our last day.

I could see the frustration etched in the face of Eldred, even while he was assuring me that we would find a good bull. That day started like all the rest, the weather warm and sunny, and the tundra, as we crossed and criss-crossed, empty. We stopped for lunch and tried to enjoy it, but we had the feeling time was running out. With mock enthusiasm we started to make one last effort, hoping for a miracle.

We had been hunting for about an hour when in the distance, beyond a stand of fir trees, we spotted two bull caribou. One had an exceptional rack, the other a good rack. Both, as it turned out, also boasted double brow points. We were much too far away for a shot with my .30-06, particularly with open sights. We managed to get the fir trees between them and us and then moved rapidly toward them and into the trees. When we again picked them up in the glasses the bull with the better rack was grazing about 600 yards off and moving away. The other bull was grazing 400 yards away. With their backs to us we chanced moving out into the open bog. Crawling on our bellies through the damp moss we remained unnoticed, but we could not reduce the distance.

Finally, in desperation, we decided to run toward a rock protruding a foot above ground 150 yards ahead. If we got that far without disturbing them I was going to rest the gun on the rock and shoot the nearer bull. We took off. We made the rock completely out of breath and with sweat running down our faces. The smaller bull was still grazing, about 250 yards ahead of us now and still moving away. The larger bull was about 450 yards away. Too far for a shot, although he was much preferred.

I focussed my attention on the nearer bull. Not wanting to shoot him through the rear, I aimed a shot at the back of his neck. The shot creased his left antler about four inches from the base. He immediately turned about ninety degrees to the right and started jogging off. I stood up and put a bullet behind his right shoulder. He hardly flinched and kept moving. I put a second shot behind his shoulder. He continued jogging. A third shot in the same area dropped him, and he was dead by the time we reached him. The three shots were in a two-inch group.

We talked about our good luck, took a few pictures, and were about to start skinning him out when who should appear on the rise above us not 150 yards away but the big bull. Apparently curious to see what had happened, he stood there a good two minutes looking at us. I put my gun on him and at that distance could easily have dropped him.

However, two thoughts prevented me. First, I was only entitled to one bull; the second, I might have shot him and put him on my Dad's or Mother's licence — but what if they had each gotten a bull today?

I couldn't take that chance. I lowered my rifle and opened the chamber to eject the bullet. The hand-loaded cartridge had separated and the powder lay loose in the magazine. What would have happened had I pulled the trigger?

245

Another thing that brightened the trip for Ken was the fine meals of trout that Leslie and Bill provided for breakfast, and the way in which they did it. After the fifth day we were done hunting, so they went trouting up to the inlet of Webber's Pond. In the shallow water the trout were teeming, but they would take neither bait nor fly. In frustration they grabbed up some flat rocks and dropped them on the surface, which temporarily stunned the trout so they could grab them with their hands. For nighttime fishing they had another technique. They would tickle them into a dishpan. At first we didn't believe this. Then they showed us. Near the camp was a small pool where we got our drinking water. After dark Bill and Leslie would go to the pool armed with a small branch, a dishpan, and a flashlight. One would silently dip the pan in the water while the other would flash the light on the trout. At the same time the one with the pan would tickle the tail of the trout with the branch and lead the fish toward the pan until he could scoop it up. These trout ran uniformly twelve to fourteen inches long and were delicious. We lived under canvas but dined like kings.

In 1960 I guided outdoor writer Jac Weller to a respectable trophy head. He was one of the finest hunters I ever met and, like Blair, an excellent marksman. After he got back to the States he wrote a two-part article on moose and caribou hunting in Newfoundland that was published in September and October of 1964 in *American Rifleman*. Because he explains the process of stalking a caribou so well, and because he says some nice things about me, we have devoted the next chapter to his description of that trip.

A Long, Hard Stalk*

Our first morning hunt began by spying out the muskeg and barrens near camp. Irregular ranges of hills rose to the north and south. There was little real timber, but the ill-defined margins of the bogs showed belts of stunted trees. Through my 10X glasses Brett examined not only the muskeg, but also the slopes of high barrens as they came into view.

Toward noon Brett sighted a caribou stag alone on the bare side of a hill about half a mile away. We saw him twice more as we approached from directly downwind. Within about three hundred yards I was ready to shoot in a comfortable sitting position. Through the scope sight his rack looked most impressive. However, Brett was not certain that the beast had a really good set of antlers.

"He's too far," Brett said. "We can get closer and make certain we want him." Reluctantly I rose and followed Saunders, who was carefully observing the direction of the wind. When last seen, the stag was grazing quietly. He could not possibly have scented us since we were directly downwind. Normally a stag's eyes are not good enough to recognize a man at distance. However, something must have spooked him. We combed the entire area carefully, but never saw him again. At dusk we returned to camp with nothing from our day but aches and appetite.

Our second day's hunt began in rain and fog. It was heavy going almost immediately. The game trails deeply cut in the peaty bog were full of water. One has trouble realizing that these paths which crisscross and go along streams are not used by men. Nor could today's caribou population possibly have cut them. But things change slowly in this landscape; a five-foot tree is perhaps fifty years old.

*The following appeared in *The American Rifleman* (September/October 1964) and is reprinted here by kind permission.

247

We discovered in a bog the bones of a caribou stag. "Some hunter wounded it and then lost it?" I asked.

"Unlikely," Brett replied. "This carcass is only four or five years old. Nobody has been hunting here since the War but me, and we haven't lost a wounded stag." Poking around in the bog with his axe handle, he pulled out a thigh bone and, a few seconds later, another.

"He became mired and starved to death," Brett said. All four leg bones were deep in the bog. Apparently this is fairly frequent after weeks of rain. The antlers, almost but not quite fully formed, indicated that this had happened toward the end of July.

Climbing higher, we began to notice fresh caribou signs. The sun had just come out, everything was truly beautiful. There was a lake in the centre of small barrens with gray rocks, green trees, and brownish-purple heather. Suddenly Brett touched my arm and pointed. A caribou stag and a doe were some five hundred yards away, across a small stream. The 10X glasses made the stag appear a fine trophy; however, Brett could find only sixteen points.

We skirted a bog and crossed a small stream to approach from downwind, stopping only one hundred yards from the caribou. We crouched behind a tiny clump of bushes too small to conceal us, though it did break our silhouettes. Because of the wind direction neither animal could smell us.

Brett now took three squares of toilet paper from his pocket and held it up to blow in the wind. To the stag this could have been only the merest flicker of white. But at this time of year they are curious. A flash of white may indicate a doe.

The beast came toward us. Brett kept the paper fluttering; we were motionless. The stag was no more than twenty-five yards away when he stopped and then began to circle downwind to get our scent. Suddenly, some cross current of air took a whiff of us to him. He was off, but ran only two hundred yards before halting and looking back. A doe joined him.

The caribou, because of their remoteness and unfamiliarity with man, are not nearly so hard to kill once they are located as, for instance, a Scottish red deer, or an elk in Wyoming. The problem was, and apparently usually is in Newfoundland, to locate an animal with the trophy that you want.

From the hilltops to the south we examined many square miles of territory, but saw no more caribou at all. It had been raining off and on all day and now we had a steady downpour. On the return across miles of muskeg and through spruce thickets, we sank into the spongy surface of the muskeg over the ankle at every step. Newfoundland has the most consistently bad walking I have ever known.

The rain changed to sleet, but just before an early dark we arrived in camp. We soon had a roaring fire in the little portable stove, took off our outer clothing and boots and toasted our feet. We wrapped cold wet hands around hot mugs of strong tea. The world was again a good place to be; a thin piece of canvas between you and the elements and the warmth of a good fire can make a lot of difference. We prepared simple but nourishing food and ate our fill.

While Brett washed the dishes, I cleaned and dried my rifle and the binoculars. I spread socks and clothing to dry by the heat of the stove and checked my cameras. We talked of sealing and trapping as Brett had known them as a boy. Then we retired to the luxury of a warm sleeping bag on an air mattress with the smell of balsam boughs in our nostrils and the sound of sleet on canvas in our ears. Before I could really appreciate it all to the full, I was asleep.

The third morning was beautiful. Bright sunlight brought out all the subdued browns and purples in the muskeg and barrens. The spruce, balsam, and fir wore their various vivid greens; the tamaracks were pale yellow. Here and there dark blue water sparkled amid gray rocks. We circled our small lake and headed northeast. Brett had my binoculars and was systematically spying out not only the country to the north, but also that which we had passed through. A single caribou can escape even the sharpest eye when shielded by a fold in the ground, a rock, or even a few small trees.

Hour after hour we went on. After lunch of tea and toast and canned sardines we lay around, discouraged. About mid-afternoon Brett was outside spying out the high slopes of hills still at least two miles away when I heard him talking excitedly.

"There's something up there," he said more to himself than to me. "I can't hold these glasses steady enough." Returning, he lay down behind a rock, rested his elbows on it, and remained motionless so long that I took a couple of pictures of him.

"There's certainly a caribou up there," Brett said. "It's so far away that I can't tell whether it's a stag or doe. Let's work along this ridge so that we are directly downwind."

I examined what Brett pointed out through the binoculars, but could see nothing that resembled a caribou.

It took us half an hour to work along the ridge to a point where Brett found a convenient dead tree to support the binoculars. This time there was no question. It was a caribou lying down facing us. However, we could not be positive at this range, about a mile and a half, as to the sex of the animal. Many females have racks.

We had to leave our ridge now to cross muskeg and a small stream flowing through spruce thickets. Then we started to climb the slope on which the caribou lay. It's impossible in that country to keep direction precisely, particularly while trying to avoid appearing on the skyline. The first barren proved to be the wrong one. But a solitary tree gave Brett an observation post from which he quickly located the animal again. It was a stag with an entirely acceptable trophy. He was facing downwind, therefore facing us. There was no danger of his seeing us unless we appeared on the skyline.

Even though we had only about eight hundred yards to go as the crow flies, we had to penetrate a fifty-yard belt of stunted fir and spruce trees. They couldn't have been much more difficult if they had been made of steel springs and barbed wire. On emerging Brett climbed another tree, but was scarcely ten feet up when he came down again.

"Right in front, about 150 yards! Walk up on him and shoot as soon as he rises." Newfoundland guides don't approve of shooting stags that are lying down.

I carried my rifle with three cartridges in the magazine but nothing in the chamber. Loading it now, I began to approach in the direction Brett had pointed out. Slowly my eyes rose to the level of the barren. I was looking directly along the tilted high surface and suddenly saw the stag's horns above the grass, moss, and bush. Two more steps and I could see the whole stag facing me. At slightly less than a hundred yards, he rose. I brought up my rifle, checked the crosshairs on his right shoulder, and squeezed. The big rifle recoiled pleasantly. As I worked the bolt I saw the stag take a few steps in a small circle.

"He's dead. Don't shoot him again," said Brett.

I preferred to put another bullet into the gallant beast so there was no chance of his coming out of his state of momentary shock to suffer. Again he was facing me, but this time with the left shoulder and side exposed. My second bullet killed him almost without another tremor.

You know how it is at the end of a successful stalk. The happiness and achievement you feel make up for all your work in cold and wet. You forget aching muscles and lonely travel.

The actual stalk had lasted an hour and fifteen minutes. We had walked well over two miles through the roughest kind of country. Brett Saunders had done a remarkable job, not only in spying out the animal to start with, but in keeping clearly in mind where he was in spite of the terrain irregularities and the detours we had been forced to take. He had ended with me in exactly the proper position to shoot. Few guides anywhere in the world could have done so well; none could have done better.

We took some pictures and then skinned out the stag. I did not want to mount the head, but did want to bring back the skull cap with the antlers and the hide. The antlers were wide, with an extreme spread of slightly better than thirty-two inches, and symmetrical with well-proportioned shovels. At nineteen points it was not even close to a record head, but, according to Brett, compared favourably with any taken in Newfoundland that year.

The two three-hundred-grain soft-point bullets had done their work well. The first had hit about halfway up the shoulder, shattered it to bits, and gone on into the lungs. The second was lower, tearing off the top of the heart and going back diagonally. Neither bullet came out, so all the enormous energy was used up in the stag. I really like the .375 *Weatherby*.

We were miles from camp with afternoon far advanced when we finally set out on the return journey. To retrace our steps around the lake would take at least four hours and put us back more than two hours after dark. We preferred to take our chances the other way, even though the territory was unknown to us. If we were lucky we would be in before dark; if we found continuous pools and streams too deep to wade, we might be forced to spend the night in the open. We did find such a stream, but managed to get around it with a two-mile detour. Finally, we came to familiar ground just as the light faded.

I have never been more tired in my life. Brett had the heavy rawhide in his knapsack, but I was carrying the antlers. They were about the most unhandy burden to carry through spruce thickets that you can imagine. I can clearly remember being sincerely thankful that I have nothing like them attached to my skull.

We finally approached the white blur of the tent and all the simple pleasures of a dry, warm, comfortable camp. The first three days had been wonderful; I was thankful for the trophy I had taken. The next three days could be devoted to learning something about the country and the animals which inhabited it. I was to find out from Brett perhaps as much as any non-resident learns about the hard, courageous lives of the men of forty years ago who trapped and went sealing and fished around Newfoundland. Brett and I spent the rest of the week quietly moving around the game trails and observing life there. I shot another caribou — one that someone else had wounded — and learned to call in a moose. I even snared a couple of rabbits with his instruction. I can still see him at about noontime each day building a fire, making tea, toasting bread, and opening a can of Japanese smoked oysters.

Members of the Saunders family have been outfitters for two generations, and have satisfactorily served scores of hunters for both moose and caribou. Brett Saunders is the most accomplished caribou stalker on the Island; he combines the superb skill and knowledge of the British and continental European gamekeeper with the friendly comradeship of the professional Rocky Mountain guide. He is one of the most interesting men I ever met.

Jac Weller

Hunters Good and Bad

Half the fun of catering is the people. In the hunting business we met our share of pleasant and unpleasant types. As a rule the pleasant ones outnumbered the rest; few hard words were spoken, and jokes were the rule of the day. Living as we did in canvas tents or camps for seven to ten days at a stretch, often just the two of you, it was the only way. You could easily get on one another's nerves, especially if the weather was dirty, the hunting poor, or the hunter was inexperienced but wouldn't admit it.

I think the best bunch I ever hunted with was Dr. John Olds and his friends. As of 1984, Dr. Olds, Beaton J. Abbott and myself are the last three living from that bunch.

After I started catering, there were many more fine hunters. Amongst the best were two taxidermists, George Lesser of Johnstown, New York, who took the world-class trophy caribou in 1951, and Stephen Horn of Mount Vernon, New York, who also took a fine head. As I did not guide Lesser myself I didn't know him quite as well. In camp he was a very religious man who knelt and said his prayers every night and slept in a long nightdress. Stephen Horn, who came in different years than Lesser, also turned out to be religious, a devout Roman Catholic.

On one trip I took Horn caribou hunting under canvas on a fly-in excursion. We arrived on a Friday afternoon and when I had the tent shipshape I started to make supper outside. I planned on having potatoes and canned ham, but when I told him he said, "I'm sorry, but I can't eat meat on Friday." I asked him if spaghetti would be OK, and he said it would be fine. Well, that didn't seem like much of a supper to offer a guest, so while he was reading I took an onion sack and dodged off to a small brook nearby. Wading up the brook to a narrow place, I made it narrower with rocks and set the sack in the gap with a stick to keep

253

the mouth open. Then I walked upstream about a gunshot along the bank, got back in the brook, and waded back down. Well sir, the trout came charging out from under the banks and the old logs where they were hiding and made a mad rush downstream — right into my trap. In a few minutes I had eight fine ones, each weighing from a half pound to a pound. I didn't call him until supper was ready. When I handed him his tin plate with three nice fried trout on it he was amazed. "How come?" he said in disbelief. "I didn't see any rod in your kit, or you fishing in the lake...?"

"Oh, the Lord takes care of his own, I guess," said I, and we shared a good laugh. He was some pleased over that, and often spoke of it. In later years I sent him a three-and-one-half-pound brook trout that Winnie had caught and got him to mount it. He did a lovely job, and it is now on our mantelpiece.

Not all my hunters were so pleasant. I had one who argued with me that I was lost. To begin with, I never have used a compass in the woods; in fact, I didn't even own one. Well, on this particular day we had tramped from early morning until noon. After a mugup we got ready to go on, but it came on rain showers and then fog. "Let's head back to camp," I said. After walking perhaps five minutes I heard him say behind me: "You're heading in the wrong direction, and I'm not going that way because I don't want to be out in the bush all night." He said this very seriously; obviously he was worried.

"Sir," I said, "you'd better trust my judgement, for I've spent many years in this territory and know every inch of it." But no, I couldn't convince him. He turned around and started walking at a fast pace in the opposite direction. Since he wouldn't listen, I let him go his own way for a spell while I continued on my original course. As soon as he was out of sight I hid behind a tree and watched him. He kept on going as before. I thought, well, I can't let him get out of my sight or I might never find him again. I hurried and caught up with him and tried again to reason with him. Still no use. Now I knew he had this fine brass compass he was very proud of, and I figured this was the problem because he didn't know how to use it. I'd used them myself timber cruising, and they are a great thing in strange country, provided you consult them from the start of each trip, trust them, and know what you're doing. By this time my patience was wearing thin, standing there in the pouring rain arguing with him.

"Let's see your compass," said I. And when he handed it over I took it and slung it as far away as I could. His mouth fell open and he stood speechless. "Now," I said, "unless you want the crows to pick your bones, you better follow me." Already we had lost over an hour. This was in November month and dark was fast overtaking us. When we got back

254

to where we left the canoe that morning I said to him: "We're some lucky to find a canoe by this lake in the dark." He never spoke. In silence we paddled across the lake to the lights of the camp, where his worried buddies came out to meet us.

"Know any of these people?" I asked him, still vexed.

For the first time since I fired away his compass he spoke. "Thanks," he said. "I give in."

But he wasn't the worst. Compared to one character I guided in 1967, after I retired, he was a gentleman. In twenty years I thought I'd run into every type, but this one took the cake. He flew in from New York on a one-week moose hunt, a pale stout fellow loaded down with cameras and gear. When I met him at the airport terminal he lost no time in telling me that at forty-two he was president of his own company and that he wanted to bag a trophy head. I loaded his gear into my wagon, picked up an aluminum boat from Calvin, and drove out toward Grand Falls and south on the new Bay d'Espoir road to the east end of Miguel's Lake. From there we steamed to an island opposite what we call The Stint or outlet to Miguel's Brook, which empties into the Northwest about three miles below Red Cliff. The day was overcast with a warm south wind. I set up our tent and tin stove, cut fir branches for a nice bough bed for each of us, and collected firewood and splits against the morning chill.

At 7:30 the next morning, while I was making a fire, he woke up, stretched, and said, "Boy, this is the life. I've never slept so sound. What's for breakfast?"

"Toast and eggs with tea or coffee," I said. "How do you like your eggs?" I said, handing him half a grapefruit and a spoon.

"Boiled," he said.

"Hard or soft?" I said.

"Three minutes," he said.

The water came to a boil. Checking my watch I put two eggs in, then started slicing homemade bread for toast. He finished the grapefruit and frowned at the saucepan with the eggs. "You know," he said, "eggs should never be boiled."

"That so?" I said.

"Yes," he said. "They should always be simmered. They taste better that way."

After breakfast he went to the lake to brush his teeth. When he came back he said, "Do you think I should take a bath in the lake?"

"Sure, if you want to," I said. "It's clean if that's what you mean."

"Are there any leeches?" he wanted to know.

"No, the bottom is too rocky. Leeches prefer mud." He went to have another look at the lake, then came back again. "I really should take a bath," he said.

"It's up to you," I said, busily packing the lunchbox. "But we really should get a move on soon if we're going to hunt moose. Early morning is one of the best times."

After a while he said, "Where's the toilet?"

"Anywhere in the woods," I said, "so long as it's not close to camp." He mulled this over for a while.

"What do I sit on?"

"Oh, you might be able to find a blowdown tree or something. But a person doesn't really need anything."

"I see. That might take some doing. I might be gone a half hour." After a few minutes he was back. I heard him rummaging in the tent and asked what he wanted. "Toilet paper," he said. I fished a roll out for him and away he went again. He was like a youngster and I wondered what would happen before the day was out.

Finally, at nine o'clock, we got going. I decided to scout the country around the west end of the lake, a three-mile trip by boat. There was a stiff westerly wind and some lop, but in less than an hour we were there. "We'll spend the day around here," I said, "and get the evening hunting as well. That way we won't have to do the lake and back twice. I've brought a lunch."

"I was planning on going back to camp for lunch," he said.

"Why?" I asked. A guide should cater to his client's wishes, but not if they're unreasonable. "The wind's breezing up; by noon there'll be whitecaps on the lake and we could take in water."

"But I always take a nap after lunch," he said, "and there's no place here to lie down. Besides, I had left my book back in camp and I'll have nothing to do all day." I asked what book. "It's a book on hunting," he said. "Anyway, wouldn't the hunting be just as good around camp? It looks the same to me."

"No," I replied, "because the wind is wrong. I'm taking us where I think you'll have the best chance."

"Well," he said, "I think you're wrong and I want to go back."

He was making me crooked. Without unloading our gear I headed back to the island. With the wind at our backs, at least the going was easier.

But after lunch, and more cooking instructions, he wanted to go back up the lake. "No, it's blowing too hard now," I explained. "We'll have to 'bide here until evening."

"Why?" he yelled. "Ever since I've been with you all I've heard is we can't do this, we can't do that. Do you think you're the only one who knows anything about hunting? You know what I think?" he sputtered, jabbing his finger in my face.

"No; what do you think?" I said, washing his plate.

"I think there's no moose at either end of this lake or we would have seen some by now. Why, I haven't even seen a squirrel in this Godforsaken place, nor a rabbit nor a deer nor a bird. And the sun, the sun hasn't shone once since I came! Explain that to me, will you?" His face was so red I feared he'd have a heart attack right there. I finished drying one plate and picked up another.

"If you really must know," I said, trying to hold my temper, "we're a bit backward here in Newfoundland. We still haven't learned to control the weather or make the sun shine when we like." I asked him how they did it in New York, and why they didn't stop the floods they were having in Texas. "As for the birds," I continued, "they're all gone south for the winter. And Newfoundland is an island, you know, and the squirrels and deer don't like to swim that far. As for the rabbits, they're too smart to stay out in the open and get shot." I picked up the pan of dishwater. I had a mind to dump it over him, but I went outside with it. After cooling off I came in the tent again. Now he had his nose in his hunting book. At 7:30 sharp he turned in, saying not a word through supper.

When I got up at six Friday morning it was still blowing, and much cooler. Now and then a shower of rain struck the tent. I knew he was awake because he rolled over quick once or twice in his sleeping bag. All of a sudden he sat up: "I've had it with this place and with you," he said. "Get me back to Gander right away!"

"All right," I said, "whatever you say. But there's lots of time. The earliest flight is not 'till six o'clock this evening — if you can get a reservation."

But no, he wanted to go right away. So I put out the fire and packed our gear and took down the tent in the rain and steamed ashore from the island and loaded the wagon and we left. Two and a half hours later we reached the airport — and he couldn't get a seat on the plane.

"Then will you drive me to St. John's so I can get a flight?" he asked.

"Certainly not," I replied. "And I want you to know that you are without a doubt the worst sportsman, if I can call you that, that I've ever come across in twenty years as an outfitter." He wrote me a check and I left. The cheque bounced.

Sometimes it was hard to resist a bit of teasing. On one occasion I guided a fellow from one of the outports in Notre Dame Bay, a man who was used to the salt water and nothing else. He came on the train from Lewisporte to Glenwood, where I picked him up for the trip up the

Northwest. He was so used to little brooks at home the size of the river dumbfounded him, but when Gander Lake opened up ahead of us he felt more at home. To boil the kettle I went ashore in Careless Cove, a place with a sloping cobble and sand beach and driftwood around, and a steep cliffy hill behind. I asked him if he'd mind fetching some water while I got a fire going on the beach. He took the kettle, started to walk away, then came back.

"Skipper," he said, "where will I find the water?"

"Oh," I said, "just dodge up along the landwash a couple of gunshots and you'll come to a brook. Dip your kettle in there."

When he came back with the full kettle I could keep a straight face no longer. "What's so funny?" he wanted to know.

"You may not believe this," I said, "but this whole lake, all thirty miles of it, is every bit fresh water!" And I'll be damned if he didn't have to go down and taste it before he was convinced it wasn't salt. Well, the water in Gander Lake is indeed very clear.

There was another time I had a bit of fun with a hunter. His name was Chalian, and he was a doctor at Notre Dame Bay Memorial Hospital, recommended by Dr. Olds I suppose. Anyway, he was a nice fellow but his knowledge of caribou was next to nil. We shot a stag on Evans Bog up on the Southwest Gander and returned to camp with a quarter each. The following day we went back for the other two quarters, and when we came out onto the bog there was a large stag off in the distance.

This was in September, the mating season, the time of year when stag caribou will come toward you from a great distance if you wave something white. Many times I've brought them in from half a mile away just by waving some toilet paper. Their eyesight, while not good for detail at long range, is keen when it comes to movement, especially anything resembling a doe. Not having any toilet paper on me, I just called out to the animal and waved my arms over my head. Right away he swung in our direction and broke into a trot. Dr. Chalian looked at the stag and then at me. He hadn't brought his gun, and although I knew the stag wasn't dangerous, the doctor did not. I waved my arms some more. The stag was really covering ground now, closing the distance fast, eyes fixed on us, head held high. He had a nice rack, too. "Are you sure this is a good idea, Brett?" said the doctor.

"Are you any good to run?" said I. He shook his head. "Oh, well," I said, "it wouldn't do you any good, anyway. He can do forty miles an hour." Which was true. At this the poor man was more frightened than ever. And at that moment the big animal hove to. He wasn't a hundred yards away, a magnificent sight with his white hump fluffed up, his shiny black nostrils flared and blowing clouds of steam, the muscles rippling along his flank and his brown antlers gleaming. I told Dr. Chalian we were in no danger, to relax and enjoy the sight.

This proved hard for him to do, for the stag hung around for quite a while. But after much coaxing I got Dr. Chalian to walk upwind of him to see what would happen. When the stag caught our scent it was as if a firecracker had exploded under his belly. He jumped straight up and came down running. "Now Doctor," I said, "isn't he beautiful?" Together we watched him canter away across the rolling bogs and barrens, tail held high.

"Yes, indeed," said he, grinning ever so little.

Animals Tame and Wild

When I look back on my life, animals have been a big part of it, bigger I think than for most people. You might say they have been a lifelong study. And although other chapters in this book have told something of this, only a separate chapter can do justice to all the animals, tame and wild, that I have known.

If I had to name a favourite I suppose it would be the dog. Nowadays dogs are mostly household pets, but in my day most people wouldn't allow a dog in the house. I never did either. But many a night in the wintertime I have slept outdoors beside a wood fire, with a bough whiffet banked with snow to windward and the two dogs behind my back for warmth. Around the small communities of Newfoundland in days gone by the dog filled a useful place, carrying the mail, taking people to hospital, and hauling firewood. The dog was a work animal and treated as such. To the trapper the dog was a companion as well, good company on the trail. My dogs certainly were. They were always glad to get home, but though I never tied them on at camp, they made no attempt to leave. On one occasion they saved me from drowning when I fell through the ice. More than once they led me home through blinding snowstorms or fog. Jack and Gelert, Spot and Sprig will always have an honoured place in my memory.

Jack was my first sled dog. A big white-and-black mongrel, he was lead dog with Gelert and Spot when my cousin Stanley and I went rabbit-canning on the Northwest the winter of 1923-24. Jim John gave me Gelert, a slender type, foxy in colour, with some setter blood in him. Both were mature then, while Spot was the junior member of the team, a thickset Labrador-type, black with a white collar and tail tip. Jack speared himself on a new fence rail while chasing something, and died on our doorstep with our young son Calvin looking on. I had just returned from a long trip in March. We wondered afterward whether he was snowblind and couldn't see the sharp rail.

Spot and Sprig were both raised on the trapline. Sprig, a medium-sized black and white collie-type male, had joined the older dog in the late thirties and learned the ropes from him. They were excellent sled dogs, and I trained them to stay clear of snares and traps by setting small baited traps around the camp when they were young. Rooting around hungry, they would get a paw or nose caught and howl to be released. A few experiences and they learned their lesson. With hunting it was different. Used to being with me all the time, they couldn't understand why they couldn't help me hunt. This caused me some anxious moments now and then.

At Gull Rocks below the Ballast Bed on the Northwest, Tom and Lewis Coates and Dick Gillingham and Roland his son had a four-man wigwam, twelve by fourteen, with a base three logs high. A beautiful wigwam. One time we stayed there in late fall, hunting, my brother Harold and I. On the south side of the River were several bogs, and we went looking in there, the dogs following behind. There was six inches of snow on the ground. When we got about a mile from camp, Spot sprang past me at full gallop, followed by Sprig. I sung out to them to stop, but they paid me no heed and were soon out of sight. A little farther on we saw the track of a caribou, saw where it had stood on a round rock to watch us and then galloped off with the dogs in pursuit.

Continuing our hunt, around noon we saw three caribou and we took the smallest one. When it was quartered we started back to camp with our meat, hoping the dogs would be back before dark. Dark came, but no dogs. All next day we waited. Thinking they might have returned to the kill we visited the place; but no luck. We came back to camp and turned in, more or less resigned to leaving without them. Around four o'clock the next morning I heard a slight rustling and fast breathing at the wigwam door. Putting a piece of birch rind on the fire embers for a light, I looked and saw Spot crawling under the door, panting and looking very sheepish. I let him crawl in beside me. And about eleven the next day, back comes Sprig too. Both were famished. How they ever found their way back I don't know, for they must have seen dozens of caribou and chased them in every direction.

On another occasion I went on a caribou hunt, taking Spot with me. I went to a small wigwam three miles in from the River and spent the night there. Before leaving camp about seven in the morning I tied on Spot with four six-strand fox slips end to end. After walking for three hours I saw the first caribou, a yearling. I killed and dressed it. While doing so I heard a noise behind me — and there was Spot. He looked very downcast and expected a licking. But it amazed me that he had been able to track me through woods, open barrens and over miles of wet marsh where one would expect no scent to linger. I couldn't punish him. I just scolded him and ordered him to stay behind me, which he was content to do.

I think Spot was my favourite. One time we were launching a house from Victoria Cove to Clarke's Head, a distance of five miles. It was Rol Gillingham's house that he bought from Frank Hoff, a big two-story house. I and several other men went down to the Cove five miles by horse and sleigh to help. Altogether there was nearly two hundred of us gathered there, and several horses. Even so, we had a tough time getting the house started, and had to sing the "Jolly Poker" to do it. And several hours later, while we were in the midst of this, Spot turned up and found me amongst all those men.

Next to the sled dog, I suppose the most interesting animal is the bear. Certainly there's enough stories about them, a good many of them hair-raising. How many are true? In all my years in the woods I've only had one bad experience with a bear, and that was the time I described earlier, the time I was a fishery warden on the River and one took my salmon I planned to have for breakfast. It did give me quite a fright to see that bear's paw come creeping in under my tent and me with neither flashlight nor gun. I was only young then. Yet since that time, although I have seen plenty of bears at close quarters by day and by night, and snared and shot a few that were making nuisances of themselves, I've never had cause to consider them dangerous.

There was one time Uncle Stan and I were muskrat trapping in to Gull Steadies and the bear came out of the camp with a rum bottle full of molasses in his mouth, holding it in his paws and sucking on it like a baby, a comical sight. There was another time when two of us were sleeping in a little log camp with a door so narrow you almost had to come in side on, and without waking us a bear came right in the door and took the butter tub off the table between us. We knew it was a bear because he left shiny black hairs on both sides of the door frame.

One time while hunting I saw a large cub feeding in a blueberry patch. To place oneself between any bear cub and its mother is dangerous. Knowing the old sow must be handy and I had only the one cartridge for my .22 *Savage*, I backed quietly out of there and hid behind some alder bushes to watch the sow if she came back. In a few minutes she did. I don't think she caught my scent, but somehow, perhaps by the cub's actions,

262

she sensed danger. Rearing up on her hind feet, she stared in my direction and sniffed the breeze. Then, dropping to all fours, she came slowly towards my hiding place. I couldn't outrun her. I was afraid to try frightening her in case she might charge. I had no choice but to shoot.

The only vital spot I could see was her forehead. I took careful aim, squeezed the trigger, and saw the hole appear between her eyes as she fell. Then a funny thing happened: she gave a loud belch and up came several gallons of blueberries. Once she stopped twitching I came forward. The cub had bolted at the sound of my rifle. A couple of pokes with the gun barrel showed she was indeed dead. The hide was no good but there was nothing wrong with the berries. Making a sack out of my shirt, I washed them in a brook and brought them home. Only after we had enjoyed a pie made from them did I inform my wife where they came from.

Sometimes a bear will look like it is charging when it isn't. Bears have poor eyesight for detail at a distance, relying instead on their keen sense of smell and hearing. One day I was with two moose hunters on the lower Gander, and as we broke out of the trees and bushes, what should we see a hundred yards upriver but a bear coming full tilt down the shore toward us. Now a bear can easily outrun a man, so I cautioned the two not to run. One of them got very nervous and raised his rifle to shoot. I stopped him, for I knew by the head-down way the bear was running that he had not seen us. "Just stay as you are and don't move," I said, "He'll run right by us." And so he did — never even saw us. Yet a greenhorn would have sworn it was a charge — and another bear story would have been born. Somebody upstream, another hunting party, had just frightened it — that was all.

When I was about sixty and should have known better, I tried to kill a bear with a stick of pulpwood. This bear had me vexed because he had made himself a nuisance at our fishing camp on Cleaves Island, dragging garbage out of the pit and all through the woods, tearing doors off hinges and the like of that. Once or twice I had glimpsed him, a rangy animal with a torn ear. And this spring when I went down to start getting ready for the fishing season, he had been at it again. His tracks were everywhere. I didn't have a gun, but a couple of days later, while out in boat collecting stray pulp sticks along shore for our summer's firewood, I spotted this same bear swimming toward Cleaves Island just upstream from the camp. First I tried running over him with the outboard motor at full speed. Two or three times I tried this, hoping the propellor would stun and drown him. Each time the bear sank, but each time he came up, still swimming, with no sign of damage.

Having gone this far I made up my mind I wouldn't let him get away.

By now he was almost ashore. Turning the canoe, I steamed in ahead of him, landed, and waited with a stick of four-foot spruce pulpwood in my hands. As he came splashing ashore, and before he got on solid footing, I brought the stick down on his skull with all my strength. The bear staggered and fell, then got up, growling. Before he could do anything, I pounded him again. And then I blacked out. The next thing I knew, my son Calvin was shaking me and calling out "Dad! Dad! Wake up! What happened?" And I told him the story. There was no sign of the bear. Later, when I asked the doctor why I experienced chest pains and blacked out, he said it was normal for my age, but not to try it again. The bear never came back.

Other animal encounters came to mind. One time I got tangled up with a cow moose and her calf that I should have left alone. I had just landed the canoe and stepped ashore this spring day when I heard a bleating sound, almost like a baby crying. "Curiosity killed the cat," they say. I took a few steps up the bank, parted the bushes and looked in. There among the alders, wobbling on long spindly legs, stood a fuzzy brown moose calf only a few hours old. Now the proper thing to do in a case like that is to get out of there. But when the calf saw me it perked up and came over. I had just started to scratch it behind the ears when I heard a faint snort. My hair stood on end. I knew what was coming. Heading for the nearest big birch,I started climbing. To reach that first branch was quite a struggle, as I was wearing thigh rubbers and the tree was wet.

In the midst of this the cow came crashing out of the underbrush toward me, letting out the bitter roars, enough to make your blood run cold. By this time I was out of reach, but time and time again she reared up and pawed at the birch with her sharp hooves. In minutes she tore the turf into muck. Meanwhile, the calf just stood back and took it all in. After a spell of this the cow moved away and started grazing. When I thought she had forgotten me I would start down. Quick as a wink she would be back, pawing and snorting and circling. It was only when the calf had wandered off for a while that I slid down and ran to my boat. Even so, no sooner had I shoved off than she was there, standing kneedeep in the water and glaring red-eyed at me. I never went near a moose calf in the woods again.

With caribou it's altogether different. You can touch their calves and the does will do nothing more than circle you and watch, alarmed and closer than usual, but making no move to attack even though they often have antlers and their hooves have very sharp edges. And the stag is nearly as timid. The fiercest I have ever seen them is one time in the rutting

264

season when Howard Thistle and I were watching two in a fight and Howard pitched my empty knapsack at them for fun. In a minute the larger stag was upon it, pumping his front hooves up and down until it was cut to shreds. Then they went back to butting and shoving one another. It was a good knapsack too.

I had a nice experience with a whale once. It scared the living daylights out of the people with me, but I got a kick out of it. This happened one spring when I was requested to take Thomas Elijah LeDrew and his wife Mary from Gander Bay to Change Islands, a distance of twenty-five miles. It was in early spring, in May, and the Arctic ice was all around, so that I was moving only at quarter speed. As we passed the south end of Change Islands a large whale surfaced about fifty feet away, heading straight towards us and spouting a cloud of steam. It sounded something like a large horse blowing through its nostrils. I don't know what kind of whale it was, but it was longer than the boat. Tom and Mary started to moan in terror. The whale dived under the boat and disappeared. As it passed under I couldn't resist placing my hand on its back. I imagined it would feel like rubber; instead it felt like it was alive, cold but alive, and seemed to quiver to my touch. Lots of times I've seen the pothead or pilot whales when they would come up in the Bay, but that is the closest I ever was to a live whale and I will never forget it.

I hate to admit it, but one of the worst scares I ever had in my life was from one of the meekest of animals. It happened this way. I was staying in a wigwam six miles down from Glenwood. It was a warm August night and the door was open. Sometime in the night I was awakened by the train whistle at Glenwood. Later, when I was almost asleep, I heard a slight noise which I took to be a bear outside. I sat up. It was pitch dark. As I went to take a box of matches from my shirt pocket, something furry hit me in the stomach hard. I made a grab for it, caught a bundle of fur in my hand, and threw it as hard as I could away from me. Whatever it was struck the opposite wall with a thump. With shaking hands I struck a match. On the floor, half-dead from the blow, lay a large buck rabbit. I went to sleep, and the next morning he was gone.

A queer sight I saw one time was a black duck trying to take off, but falling back into the water each time because it had something on its neck. Paddling closer I saw that this something was a weasel. Although the weasel seemed to have a death grip on the duck's throat, after two or three more tries the duck mounted aloft and the weasel let go and fell out of the sky. Feeling sorry for the little hunter I swung the canoe over to where it was swimming along and stuck out the blade of my paddle. Without a moment's hesitation it climbed on. Gently I lifted it aboard.

265

Directly the paddle touched the bottom of the canoe the weasel darted forward and hid in the dark of the cuddy, where it groomed its soggy brown and white fur and watched me with black, beady eyes. The minute the canoe struck the beach it was over the gunwale and gone. I often wondered if the duck survived.

Once when we were young fellows, eighteen or nineteen, myself and Harold and Roy Reccord went up the Venison Path to Mount Peyton for a look around. I guess we were hoping to get a caribou. I don't recall that we did, but one night we slept by a bog with a little pond and in the morning when we woke up we saw two goslings feeding there with their mother. She flew when she saw us move, but they couldn't because their flight feathers weren't grown in yet. So two of us drove them towards the other fellow and we caught the both of them and brought them home. They learned to fly, but would always come back. When it came around December month they were still hanging around, looking to be fed, not too happy with the snow and ice — so we had them for Christmas dinner.

And I mind one time we caught an owl in a trap by mistake. It was about 1927 and it happened up around Third Pond. This was a great horned owl and it was caught by one leg, which wasn't broken. In fact, it wasn't hurt at all. Wanting to free it, I tossed my jacket over it as it sat there glaring at me with its big yellow eyes. But when I took hold of the trap to open the jaws the owl shot out one foot and sunk its talons into my wrist clear to the bone. The talons of a great horned owl are over an inch long. I forget who was with me — I think it was Jabe Hart, Winnie's brother-in-law — but I remember the pain and the blood. It was some job to pry that bird loose from my arm, but he did. Then we took a snapshot and let it flap away. The wings hardly made a sound. It gave me some notion of how a rabbit feels when it sees an owl's shadow cross the moon. Sometimes, snowshoeing back from the trapline at night and hearing an owl hoot, I've fooled it by sucking loudly on my palm to imitate the sound of a rabbit in pain. Seeing this big bird come sailing over, not making a sound, scanning everything below as if in broad daylight, was unforgettable.

While on the subject of birds of prey, I must tell you about our tame eagle, Jack. The whiteheaded or bald eagle was a common sight along the Gander in my day, when there were still many tall pines for nesting and fishing, and the salmon were plentiful. At Jonathan's Pool in Third Pond one time my youngest brother Don, guiding a sport, watched an eagle soaring. Suddenly it dived, struck the water, and came up with a salmon. The salmon being too heavy for it to lift, the eagle battered its way to shore where it proceeded to devour it. Don didn't like this bird taking fish from under his nose when his sport had been unable to raise one, so he started up his motor, went down to where the eagle was having its meal and took it away from the bird. The salmon, minus a few chunks, weighed four pounds.

The tame eagle Jack came to us in this way. One day around 1931 my brother Harold and his chum Ronald Francis were coming down the River in boat when they saw an eagle's nest in the top of a large dead pine, with an eagle perched on the rim. Being just young fellows and wanting some sport, they cut down the tree. Of course the nest, which was over six feet across and two feet deep and made of sticks, was smashed to smithereens. But somehow the eaglet in it survived, though it couldn't fly. Harold took it home, kept it in a pen and fed it daily with flatfish they stabbed with a hay prong. Since it grew and thrived we decided to give it a name, and Jack it was from that time on.

Jack got so tame they let him out of the yard and gave him his freedom. Soon he would follow them around everywhere. After he learned to fly, Jack would cruise around the Bay, and before long he was catching flatfish and sculpins and eels himself. Sometimes he would be gone for a day or two at a time. Everyone around the Bay knew about him; we would hear reports that he had been seen at George's Point or down to Tibby's Cove. Sometimes we worried about him, for in those days some people still thought that eagles would carry off lambs and babies, and without the white head and tail of the mature eagle he might be shot for a hen hawk. But he always came back.

Sometimes I would see him resting on his favourite perch on top of Dad's woodhouse, about two hundred yards from where Winnie and I lived, and I would grab a prong and toss a flatfish in the air. Before it struck the ground Jack would have it in his claws.

Jack's capture took place about a year or two after we came home from Buffalo — Calvin was only three or four at the time. And one day — it was summertime and he was wearing short pants and a sleeveless shirt — the screen door slammed and we heard him crying. Rushing out, Winnie found him looking out through the screen door at Jack, who was glaring in at him. Calvin said Jack had chased him across the yard. There were no marks on his skin, so we didn't know what to do. As it happened the problem was solved by Jack himself. Separating our yard from my parents' was a wire fence, and on our side we had a flock of hens. One of the hens had a brood of chicks that followed her about. A couple of days later, hearing a commotion and a squawking outside, we went out to find the hens and chicks running every which way and Jack lying by the fence on the far side. It seemed that he had swooped at the chicks and slammed into the wire fence, breaking one of his wings. I took a pole and made away with him then and there.

There was one more incident that I'll never forget involving a bird, a whiskeyjack or Canada jay to be exact. They're supposed to be related to crows, and whether they are just as smart I don't know, but this one certainly was. I was up to Little Gull River trapping alone, and for company I would feed these jays that hung around my camp. Bits of bread, or some fat scraped off a pelt, was what they liked. But one got caught by the left leg in a trap I'd set handy the camp for a weasel that was using there. The leg being only held by a bit of skin, there was no way to splint it, so I cut it off and the jay flew away. And in March, as I was heading back there to lift my traps for good, and while I was still a few hundred yards from camp, a jay came flying, then disappeared. I paid it no heed, but when I laid down my pack on the doorstep a one-legged jay landed on it. The bird had been riding on my cap. And this jay was missing its left leg. Until I left for home a week later he came for crumbs and suet every day. I guess he never held it against me.

AFTERWORD

A Short Family History

Afterword:

A Short Family History

I was born at Gander Bay on February 15, 1904, the second son of Frank and Mary Saunders. My brother Gordon Earle had been born on the exact same date two years previous, but only lived six days. The midwife who brought me into the world was Mrs. Henry George Peckford — Sis Peckford everybody called her. She lived at Harris Point, which is almost opposite Clarke's Head. I was christened Evelyn Brett — Evelyn being after our Church of England clergyman at the time, the Reverend Evelyn Cleveland Clench — but they always called me Brett.

Mother's maiden name was Mary Matilda Gillingham. A tall, handsome woman with dark hair and warm brown eyes that often twinkled with mirth, she came from three generations of Gillinghams going back to Robert Sr., one of the first permanent settlers in Gander Bay. She was born in 1882 to William (Billy) Gillingham of Clarke's Head and his second wife, Sarah Ann Hodder from Horwood, who belonged originally to Hare Bay, now known as Deep Bay, on Fogo Island. Like many of his time, Grandfather Billy very likely had codtraps down around there in the summertime — they called it The Outside — and probably met her in that way. His first wife died fairly young. I can't mind about him, but Aunt Sarah Ann I can, because she would say to me, when I got old enough to use a gun, "Go shoot me a mess of robins for a pot of soup." And once in a while, to please her, I would do it, for she was an old lady. That would be around the time of the First World War. Three of William's brothers were Isaac, John and Richard; there was also a sister named Frances or Fanny.

Mother had three brothers and two sisters. John, the oldest, was a half-brother by William's previous wife. He was born about 1865. The

271

true brothers were Hezekiah (1876) and Stanley (1892). Stanley, or Poor Stan, drowned on the Northwest Gander on a muskrat trapping expedition in April of 1924 at the age of thirty-two, leaving a young wife Dorothy (nee Bauld) and their daughter Nellie. My mother's two sisters were Victoria Jane, who died unmarried at twenty-four on April 20, 1910, probably of diphtheria, and Louise, who married Jaspar Sherring of Glenwood and bore one son Douglas before being widowed. Aunt Louie later married Jim Shea. She had nine children by him. Uncle Jim was drowned near Glenwood trying to swim ashore from a sinking motor boat. She died in 1961 at eighty-one.

We have an Indian connection. Aunt Fanny Gillingham married Charles Francis Sr., a Nova Scotia Indian. And through this connection comes a story concerning one of the last Newfoundland wolves in Notre Dame Bay. In the bounty records of the then-magistrate for Twillingate District, John Peyton Jr. of Twillingate, the last entry in his book is for the payment of a £5 bounty to one Charles Francis of Gander Bay for the skin of a wolf killed on April 5, 1876 at Gander Bay. And it so happens that Grandfather Billy's mother Eliza did kill a wolf one time when she went for a turn of water. In those days many people wintered in a log cabin away from the shore. She lived near Big Hill, about a mile in the woods, and they got their water from Cow House Brook nearby. The wolf was lying there beside the pool, blocking her path and growling, but unable to stand because it was bloated. Someone had left a string of salt herring in the brook to soak and the wolf had gorged itself and then tried to quench its thirst. Anyway, Eliza grabbed the axe they kept there for chopping out the ice, killed the wolf, and brought home her two buckets of water as planned. At the time she would have been fifty-five or sixty. There's a good chance that it was the skin of this wolf that her son-in-law Charlie Francis Sr. turned in for the bounty. Eliza was a Goulding from Greenspond, then a prominent centre for the early cod and salmon fishery in northeastern Newfoundland.

Uncle Charlie was a full-blooded Indian from Nova Scotia, but perhaps with New Brunswick or Quebec connections. I can just recall as a boy seeing an old man, dark complectioned, nearly blind, coming to our house and rapping on the windowpane, then on the door, saying "Is dis de post office? Any mail for me?" At that time the post office was by Gander Stores on Burnt Point, about a quarter mile farther on. After Mother gave him directions he dodged off down the road, feeling his way with a stick. Some time later — my brother Harold can mind this — somebody came to borrow our wheel barrow to carry him home: the old fellow had taken a fall and hurt himself. Uncle Charlie never walked abroad again. This would be about 1917. He and Aunt Fanny had five or six children, four boys and one girl that I know of. Charlie Jr. and Tom became Anglicans like their mother, but Andrew, Peter, Edward, and the girl remained Roman Catholics like their father.

My father, Frank Saunders, was a Change Islands man himself, born at Paynes Cove in 1876. The house is all gone now. His grandfather was an Englishman, Edward Saunders, from Poole in Dorsetshire, England. His dates seem to be 1826-1892. Two of his sons were Edward James, who died in 1892, and Samuel (1851-1907), both probably born in Change Islands. A brother or uncle of Edward James served with Lord Kitchener at Khartoum in the Sudan, leaving a sword which is still in our family. Dad's father Samuel (or Sammy) married Thurza Porter, whose family may have come from Exploits, and they raised three boys and three girls. The other two sons were Henry and Ned. Henry (or Harry) became a master carpenter in Buffalo, but for years made his living during the winter playing poker. He never married. Ned married Jean King who bore him one daughter, Marjory, before he died in 1915 at age thirty of TB. The three girls were Edith, Eliza and Emily, and they married Frank Lockyear, Harry Oake, and Alec Scammell respectively. Alec and his father Frank were drowned off Fogo Islands around 1917. Samuel's father moved back and forth between Poole and Change Islands for years trading in fish and rum. He is buried in the Church of England cemetery at Change Islands beside Uncle Ned. Grandmother Thurza, who died in 1904 at fifty-two, is also buried there, but Samuel, said to have died in St. John's at the mental hospital, has no stone in Change Islands.

After attending school in Change Islands and at Methodist College in St. John's, my father went to Twillingate to apprentice with the firm of Owens and Earle, fish merchants. This would be about 1895. Saltfish went from this area to the Caribbean and the Mediterranean, and names like Port-au-Prince, Alicante, Lisbon, and Madeira would have been familiar to him. From Twillingate he moved to Big Burnt Bay (now Lewisporte), where he hoped to buy a piece of land and go into business. With him in a leather bag he had $300 in silver fifty-cent pieces which his father had given him when he left home. The land he wanted was soon to be the site of the terminus for the branch railway being built from Notre Dame Junction to ship pine lumber from Lewis Miller's mills at Glenwood and Millertown. The asking price was $700. Disappointed, he may have worked for a time with pick and shovel on the line before moving on to see what he could do in Gander Bay, then a fairly prosperous centre for salmon fishing and sawmilling. Years later, after the Miller lumber empire had collapsed and Dad was an established businessman and could afford it, he got the chance, through his brother-in-law Jim Shea, to buy a strip of land extending from Woolfrey's to Hann's Point in Lewisporte for $5,000. He foolishly turned it down saying, "What would I do with Big Burnt Bay?" He did buy a piece at Norris Arm, however.

Around 1896 he came to Gander Bay and set himself up in a small shop selling general merchandise on Big Salt Island, home of the oldtime salmon fishing families the Hodders and Gillinghams. He probably boarded with the Hodders, who with the Gillinghams had a grant from Queen Victoria to fish salmon there. A year or two later he built or bought a store of his own at nearby Shea's Point on the south side.

The south side at this time was growing in population, thanks to a boom in lumbering brought on by the decision of the Phillips lumbering interests of Maine to establish a large steam sawmill at Barry's Brook near the mouth of the Gander River. The mill, built in 1890, was managed by old man Phillips' son, George Leamington. To build it they brought in tradesmen from Nova Scotia and New Brunswick. It was two storeys high, with two rotary saws — one above the other — to split the big logs, and gang band saws to make the lumber. Father told me it had some of the best shipping facilities anywhere. The lumber was loaded directly on trolleys which ran on narrow-gauge tracks to a wharf a quarter mile down around the shore where schooners could dock. For larger vessels they used two steam tugs, the *Annie* and the *Claude*, to tow the lumber in rafts or scows out to the deepwater anchorage, five miles away at Sandy Cove. The *Annie* was made of wood, and the *Claude* — named after one of the Phillips' boys, born in 1894 — was steel. The ships that came were large square-riggers with two and three masts and special hatches cut in their bows for pushing the lumber in through. This lumber was not like you see today, it was made up in what they called deals, heavy four- and five-inch planks up to a foot wide and ten, twelve, or more feet long. They resawed it overseas.

By the time Father arrived a small village, known as George's Point, had grown up around the mill. Besides company housing, it had two stores selling general merchandise, blacksmith and carpentry shops, barns for the oxen and horses, and a post office. In 1886 a telegraph line had been put through from Gambo to Port Albert, with connections to New World Island, Twillingate, Fogo and Change Islands. The postmaster was Charles S. Rowland, who moved there with his wife from Point Leamington, where old man Phillips had another sawmill run by his son George. So that makes two Notre Dame Bay places named after the same man. At night the Point was lit up by electric lights run off the mill's wood-fired generator.

The mill meant year-round jobs and ready cash for a good many people. There was work, not only in the mill and lumber yards, but in the woods as well. At one time or another the company logged pine on all the major tributaries of the Gander, including the Southwest and Northwest, and around Gander Lake. On the Lake, in fact, they operated a steam tug, the *Dominion*. And for a time they had a sawmill in Glenwood. Two of my uncles worked for them in Gander Bay: Jim Shea was their horse doctor and Hezekiah was tallyman and likely cruised timber for them in the wintertime. And my mother, as a young woman, kept house for Mrs. Phillips' sister, a Mrs. Eastman.

With so much activity my father expected to do well. And he would have, if the pine had held out. Oh, some very fine logs still came down the River. I've heard Uncle Hezekiah say that even in his time some were over three feet across the butt. The highest tally they ever sawed out of one log, he said, was 1,100 board feet. Ten or a dozen like that would be enough to build a small house. A few big houses were built. Rowland, the postmaster, had a mansion, and so did Phillips. My mother said that there were doors in Phillips' house made from a single pine board.

But by 1900 or so they had cut the best. Cull logs — logs with butt rot or heart rot or else windshook with cracks in the wood — began to show up more and more. Uncle Hezekiah said that in the latter years it was common to have to discard half the logs. On top of that, in 1900 the Scotsman Lewis Miller had built a big mill at Glenwood and another on Red Indian Lake. Together those two mills sawed more lumber than all the other mills in Newfoundland combined, and a lot of it went to the same markets. Then a speculator from Nova Scotia, Harry C. Crowe by name, started buying up Newfoundland mills right and left. It wasn't the mills he was after — it was their timber limits. In 1902 George Leamington Phillips died. Soon afterwards the mill closed and the lands went to the Anglo-Newfoundland Development Company, which started hiring men in 1905 to cut pulpwood for its new Grand Falls mill.

Today all that's left of the George's Point operation is some piles of sawdust and slabs, the remains of the rock piers that held the log boom, and a ringbolt in a rock on Ludlow's Point.

Watching George's Point fail, and seeing a market for local construction, Father made up his mind to go in the lumber business himself, with a water-powered mill sawing local spruce and fir. Around 1900 he met and married my mother, and about the same time he launched his house and shop across the Bay over the ice to Clarke's Head. From her step-brother John Gillingham he bought a strip of land on the south side of Clarke's Brook running from the shore nearly a mile up the brook. According to records kept by Harold and his wife Kathleen, in August

1901 he paid $30 for a lease to operate machinery in the brook, followed by a rent of $5 each year thereafter. The formal lease is dated the third year of the reign of Edward VII, which would be 1904, the year I was born. It was like a land grant and it was good for twenty years.

An old time-book shows that in May of 1903 he hired Henry Collins of Gambo, a millwright, to supervise construction of the sawmill. For 51½ days' work on the mill, dams, and chute or flume, Collins received $103. The job of locating the two dams and marking a route for the flume went to his brother-in-law Hezekiah. Hezekiah was paid $18.80 for a total of 188 hours work. The first dam was a mile upstream where the brook runs out of Clarke's Pond. The second was at Steady Water, 1,700 feet from the turbine. The men who built them got eight cents an hour. At the lower dam Hezekiah started the flume and, letting it drop one inch every four feet, he brought it out with plumb bob and twine by the best route, over cliffs and across bogs to the mill site. To minimize leaking it was made of matched or tongue-and-groove lumber; its dimensions were three feet wide by two feet deep. The men who built it received five cents an hour. Where it came out of the woods the chute, supported on round spruce trestles, had to cross Uncle John's hayfield and garden. There is a signed agreement dated 1904 giving Father the right to do this, provided Uncle John, who had salmon nets off Burnt Point nearby, could land his catch at Father's wharf.

Meanwhile my father had set up shop again and was soon open for trade. While there were not many people on this side of the Bay, he had the advantage of being the only merchant — at least until the Horwood Lumber Company moved in and built Gander Stores Limited some years later. The principal families on the north side at that time were the Gillinghams — by this time quite a clan — and those of Charlie Francis Sr., Esau Harbin, William Head, George William Coates, and a few others. These were his customers.

I wish I had been around to see the mill start up. The flume, about twelve feet high where it crossed the road, delivered a twenty-seven-foot head of water which was funnelled into a headbox to drive a vertical steel turbine geared to a horizontal shaft on the floor of the mill. The name of the turbine was "Little Giant." The falling water struck a series of buckets arranged in a spiral on the shaft, causing it to turn. This end of the shaft was twenty-four inches in diameter and sat inside the headbox, which was bolted to a timber floor, called a penstock, in the brook. My father bought the turbine from J.C. Wilson & Company of Picton, Ontario. Very efficient and reliable, it developed about twenty-five horsepower.

With Hezekiah as sawyer, they started sawing in September of 1903 and continued through part of November. The time-book shows that for those three months Dad paid out $248.45 in wages for up to nine men. In October 1905 he had nineteen men on the payroll, most of whom got a dollar a day for ten hours of work. Uncle Hezekiah, who had been paid fifty cents a day at Phillips' a few years before, now received $1.80 a day. Uncle John's son Doff, or Theophilus, then fourteen, got fifty cents a day for running the shingle machine.

How long the water mill ran I can't remember. But it probably sawed well into the First World War because Harold, who was born in 1910, recalls seeing the lumber piles. I was six then, and I can mind, just barely, the little schooner or bulley boat that Father bought some years before up Exploits way for transporting his lumber to the merchants at Change Islands and Fogo and places like that. She was black with brown barked sails, about forty feet long and eighteen tons. He and George Bursey made many a trip in her. He always wanted a schooner, but a bulley boat would do. She drew too much water to tie up at the wharf, which was on the south side of the brook at the end of the sawdust piles, about where the big rock is now. Instead, they would take the lumber out in a scow to where she was moored off on her collar in midstream. One thing I recall about the sawmill years is a big storm with an easterly wind that washed away the end of the sawdust dump and with it thousands of shingles piled there. The same storm took away part of the little graveyard by the church on the north side of the brook, as well as some boards stored under the new shop, which extended out over the water a bit. Years later we found a few human bones in the landwash nearby, driven there by that storm.

During the War there was a big demand for pitprops for the British coal mines. Dad got a contract to cut some too. About this time he saw there was more money to be made in the shop if he expanded, so in 1919 he had his brother Harry build a much larger shop. By then our family had grown to four — Aubrey was born that year, and Marion in 1913. I was getting old enough to help Uncle Hezekiah in the shop. Dad and Mother kept a big garden and most years they had a pig or two, and sometimes we had a cow. He built an ice house so he could sell a bit of fresh meat, pork or beef or venison in season. With the cream we could make and sell some ice cream in the hot weather. That was my job and I was allowed to keep the profits.

As business picked up, Father hired a clerk, Charlie Fookes by name. There was talk of a pulp and paper mill being established somewhere in Newfoundland. The Reid Newfoundland Company surveyed the Gander watershed for timber. Rumour had it that Gander Bay was being considered, that there would be a townsite laid out in Sandy Cove and a big dam built just above tidewater. Sir Richard Squires and his Liberal Reform Party were promising to "Put the Hum on the Humber" and "The Gang on the Gander." My father, always alert to the chance to make money, followed the rumours and bought up pieces of land here and there — a few acres of shore frontage at Tibby's Point, a bit at Dawson's Point at the mouth of the River, a piece at Norris Arm. He even got hold of the townsite plans for Sandy Cove. But Gander Bay was passed over in favour of Corner Brook.

In 1921 Donald, their last child, had been born. By now my parents were respected members of the community and of the Church of England. School teachers stayed at our house; as did the various clergy on their travels around the parish. Mother kept a servant girl. Father was a lay reader in the church and one of its principal supporters. All of us were expected to attend divine service, to say our prayers regularly, and not to throw rocks or do any work on the Sabbath. My parents, although God-fearing and strict on religious matters, were also fond of company and fun. Although I was growing restless with home, it was good to be part of a large family with plenty of uncles and aunts and cousins, and to live in a place where everybody knew everybody else. This was the life my father and mother made for us.

Father passed away in 1954 at seventy-eight. His shop had burned not long before and he was never the same after. Mother outlived him by nearly twenty years. In 1968 Premier Smallwood was looking for someone to open the causeway connecting Gander Bay South with Gander Bay North. She was the oldest person there so he got her to cut the ribbon. She was still fit and alert when she died in 1979 at ninety-seven years of age.

APPENDICES

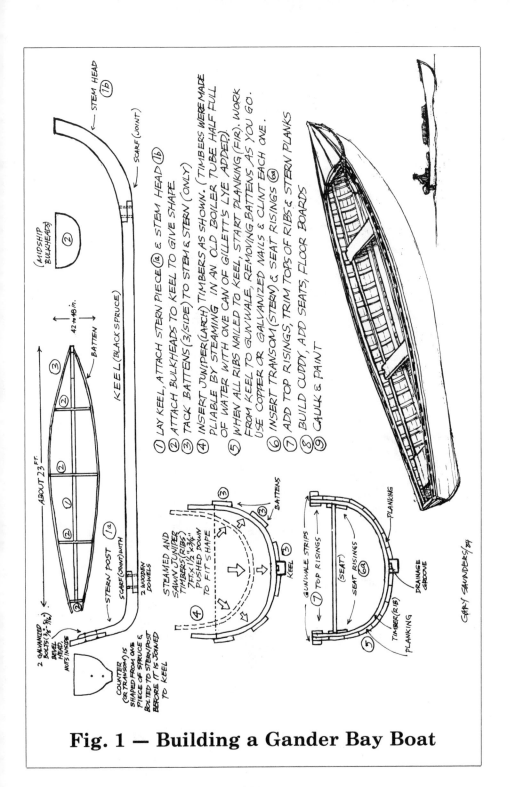

Fig. 1 — Building a Gander Bay Boat

281

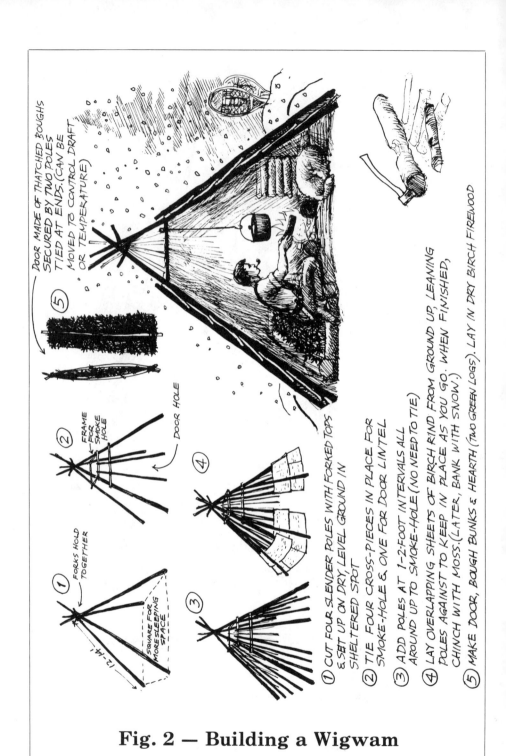

DOOR MADE OF THATCHED BOUGHS SECURED BY TWO POLES TIED AT ENDS. (CAN BE MOVED TO CONTROL DRAFT OR TEMPERATURE)

⑤

FRAME FOR SMOKE HOLE

②

DOOR HOLE

④

FORKS HOLD TOGETHER

①

SQUARE FOR MORE SLEEPING SPACE

12-14'

③

① CUT FOUR SLENDER POLES WITH FORKED TOPS & SET UP ON DRY, LEVEL GROUND IN SHELTERED SPOT

② TIE FOUR CROSS-PIECES IN PLACE FOR SMOKE-HOLE & ONE FOR DOOR LINTEL

③ ADD POLES AT 1-2-FOOT INTERVALS ALL AROUND UP TO SMOKE-HOLE (NO NEED TO TIE)

④ LAY OVERLAPPING SHEETS OF BIRCH RIND FROM GROUND UP, LEANING POLES AGAINST TO KEEP IN PLACE AS YOU GO. WHEN FINISHED, CHINCH WITH MOSS. (LATER, BANK WITH SNOW.)

⑤ MAKE DOOR, BOUGH BUNKS & HEARTH (TWO GREEN LOGS). LAY IN DRY BIRCH FIREWOOD

Fig. 2 — Building a Wigwam

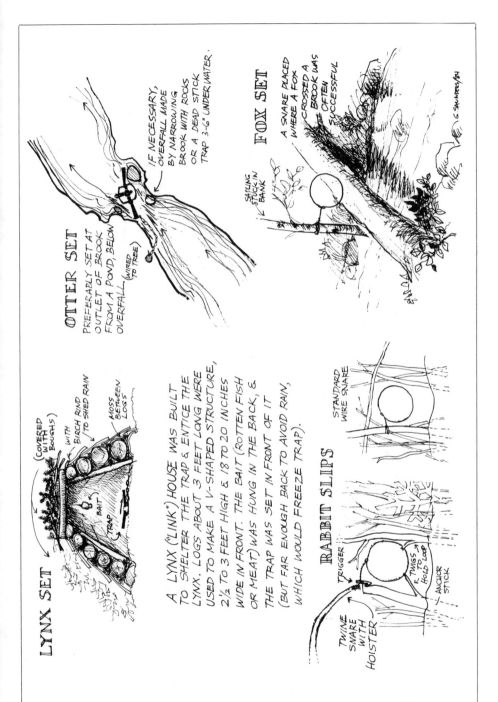

OTTER SET
PREFERABLY SET AT OUTLET OF BROOK FROM A POND, BELOW OVERFALL (WIRED TO TREE)

IF NECESSARY, OVERFALL MADE BY NARROWING BROOK WITH ROCKS OR A DEAD STICK TRAP 3-6" UNDER WATER.

FOX SET
A SNARE PLACED WHERE A FOX CROSSED A BROOK WAS OFTEN SUCCESSFUL

SAPLING STUCK IN BANK

G. SAUNDERS/84

LYNX SET
(COVERED WITH BOUGHS)
with BIRCH RIND TO SHED RAIN
MOSS BETWEEN LOGS
BAIT
TRAP

A LYNX ("LINK") HOUSE WAS BUILT TO SHELTER THE TRAP & ENTICE THE LYNX. LOGS ABOUT 3 FEET LONG WERE USED TO MAKE A V-SHAPED STRUCTURE, 2½ TO 3 FEET HIGH & 18 TO 20 INCHES WIDE IN FRONT. THE BAIT (ROTTEN FISH OR MEAT) WAS HUNG IN THE BACK, & THE TRAP WAS SET IN FRONT OF IT (BUT FAR ENOUGH BACK TO AVOID RAIN, WHICH WOULD FREEZE TRAP).

RABBIT SLIPS
STANDARD WIRE SNARE

TRIGGER
F. TWIGS TO HOLD LOOP
ANCHOR STICK
TWINE SNARE WITH HOISTER

Fig. 3 — Some Common Trapper's Sets

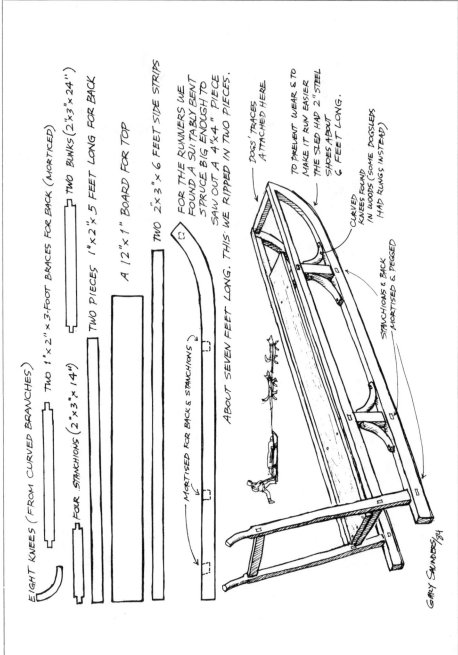

EIGHT KNEES (FROM CURVED BRANCHES)

TWO 1" x 2" x 3-FOOT BRACES FOR BACK (MORTICED)

TWO BUNKS (2"x 3"x 24")

FOUR STANCHIONS (2"x 3"x 14")

TWO PIECES 1"x 2" 5 FEET LONG FOR BACK

A 12"x 1" BOARD FOR TOP

TWO 2"x 3" 6 FEET SIDE STRIPS

MORTISED FOR BACK & STANCHIONS

ABOUT SEVEN FEET LONG. THIS WE RIPPED IN TWO PIECES.

FOR THE RUNNERS WE FOUND A SUITABLY BENT SPRUCE BIG ENOUGH TO SAW OUT A 4"x4" PIECE

DOGS' TRACES ATTACHED HERE

TO PREVENT WEAR & TO MAKE IT RUN EASIER THE SLED HAD 2" STEEL SHOES ABOUT 6 FEET LONG.

CURVED KNEES FOUND IN WOODS (SOME DOGSLEDS HAD RUNGS INSTEAD)

STANCHIONS & BACK MORTISED & PEGGED

GARY SAUNDERS/84

Fig. 4 — Building a Dogsled

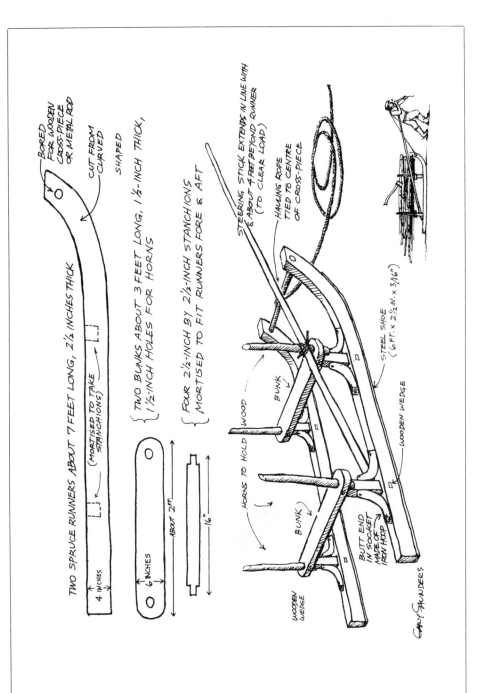

Fig. 5 — Building a Handslide

SAUNDER'S CAMPS

P. O. BOX 435   **SAUNDER'S CAMPS**   *TEL. 8-3361*

Fishing & Hunting

GANDER, NEWFOUNDLAND

Dear Angler:-

To speed our correspondence, the following data has been compiled for your information. Please feel free to enquire further.

FISHING: The Gander is Newfoundland's second largest river, and one of the island's most productive salmon streams producing annually an average of 2500 fish. ranging in weight from 5 to 20 lbs. Trout fishing is also available throughout the season. Fly fishing only is permitted, most fish are caught on wet flies. Licenses and suitable salmon flies are sold at camp.

FACILITIES: Saunder's Camps are located 15 miles from salt water, with good pools nearby, upstream and down. We can accommodate 10 persons in comfortable Government approved cabins, a good cook and competent guides ensure an enjoyable stay. We have electricity and refrigeration in which fish may be kept to take home.

RATES: Our rate is $35.00 per person per day which includes meals, accomodation, guide, boat and motor for each person, and transportation from Gander Airport to camp and return. Bring only your rods, tackle and personal kit.

TRAVEL INFORMATION: Trans-Canada Airlines operate two flights daily to Gander from Montreal, also a direct jet flight on Mondays only. Guests are met at the airport. Gander has one of the best hotels in Newfoundland.
The camp is reached by car and boat in two hours, or by chartered float plane in fifteen minutes, the fare for a 3 passenger plane is $11.00, 5 passenger $20.00.

MISCELLANEOUS: The Gander river is one of our beauty spots, its waters are uncontaminated by any industrial waste. Apart from fishing, the canoe trip with experienced rivermen affords memories and movie footage that are priceless. Moose are frequently seen. Daytime temperatures average 65 degrees, nights are cool and hayfever is unknown. Finally there are no telephones to disturb the peace.

Sincerely yours,

Brett Saunders

(Left)
Sample of an advertising flyer for Saunders Camps from the 1960s.

(Below)
Copy of a $50 share in a Nova Scotia fox farming venture dated 1915.

Facsimile of pages from wolf bounty record book of Magistrate John Peyton Sr. recording payment to Charles Francis of Gander Bay for a wolf killed there on April 5, 1876. *(Courtesy Edgar Baird.)*

THE HORWOOD LUMBER COMPANY
by
Sam Blake*

In the year of Nineteen Twenty-two
I'll have you all to know,
When the men of Gander Bay
Ploughed through the frosty snow;

In search for logs and pulpwood
Each tried to do their part;
The way those men were treated
'Twas enough to break your heart.

They worked away contented
For a month or so,
And soon as the freight was landed
Off to the store did go.

Going in the office,
Mr. Burden there they found;
They asked for goods they needed;
He quickly wrote it down.

Upon a piece of paper
So very small and rare.
"Give this to Joe Peckford,
Same as you did last year."

The goods you got was just enough
To last you for a week;
Before that much was paid for
You were cripple, sore and sick.

As for your horse, she would
Look in wonder and dismay --
"You must be a cruel teamster
To treat me in this way.

"The logs I have pulled out for you
Amount to dollars and cents;
I got hay and oats when I started,
And not a mouthful since.

"As for Mr. Horwood,
Such a man could not be found;
We'd live just as well in Gander Bay
Were he twelve feet underground."

*Samuel Blake was Gander Bay's official bard and composed many ballads
and poems about life there, most of which are now unfortunately lost. This
one was preserved by Mrs. Jaspar Vivian, who kindly wrote it out for my
sister-in-law Kathleen Saunders in 1984.